Get Outta Town

A tale of the Grateful Dead,
the IRS, and Coffee

Get Outta Town

(A tale of the Grateful Dead, the IRS, and Coffee)

by **Ted Ringer**
Illustrations by the author

Acid Test Productions
Petaluma, California

Book Design by Timothy Harris,
© 1997 Cover Design by Tim Harris and James Nichols
FINE LINE DESIGN
845 Olive Avenue #210,
Novato, California. 94945
415•897•2575
e-mail fnlndsn@hooked.net

ACID TEST PRODUCTIONS
1370 Industrial Avenue, Suite G
Petaluma, California 94952
707•769•7484
Fax 707•769•7409
email AcidTest@ix.netcom.com

ACKNOWLEDGMENTS

Many people helped nudge this book to
and through creation and I want to thank:
W.S. Sutton, Valari Jack, Emily Hunter,
Sarah Fitzsimmons, Daryl Manes, Rob
Wilder, Eddie Lewis, Natalie Goldberg,
M.L. Fisher, Brad Carlson,
those Acid Testers,
the guys at the bar, and,
especially, Minnie.

TABLE OF CONTENTS

Chapter One - Hit the Road, Jack

The omens were dark. The vibrations bad. The diagnosis grim. The customers were angry and the employees irresponsible. Deliveries were uncertain and the cleaning crew had quit. The front window had been broken the night before by a big guy in a suit who mistook it for a door. The change was not adding up and the partnership was feeling shaky. Minnie thought it might be time for a vacation.

Of course, it was always time for a vacation, but responsibility lay like a bad dream in his bones and he carried it around with him everywhere. It was just a job, wasn't it? But maybe it was more than that. This bar had been his place of ungainly employment, his office, his stage, his throne for seven years. Not to mention the scene of long nights, painful diversions, and moments of bad judgement.

The other night a customer had said, with that special emphasis given to everything by an excess of alcohol, "Minnie, this place is like a big adventure every day."

Minnie, the boss, the man who knows, had turned to the drunken innocent and answered, "This is not an adventure, asshole, it's angina."

It was at that moment that the actual plans for vacation began to form. They weren't extensive or elaborate or complicated. As he said to himself, in a quiet, reflective tone, "Time to get the fuck out of Dodge."

It didn't take him long. He had never been big on forethought. Action was more natural and a decision, once made, instantly gathered momentum. What was decided may not have been advisable or often even coherent, but it had always proven wise for anyone who valued their safety to get out of the way once the process was set in motion.

A rumbling started deep in his mind. He had worked nine

days in a row, all double shifts, and it was making him crazy. Claustrophobic. The mirror behind the bar kept showing him a tired face he almost recognized as his own. He thought that if one more employee asked him what to do or if just one more customer pretended to be his friend, he would explode. And it would not be a pretty sight. He surveyed the customers who lined the long bar and those at the small tables.

He muttered to himself, "I've had it. This is it. I've been here too long." Then he spoke up and ordered another shot of tequila from the foreign-looking bartender. All the bartenders were followers of Islam. Most of them from Morocco. Their English wasn't very good but they didn't drink. It was policy. And it was a policy that had always saved the bar money.

He ordered a shot and threw it down with a quick tilt. Minnie looked at the bartender, clearly, for the moment, and said in a gruff voice, "You're in charge. I'm leaving."

The bartender shook his head in pity at the ways of his American boss as Minnie walked to the end of the bar and grabbed the phone.

He called his friend, Ricky, at Bluebeard Motors and rented a big red Chevy convertible, wide and powerful. He then asked his kitchen crew to make up a few days worth of sandwiches and a gallon of green chili.

He gathered his staff and issued orders.

"I'll be gone for a while, but I'll be checking up on you guys and just because I'm having fun doesn't mean you jailbirds don't have to work. Beaver will be keeping a close eye on you, so don't fuck around. Don't let me down. You guys are professionals."

He thought about it for a moment and said, "Hell, I'm a professional." He rolled his eyes and started laughing in a big way, his large yet purposeful belly shaking in agreement.

The Beaver he referred to was his partner, another big guy. It seemed no one had a regular name in this place, except for the waitresses who were completely civilized and had names like Barbara, Cathy, and Diane. As for the guys, there was Beaver and himself, the two head honchos, and then assorted helpers who went by names like Noodle, Baby Fay, and Cowboy. Smiley, Dutch, and Bubba.

He looked through the heat of the kitchen at this motley bunch and said, "Don't try anything funny. I'll be back before you know it."

They heard him laughing as he went down the stairs to what passed for an office. He sat down at the heavy metal desk, elbowed clear a spot in the center, and wrote out a big check to himself. Then he scribbled a note to his partner which said,

Beaver —
Taxes on the 31st. What do we do about Gin's
mother? Bratwurst order on Tuesday. Centennial
called. You take care of it. I'm out of here.
I'll call you. Vacation Time!

He stuck his note to the bulletin board, then pushed the creaking chair back and stood for a moment in thought.

Both he and Beaver had done this before. It was the nature of the business. You worked your ass off and kept everything together for a long stretch and then one day you cracked. You couldn't take it anymore and vacation became inevitable, necessary, and immediate. This was a partnership. They were used to each other and somehow it worked. Minnie loved this place, but he needed a break. It was either that or go crazy.

He grabbed an armful of t-shirts from a box in the corner.

He'd need some clean clothes. The shirts had the bar logo in fancy script on the back — an official-looking seal with the name, Moonbeam Tavern, Boulder, Colorado. A small quarter moon was on the front, positioned over the heart. On his way to the door, Minnie ducked beneath a big, black, hot water pipe with a grace acquired from years of practice. He took a last fond look at the chaos, and said, "So long, suckers," kicking the door shut behind him.

It slammed with a satisfying bang, shaking the walls, and then he heard a crash. Minnie walked down the narrow hallway past the bathrooms and knew that, once again, the board with all the important notes, including his latest, and all the dated postcards, overdue invoices, and announcements of events long past, had fallen to the floor, testimony to his partner's mechanical ability. He hoped Beaver would find his message.

He went out the basement door and up the steps to the parking lot. He threw his stuff into the back seat of his car, an old, beat-up, mini-pickup. He always said it was a collector's item. Who, exactly, might collect this vehicle, besides himself or some tow truck, was open to speculation. He gunned the engine, backed into the alley without looking, and sped off into the dark night toward freedom. As he squealed onto Broadway, he honked the horn and shouted out the window into the cool air, "Let the vacation begin."

Chapter Two - Sue Me, While I Kiss the Sky

His first stop would be Oregon to see the Grateful Dead. There were two shows that coming weekend. He had been a fan since high school and though he had a real aversion to groups, he would not have objected to being classified a Deadhead. That's how much they meant to him and how inherent a thing it was; just like he couldn't avoid a grouping with other redheads or forty-two year old Jewish guys from New Jersey or those who fit into size 11 1/2 D shoes. He couldn't and wouldn't disavow being a Deadhead. It was a fact of nature.

To Minnie, rock-and-roll was a religion. Tutti Fruiti Aw Rootie was a zen-like pronouncement, a koan that, with study, would reveal all. Do Wah Diddy, if you felt it deeply and truly enough, would save you. Rock-and-roll was here to stay and the Dead were carrying that spirit forward. He believed that if the dancing was hot enough, if everyone could imagine and believe it, then paradise would manifest here on Earth. Of course, it helped to be high.

Vacation was just what he needed. Oregon would be a start. First a couple of shows, then up the coast for fishing and whatever else turned up. He could picture it now. The ocean on his left, the mountains on his right. Streams, creeks, and rivers calling to him from within their green cloaks. Water bubbling, a reason to stop, take a deep breath, and partake of the wonders. The fish would thumb their fins at him, daring him to cast his line in their neighborhoods. They'd laugh among themselves that they already knew all of his tricks, but he would, nonetheless, pull them out, one after another. All of this — the rivers, the fish, the wonders — would flow toward him and the sea as he sped by, waiting for the instinct, the intuition, the billboard that would tell him that this was the place to stop, that this was the moment.

He pictured himself speeding northward, a warm salty breeze rushing past, a beautiful blonde by his side, maybe two blondes, admiring him with wide eyes, the border and the unknown before him. He longed for a mystical trip, one where he would learn all, know all. It seemed he need only to point himself forward with an open heart and an open wallet.

His troubles at home were numerous and included leaky pipes in his cabin in the mountains, guys who wanted to borrow money, miscellaneous bodily aches and pains, and old girlfriends who now thought of him as a brother. On this trip he would forget about being lonely in the midst of these people, take a break from his problems, and leave behind the responsibilities of the bar and everything that plagued him. He would concentrate on the wonderful something, complete with naps, that lay before him.

These thoughts filled his mind as he headed home. But mostly he was tired. Tired of the same old thing. The same old way.

Once back in his apartment, he phoned his cleaning lady.

"Gorgeous? Min here. I'm leaving in the morning. Will you take care of things while I'm gone? Yeah. Don't worry about that shit. No, I'll call you. That cat will eat anything. How's what's his name? Uh huh. I know what his name is, I just don't like to say it. Why don't you come with me? We'll have fun. Music, champagne, romping under the stars. Okay. Okay. Okay. I understand. Yes, I think marriage is a wonderful thing. The money will be in the same place. Take all you want. Yes, dear. I will. Of course. I'll call you. Bye."

He made a list. A short one of errands to do before he left the next morning - Reservations, Loose Ends, Bank, Clothes, Gas. That ought to do it. The phone rang, but he ignored it. He opened the refrigerator and examined the pathetic collection of forsaken crumbs and half-filled containers and closed the door with a groan. He grabbed one of the sandwiches he had taken from the bar and, in honor of the vacation, he put on the Dead. "Cumberland Blues."

> *I can't stay much longer, Melinda*
> *The sun is getting high*
> *I can't help you with your troubles*
> *If you won't help with mine*

He turned the music up, and sat in the big chair. He chewed, a bit dazed by things, and looked out the window at the lights of town.

That night he had a dream. It was one he often dreamed. It was dark and he was under attack. When he went to defend himself, he found that he couldn't move. A bird flew by, as it always did, at the moment the fatal blow was about to fall. He looked up at it, wistfully, but this time he began to whistle to it.

The next morning he packed, which meant pulling the duffel bag from the bottom of the closet and throwing all the t-shirts, a bunch of socks, and a few other things in it. He grabbed some tapes for the ride and put them in a box — Beatles, Hendrix, Clapton, Santana, a few others. And, of course, the Dead.

Minnie liked that electric guitar. In his opinion, it was the perfect invention. It was a thing you could hit as hard as you wanted without hurting it and, in reaction, it would make the loudest sound possible. If you were talented, it could make the loudest music possible. And the sweetest. It could express, in a way no other instrument could, a whole range of feelings — frustration and beauty, tenderness and anger, ecstatic joy and the deepest regret. Harmony, melody, and love were all possible. There was no sitting still. You had to get up and dance. This was a gift from the gods.

If anyone had pointed out that these songs were more than 25 years old, Minnie would have countered that they were timeless. He would have said, "So sue me. This is real hippie music."

The morning was bright and beautiful. He picked up his convertible at Bluebeard. He had known Ricky since New Jersey. He told Minnie to keep the car as long as he liked, but to keep it on the road and out of the ditch.

Minnie was feeling good as he finished his remaining errands. The highway was calling and the tank was full. He was leaving the old and the known behind him and heading off into a future that could become anything. He welcomed the path of asphalt that stretched out in front of him. No irate customers, no bills to pay, no demands on his time. Just new scenery, a little peace and quiet, and endless possibility. Maybe a few fish and some girls.

As he went through the last light in town, Minnie stuck his hand up into the air rushing by at 50 mph and threw a wave backwards to all he was leaving behind. He took a deep breath of the exhaust of the truck in front of him and, with a smile on his face, reached for the knob of the tape player and turned it up. He had the key to the highway and he wasn't going to waste this chance. He had two days to make it to Eugene before the shows. Minnie pushed the pedal toward the floor and began whistling.

Chapter Three - Like a Highway Sign

The miles were flying by. Minnie soon settled into the rhythm of freeway driving — long straight-aways and gradual curves. He put his red bomb on cruise control and pulled another joint out of his pocket. He steered with his knees as he lit it and took in a big lungful. His eyes opened wider and they twinkled with the slight shift to a different gear. He sank a little deeper into the comfort of his big Chevy as it rolled forward.

Pigpen was singing.

> *Baby, here I am*
> *I'm the man on the scene*
> *I can give you what you want*
> *But you've got to come home with me*
>
> *I got a whole lot of good loving*
> *And I got some in store*
> *When I get through throwing it on you*
> *You've got to come back for more*
>
> *Hey, let me light your candle*
> *Cause Mama I'm so hard to handle*
> *Yes, I am.*

This music, as always, put him into a different state of mind.

There were mountains to his right, for the moment, but the further west he went, the more everything spread out and the flatter it became. The bigger the landscape got, the more it felt like he was going slower, so he took the car off cruise control and sped up. Traffic was sparse. He left Steamboat and Craig behind him and was now headed for exotic places like Maybell and Elk Springs, Blue Mountain and Dinosaur.

He didn't know how or when dinosaurs had roamed this area. It was a little before his time and must have been different then. As the miles drifted by, 80 of them an hour, he had a few more hits and transformed his surroundings from dry, uninterrupted plains into a scene of green lushness, dotted with groves of palms. At respectful intervals, he saw groups of huge dinosaurs moving slowly forward. They, too, were on vacation, covering great distances with a few footfalls, their long necks moving slowly from side to side, at one with the prehistoric landscape, not thinking, not worrying, not wanting, going about their king-size business with no regrets, only clear minds and clear hearts.

Minnie envied them. This was a state he had tried for years to reach, only to find that his heart, though smaller in some ways, beat much faster and his brain, by all accounts larger than theirs, could not slow down. Some had left their bones behind, some only footprints. Minnie decided he was the kind who would only leave footprints.

Suddenly, Minnie heard a prehistoric blast from behind and a huge diesel blew by with a wave of air that shook him. He gripped the wheel tighter and directed a fair sample of profanity at this interruption to his thoughts. He looked down and saw that he was only going 40. On the tape player, Jerry was going into a solo on "Big Boss Man" and Minnie brought the red Chevy back to the present and up to and a little beyond the speed limit.

He was glad to be on his way to the show, where he would feel at home. It was one of the few places he did anymore. He had always considered himself a freak and an outsider. At one time, 25 years ago in Boulder, he had felt like he belonged. There was plenty of long hair and music and dope. And even though the world was in a mess, it had been a time of peace and love and hanging out. He had believed back then that if you got high enough, you might just stay there.

A gathering of the tribes seemed to be happening in the late sixties. The world was changing and it was at the concerts and dances that you looked around and knew that you weren't alone. They were all freaks and every new record, song, or written word was a signpost pointing the way.

He got excited remembering all this. He turned the music up and lit another joint.

But Minnie knew things were different now. He was different, too. He had seen the narrowness, the cynicism, and the limita-tions of that scene, yet he knew that all of those dreams had meant something. He knew that there had been magic there and that it was still real. If you believed it, it could transform you. It had been a step forward. He carried the values of that time within him. He knew a lot of it had been bullshit, but a lot wasn't and he wasn't about to let it go.

The Dead concerts were one place where it seemed all that stuff still held true. At the shows that spirit lived on, the music blasting and everyone going higher, if only for one night.

He wondered what was wrong with him. Was he just worn out from all the work at the bar? Or had he lost the spark he had 20 years ago. Hell, he had it 10 years ago. Was he now an old fart? Was everything going downhill? As the bleak landscape flew by, he wondered if he had any meaningful future. Was all that was left to him just a lot of lonely nights and another shot of tequila?

What had happened? The girlfriends never worked out. The bar had, but so what. All his friends were married, had children, were too busy for him. Every relationship had been a mess. The girl always leaving him for someone else. He thought he ought to be used to it by now. He still wanted to rock-and-roll, but it seemed everyone else was getting older. He was too. He couldn't help it.

He glanced at the bundle on the seat next to him. It contained the sandwiches and chili from the bar. At least, he wouldn't have to worry about hunger. He had a box of t-shirts in the trunk, so he didn't have to worry about laundry. This was the kind of carefree vacation he liked.

Minnie thought about Rhonda, his cleaning lady, and her great charms and skills. He had thought about her often, with admiration and longing. The trouble was that she was married. What a shame. And, while he was on the subject, he thought about the waitresses at the bar. They were all so good-looking, so sexy, so nice, but so young. That was the problem. He kept getting older while they always stayed the same age. They would work and he would woo, in his manner, and then they would go on to something else and other young, beautiful girls took their place.

Minnie shook his head and looked at himself in the rear-view mirror. Enough of this shit. He raised his eyebrows and turned his head from side to side to check his profile. He glanced at the highway, responsibly, and then returned to the mirror. He wiggled his eyebrows and smiled. He tried to adopt a faraway, romantic look. It made him laugh. He shook his head again and ran a hand over his bald dome and grabbed the long, thin, red locks that clung, hopefully, to the back of his head. As he sat there in the driver's seat, his imposing, reposing stomach hid his seatbelt. He gestured to the world at large and said, with a touch of resignation, "Here I'm is. This is it. That's all there is."

He was quite distinguished in his own way. His bulk, his dome, his relaxed manner of dress, his wise, extravagant visage, handed down from the ages, all combined to give him a strong resemblance to Mr. Natural. And this resemblance was reinforced by personality. He was easygoing, but could always make his point. Beneath his flab and harsh words and bluster beat a large and true heart. You only had to look to see it. He was honest in everything that mattered, faithful to his friends, and generous to the bottoms of his pockets.

His personality transformed any limitations in the way of appearance and he shone with an individuality that could not be denied. He was not quiet and he was not always polite, but he was always himself and no other. He gave himself the right to be here and added a dash of hope for the future, but beyond that he wouldn't elaborate.

Later, as he passed through Salt Lake City with its narrow Mormons, he couldn't help contrasting it to the islands, his old haunt. Though improbable, the Caribbean felt like home to him. He had spent several wild years there as tourist, bum, manager of a resort, and purveyor of mosquito-netting, and its turquoise waters, swaying palms, white sand, and blondes still called to him.

For the moment, however, it was full speed ahead. Salt Lake City fell behind him, tumbling in his wake, gone in a puff of smoke, and forgotten. He bent low over the steering wheel and lit another joint as he drove through the Great Salt Lake and past Bonneville Speedway. Oasis, Elko, Battle Mountain, and Winnemucca lay ahead. He was pushing it and when, at last, he couldn't distinguish between dinosaurs, giant rabbits, and the bridges and overpasses of the freeway, he decided he had better call it a day or a night or whatever it was.

He took an exit labeled Dunphy, which at that moment sounded right, and in a fog of long distance, loud music, and limited resources, he rolled to a stop in front of the El Rancho Hanson Motel and slowly separated himself from the car.

Chapter Four - Make Mine Black

Minnie registered at the front desk and was welcomed warmly, despite the late hour and his imposing appearance, by a young man who resembled an accountant with acne. He seemed eager to talk and if Minnie had been less tired and more alert, he would have recognized a desperate night-clerk-middle-of-Nevada loneliness beaming at him from every pore. For all that, the clerk was shy.

"Hi ya, Mister." He pushed the registration form across the counter. "Kind of late night for you?"

Minnie grunted, grabbed a pen, and, with the room whirling, tried to remember how to write.

"Where you headed?"

"To see the Dead."

The desk clerk drew back a bit at that but kept on. "It's a long road, isn't it?"

Minnie looked up at the kid for a moment, studied him closely, and said, "Not only that, but it's a long strange trip. That's why we need our sleep." And then he smiled, putting the clerk at ease. "See you in the a.m."

The clerk said, "Sure, Mister. Sleep tight."

Minnie turned and walked out into the cool night air. The bright light in the parking lot shone down on only one other car besides his Chevy. It was an old Volvo station wagon with Colorado plates. It was full of junk and covered with a thick coat of dirt, dust, and mud. As he crossed the lot to his room, Minnie said, "Small fucking world." He entered room 14, didn't even look at the TV, and went straight to bed. In the moments before sleep, the white lines kept racing toward him and he repeatedly and involuntarily flinched. Then, as he turned onto his side, the world went black and he began snoring in a peaceful though substantial way.

It would be idle speculation to guess how long he might have slept had he not smelled the coffee. And not in the metaphorical sense, either. The thick, brown scent crept into his dreams and got him going. It was real and it kindled a craving in him. Minnie suddenly woke up. He looked around and realized he had a full day's drive ahead of him. He promptly got out of bed and prepared for departure.

The sunlight hit him when he stepped outside and made him cringe, but then he smelled the coffee again and he pulled himself together. The Volvo was still there and he went to the door in front of it. As he gave it a loud thump, he shouted, "Bowman, I know you're in there. Open up."

The door opened a crack and rested there a moment. An intense aroma of coffee escaped. Then the chain rattled and a tall skinny guy popped out. He had big brown cow eyes and bushy eyebrows. These eyes were wide open despite the early hour. He was obviously wired.

"Minnie! Don't scare me like that."

He said it with a smile and it was obvious he was glad to see him, but his tone said he was a little nervous. They attempted to go through an elaborate handshake which broke down on the fourth variation.

"Aw, fuck it," said Minnie. "How the hell are you?" His voice boomed in the Nevada morning.

"Good, Min. And you?"

Minnie put his arms out. "I'm on vacation." He did a little dance which explained it all. "You?"

"Another trip to Guatemala. On my way back."

Minnie looked at the dirty Volvo. He threw some sarcasm at the station wagon, saying, "Nooo?" and resumed smiling.

Bowman felt the need to explain. "Vacation for me too. Things are different now."

Bowman was an old Boulder fixture. His main business was repairing Volvos, nothing newer than '72. In the Yellow Pages it said - *Serving Boulder from the same low rent location for 20 years. Honest. Cheap. Imaginative. Talkative.*

A long time ago, Minnie and Bowman had been dealing partners. It had been business, but it had also been friendship. It still was. They had started small, just to maintain their stash, but it eventually grew into endless deals and big money. As time went on, things got crazier - too many headaches, too many weirdos, too much dough. Bowman started doing more coke than he could handle and began to get careless. Minnie couldn't take the low life anymore and broke off the partnership. Three weeks later Bowman was busted. Minnie took off for the islands. They might not be able to get their handshake together, but they were still close friends, even after everything that had happened and all the years in between.

Bowman put up a hand indicating that Minnie should wait. He went inside and brought out an elaborate and obviously portable coffee-making apparatus that looked like it had been developed for astronauts. He poured Minnie a big mugful. He returned the device to the room and then they sat on the hood of Minnie's car.

Minnie asked, "Got any sugar?"

Bowman winced. "Minnie, sugar isn't good for your health."

At this, Minnie made a face which showed how much difference that made to him.

"Besides," Bowman said, "you wouldn't want to insult the purity of these beans."

"What?"

"Check it out. This isn't Folgers."

Minnie took a sip. His eyes lit up. He gave Bowman a shrewd appraising look as he slowly savored the rest of the mug. There was a respectful silence. Then Bowman handed Minnie a bag which contained the blackest, shiniest, most pungent beans Minnie had ever encountered. He stuck his distinguished nose into the bag.

He pulled it out, impressed. "Almost like taking a hit."

Bowman nodded. "Keep the bag." He looked around the empty parking lot cautiously and said in a conspiratorial whisper, "I've got a load in the car."

Minnie gave it a look. In the early morning light, the old station wagon appeared to be almost quivering from all the caffeine it contained. He asked, "From Guatemala?"

Bowman made an almost imperceptible movement of his head.

Minnie couldn't figure out why he was acting like this and said, "Hey, what? Like it's illegal?"

Bowman stared at him and then raised his left eyebrow. "Minnie, you just don't know. How do you think I pay for these trips? This isn't just any coffee. This is Altos Ladino. People will kill for this. This is the most expensive coffee in the world. A couple of cups and you see God."

"Come on. These are coffee beans, not fucking marijuana."

"I get this stuff for the Dead."

"No way."

Bowman shrugged. "It's a different world now. Don't tell anyone where you got it. Just enjoy it."

Minnie eyed him closely. First coke and now coffee. There wasn't much difference, except that one was legal. "This isn't like old times, is it? You seem a little jumpy. You shouldn't drink so much of this stuff."

"It's not that. It's just that things are getting kind of hot. People are following me. They're on my ass." He took a breath and then made a visible effort to relax and shrug it off. "Nothing I can't handle."

Minnie said, "You're not in business, are you?"

"Nah. I just do this for fun."

"Don't fuck with me."

"I'm not. I mean it. You know, I just go down and hang in the jungle for a while and then bring some back for my friends. Nothing big."

Minnie was not completely convinced.

"I'm not. Okay?" Bowman bared his teeth at Minnie and then smiled. "But I've run into some weird stuff. I heard some things and I've seen a couple of things I shouldn't have. You know me, sticking my nose in where it doesn't belong."

Minnie checked the nose. It looked almost normal, but the more he looked at it, the odder and more suspicious it appeared.

"Min," Bowman said. "Back to Earth."

Minnie shook his head. "It's early, goddamnit."

For Minnie, all the dealing days were over, but here was a reminder of how things had been at one time. The endless paranoia. He was glad he was out of it.

As they talked, the sun got higher in the sky and, between that and the coffee, the day was warming up.

Then Bowman asked, "Do me a favor?"

Minnie looked at him closely. "As long as it's not something completely stupid."

"Stupid? Min, come on. Moi?"

Minnie rolled his eyes.

"Okay," Bowman said. "Two favors. But no big deal. One, keep this key for me."

Minnie took it. "Uh huh. Then what?"

"Meet me at the show. I'm going to talk with a guy and I want you to check him out. Tell me if you think he's okay."

"What's this about?"

"I can't really tell you and it's better if you don't know."

"Oh great, first you tell me people will kill for this shit. That makes me feel really good. Then you tell me people are following you. And now you want me to hold this fucking key cause you're freaked out. And, you want to mess up my show so I can meet some fruitcake. That's no big deal?"

"Min, it's nothing really. Just do this as a pal, okay?"

"Oh sure. Look, we've done this before. You've got to tell me more than this. What's the real story?"

Bowman heaved a big sigh across the parking lot.

"Well, some of this coffee I get for the Dead. As a favor. And, like I said, this last time I was in Guatemala, I saw some stuff I shouldn't have and I heard things from the people I know down there. These coffee guys are hard-core."

"Coffee guys?"

"Yeah, the guys who really deal it. We call them the Coffee Cartel. It was a joke at first, but now.... Anyway, I feel like I need to do something about it."

"What the hell happened?"

Bowman waved the question away and continued. "You know I can't go to the cops and the Dead know a lot of people. They have guys working on stuff."

"What do you mean stuff?"

"Rainforest issues. Stuff like that. I've talked with some of them."

"Like you're an environmentalist now?"

"Will you let me tell you the fucking story? I just want you to meet this guy I've been talking to, you know, give me a sanity check, tell me if he seems straight to you."

It was becoming clear that Bowman was right. Minnie didn't want to know.

"Look," Minnie said, "I'm on vacation. I'm trying to relax. The last time we did something like this, I had to leave the damn country." He paused, feeling like he was losing control. He took a deep breath. "You are really working me. I'm your buddy and I'll do it, but just until tomorrow. After that, forget it. You get the key back, I'll check the guy out, and that'll be that. Okay?"

A look of relief came over Bowman. "Thanks, Min. I've got to go do a few things on my way to Eugene, but I'll meet you first show at the break, outside the bathrooms on the west side."

Minnie was about to ask him what he had to do when Bowman's eyes narrowed and he said in a voice that made Minnie nervous, "Don't give this key to anyone. Don't let anyone know you have it. Okay?"

Minnie looked at the key in his hand. It was obviously the key to a safety deposit box - long, with only a number, 2451, engraved on one side of it. Otherwise, no markings, no nothing.

"What's in the box?" Minnie asked.

"You don't want to know."

The past was all coming back again. "You're such a jerk."

"Min, it's only until tomorrow afternoon. I'm just a little paranoid."

"Like I don't know that?" Minnie had to laugh. "Okay, okay, okay."

They talked a little while longer about people they knew and the bar and old adventures and about the way things had changed back in Boulder. Things definitely were different, but despite all that and despite Bowman's story and all the weird things that had happened to them, Minnie knew they would always be friends.

Finally, they attempted to shake hands again and Minnie climbed into the convertible. He gunned the Chevy, honked the horn, and spit a little gravel. Bowman was beside the Volvo, waving.

Minnie eased onto the freeway and, as he did, he glanced at the aromatic bag of beans on the seat beside him. He shook his head at the thought of Bowman. It took a character to appreciate a character.

Chapter Five - Watch Your Speed

It felt good to be moving. At the bar, he was either working down in the office, sitting at the bar, or shuffling between them. Although you couldn't call driving exercise, it was definitely movement. And it was all the exercise Minnie wanted.

With the music blaring and the miles flying by, he thought this is the life. The long, clear highway leading wherever I choose. And right now he was choosing Eugene and the Dead. The Cascades, which had been only a rumor on the map, edged up over the horizon and presented themselves as a growing, living thing which eventually swallowed both him and his car. The air had a hint of altitude and, because the sun had shone the whole way, he had yet to put up the top. He was excited. He hadn't been to a show since January.

On the box, he had a tape, one of the last with Pigpen, 5/25/72. Pigpen was singing,

> *Without a warning*
> *You broke my heart*
> *You took it Baby*
> *And tore it apart*

It made him think of one of the first Dead shows he had seen in high school, back in 1968. He and his buddies had driven through a blizzard to Scranton, where the band was playing at a Catholic youth center.

Everyone, except Minnie and his friends, was in coats and ties. He and his buddies felt as if they were in a foreign country. The worst part was that the audience simply sat there, motionless and uptight.

The band did a few numbers and the energy just wasn't right. Weir looked out over the lights and said that it seemed like people were tired, a bad night, nasty weather, etc. and ended the show early. The Catholics clapped lamely and started to get up to leave. Minnie looked at his friends. They couldn't believe it. They hadn't driven hours for this. Minnie's gang grabbed their chairs and went to the front of the small auditorium. They plopped them down in the center and jumped up on them. They screamed. They yelled. They clapped and whistled. They were going to stay on their chairs making noise until something happened, until either the band started playing again or they got thrown out.

After a few minutes of this, the band came back out to see who these crazies were. After a moment of watching, both Jerry and Phil were laughing. Weir pointed at Minnie and said, "This is for you guys," and the band went into "St. Stephen." Minnie and his pals went wild. Four good Jewish boys in bluejeans in the front row, standing on their chairs, tripped out of their minds, with a crowd of Catholic youth behind them, in coats and ties and proper clothing, finally awake, and asking them, telling them, shouting at them to sit down.

"Down in front!" they yelled.

Minnie turned toward them and answered, "No. You stand up. Loosen your ties and shake your ass. This is rock-and-roll!"

Things hadn't changed much since then. Minnie saw music as a sacred privilege you shouldn't abuse. You had to get off your butt and participate. Just like the song said, "If you get confused, listen to the music play" and there you were. The bus came by a long time ago and he got on. That's when it all began. "It's coming, we're coming, coming around." He knew they didn't make that stuff up out of the air. These weren't just poems. This was like explaining a dream. This was what they really meant. This was serious. This was the truth. It had to be true or the Boys wouldn't be doing it this long. It was more than a job.

There was no denying when it was happening, when things were working. It was definite electromagnetic energy that was real, that everyone was a part of, that the audience had an effect on. That's what air guitars were for: to nudge the energy. It was a responsibility, an energy ride. You surfed that energy and could give it a push one way, to help it along, or drag it down another, if you were being negative. There was no way to control it and it was better if you didn't, if you just went with the flow of things. But you definitely had to participate or you would miss the bus and that would be no fun.

It was early evening when he rolled into Eugene, a small, quiet college town that was now full of tie-dye and vans and long hair and clumps of kids just sitting on the sidewalk on top of sleeping bags and packs. It was a party. By the stadium, a village of fans had already formed. As Minnie drove by, he could hear music and see small groups of people dancing. Everyone was there to see the Dead, to listen to the music, to be together. He took a deep breath. This was a scene he knew well and he was a sentimental guy.

While driving toward his hotel, Minnie imagined that all of the people on the street and in the shops and in all the houses that he passed, all these people, whether they were young, like most of those he saw, or not, like that old man at the light, the woman with the baby stroller, even that policeman, he imagined they were all in town for the music. The show wasn't until tomorrow and you could already feel the energy.

He found his hotel, the Eugene Holiday Inn. He was lucky to have gotten a reservation. There were two shows — Saturday and Sunday — and both were sold out. Probably 60,000 people in town for them and the woman on the phone had said things were booked up for 50 miles around.

The hotel was expensive and, as he drove up, he could see that it had a pool out in front. That was a good sign. It was hotter than hell. He could use a swim. And then a big meal, a little music somewhere, adventure, girls, and a good night's sleep. That would be plenty. The show was the next day.

He entered the lobby and saw a small crowd of longhairs and headbands and bluejeans. Everyone was talking and hanging out and it appeared that more than a few were trying to get a room. Eventually, he gave his name at the desk. This clerk was the opposite of the shy guy in Dunphy. His hair was slicked back and he had a fancy tie and a long nose. He also had an air of impatience and disdain. He wasn't used to Deadheads. He gave Minnie the once-over and consulted his reservation book.

It was taking him a while and Minnie turned to a couple standing behind him, a tall guy with a shaved head and a short girl in a striped tube top and cutoffs. The three of them exchanged names and points of origin. They speculated on the weather, compared notes on the last shows they had seen, and generally yakked it up. Minnie had driven a long way and was ready for a little nap. He looked back at the clerk, who was now in conversation with another man behind the counter.

Finally, the clerk returned and said, "Mr. Minion, we don't seem to have a reservation for you."

Minnie looked at him calmly and said, "Would you check again? I made the reservation two days ago."

Without checking and without apology, the clerk said, "Mr. Minion, I've looked and you have no reservation."

"Well, any room will do."

"We're booked up."

This was the kind of slight Minnie had no patience with. He took action. His voice grew in volume as he said, "I have a reservation. It's on my credit card. Don't fuck with me."

The lobby was still. Everyone had turned to watch this encounter.

20

"Mr. Minion. . . ."

Minnie's voice dropped to a more normal level. "I'm easy to get along with until you make me angry. Then I go a little crazy. You know what I mean?"

Minnie had his face right up close to the clerk's. He smiled in a way that was open to interpretation. The clerk had suddenly lost his haughty manner.

Minnie's voice was emphatic. "I'm angry now." He pounded his fist on the counter. "Either get me a room or call the police."

The clerk hesitated for a moment. Then he turned and reached for a key. Minnie's reservation had been confirmed.

Chapter Six - Sitting on Top of the World

This was the day. The show. The first of two and Minnie had a backstage pass that would let him in free and allow him access to everywhere except onstage, in front of the microphones.

He had to pick up his pass at a special ticket booth on the east side of the big football stadium where the concert would take place. It took him an hour to find a parking place. The traffic was unbelievable. Even though it was only eleven in the morning, at least half of these people should not have been driving. You could see their dilated pupils from the sidewalk. He finally found a place in the driveway of the National Guard Armory, across the street from the stadium. He thought it was odd that there would be such a prime spot free, but wasn't about to pass it by.

He walked through the swirling crowd admiring the outrageousness of it all, looking for people he might have met before, and stopped to buy a brownie from a beautiful girl with a ring in her nose. It seemed like every other person was after a ticket. "Need two tickets." "One for Sunday." "Just one." They repeated their requests patiently and endlessly, waiting for a miracle. The people moved lazily and were mellow. It was another hot day and Minnie was glad he had brought his hat.

He saw a pay phone up ahead and went to it. A young man with stringy hair was talking. "Yes, Mom. Don't worry. I'm eating well. You know, tofu. The car still works. I'll be home in two weeks. Uh huh, well, I could use a little more money...." Finally, it was Minnie's turn and he punched in the required numbers and after a moment, he heard a ring. On the other end, a voice answered, "Moonbeam Tavern." He recognized it.

"Katherine, darling. Minnie here. How's every little thing?" He got a short report. "Is Cowboy working the kitchen? Let me talk to him."

There was a long pause as Cowboy was summoned to the phone. A very long pause. Minnie looked around in the hot sunshine. His feet hurt. The people who passed by in an endless flow were smiling, laughing, and talking in a friendly way. He couldn't believe the tie-dye. And everyone seemed so young. For a moment he felt like someone's father.

Cowboy finally got on the line and said, "Boy, am I glad you called. This place is falling apart. Slider had a bike accident and can't work. The fryer cuts in and out. It's hot here and we're getting slammed. Dutch is breaking up with his girlfriend and is burning the burritos. The order from Kraft is..."

Minnie held the phone at arm's length and shook his head. Then, he said, "Cowboy, enough already. You're making my ear ache. Talk to Beaver about all that stuff. I just wanted to see how you were getting along. Everything sounds great."

Cowboy asked, "When are you coming back?"

"Oh, fuck. Cowboy, I'm on vacation. You remember what Superman said to Lois Lane when she asked him when she would see him again? He said, 'Perhaps tomorrow, perhaps never.' Okay?"

He hung up the phone, bought a beer from an enterprising guy standing next to the sidewalk with a cooler, and walked toward the stadium.

Minnie had the inside track on a backstage pass because of an old grade school friend of his named Buddy Levine. Buddy had come back from jail in Thailand and, because Minnie had a bad back and had suggested it, he had gone to school to become a chiropractor. At the time, it seemed like a good idea. In school, Buddy had been the friend of a guy, another Deadhead, who became the chiropractor for the guy who was the Dead's doctor. It's a little complicated. Over the years, Buddy and Minnie had been to many shows with these guys. They had all become friends and so, now, when Minnie wanted to go to a show, he simply called The Doctor and he put Minnie on the list. That's the way things worked. It was who made sense. Who you could relate to.

With his pass visible, Minnie waded with the line into the back of the stadium. It was a beautiful day. Blue sky with big puffy white clouds on the horizon, promising eventual relief from the heat. As he came up even with the top of the lower level of seats, Minnie saw a sea of bodies, a blur of colors and movement, both in the seats and on the field. At one end was a huge stage anchored by 50 tons of equipment.

The speakers towered 40 feet over the stage and, out in the crowd, there were four more speakers on the top of huge cranes, just in case anyone missed the sound from the others. Huge tie-dyed banners draped the stage. Recorded music drifted over the dense crowd. People had staked out their spots on the field with blankets and baby carriages and coolers. There was barely room to get by, yet there was constant movement.

Minnie thought it best to be close to the stage and he made the long hike across the field. He wanted to check out the scene and, besides, it would have taken him about an hour and a half to go around the other way. Even though it was all familiar, he never tired of this kind of crowd. They were friendly, generous, and everyone was in a state of great anticipation. Excited, but endlessly patient. This hanging out was a part of the whole experience. Beach balls and balloons bounced through the crowd. Frisbees sailed as if on independent missions. People were looking toward the stage, waiting, or they were embracing or toasting each other or laying back getting the beginnings of a sunburn.

Minnie found a place halfway up in the stands on the left side of the stage. The sound would be good, he could see everything, and he calculated that in about two hours he would be in the shade. He was already soaked from his trek across the field and his face was even redder than its usual high color.

He looked out over the sea of people. The stadium was filling up and he saw thousands of bodies moving as if one huge organism, with uncountable arms, and the whole mass of it appeared to be breathing in its multicolored outfit. It was as if he were having a flashback. He wasn't tripping, but it was one of those hallucinations. He ran a hand over his red dome and took a long gulp of water from the bottle in his pack. The show hadn't even started and he was already getting off.

Just then, three young girls, about 18 years old, made room for themselves right in front of him. They were giggling and talking and had on shorts and tank tops that could only stimulate an imagination like Minnie's. They arranged themselves for the long afternoon. As he took a deep breath of early afternoon air, everything started to feel right — the weather, the vibe, the entire day. And the show was about to begin. Minnie leaned forward, smiling, and introduced himself.

Chapter Seven - Now That I Can Dance

Minnie and the girls got to jive around and talk long enough for him to find out that the cute one, with the flower painted on her bare stomach, was named Susan. Minnie thought that she was really something, though he feared that that something might be too young for him. Hell, he could have been her father.

It didn't seem to matter. He was just a guy sitting behind her and she was cute and friendly. She offered him a joint. It was a promising start. The girls and Minnie were in the middle of smoking it and Lisa, sitting next to Susan, was coughing like crazy, when the band came on stage.

Even though the seats were fairly close, when the Boys walked on, they looked pretty small. They were dwarfed by the equipment and seemed a long way from each other on the huge stage. It was Jerry who stood out. He was wearing shorts, his white bird legs holding up a rather large and relatively old torso. His black shorts, black socks, and black high-tops set off his white skin as if shorts were a discovery new to him. The black t-shirt and dark sunglasses emphasized the mass of white hair and white beard and was a reminder of his age and recent bad health. He looked fragile, but that impression faded quickly as he struck a few warm-up chords on his guitar.

This sound was raw power. From his place in the stands, Minnie could feel it in his chest. It was that loud. The tower of speakers were transmitting the notes directly to each member of the audience with a clarity that was personal and impossible to overlook. Jerry nodded at the other members of the band, counted off the beat, and launched into "New Minglewood Blues."

I was born in the desert
Raised in a lion's den

Forty-seven thousand people rose to their feet, screaming. Arms were thrust upwards in an effort to express something that words couldn't contain: a joyful release of all the anticipation that had been leading up to that moment.

This was a vacation, not only for Minnie, but for everyone else at the show. They were being taken on a trip and they willingly let go of any worries they might have had about where they were going or when or how they were going to get back. Everyone was giving themselves to the music, just like the band was. They were all partners in this beautiful sunny afternoon. A typical city involved in a typical daydream.

The band was in good form and when Jerry went into a solo and it really began to take off, the rock-and-roll energy of it could be felt by everyone. Thousands of arms waved in the air. The crowd reacted with their own wild sounds and wordless exclamation, answering the series of notes that Jerry was playing. Each note seemed to rearrange their DNA. The music was loud. It was one of those days where everything was working together. People danced with each other. They danced with themselves. They sang along. It got better and better. Twirlers twirled, joints were passed, and the tunes rolled on. All through the crowd, people turned to each other to make sure they weren't dreaming and to confirm the fact that the unbelievable thing they had just heard had really happened.

At moments throughout the afternoon, there was an overwhelming poignancy when Jerry sang certain lyrics like "I will survive" or "When I'm gone" or "I'll stay with you." Everyone knew he had been in a coma and had almost died. Everyone knew these guys had been playing together like this for 30 years and they knew that nothing lasted forever — not Jerry, not the band, not themselves, not this moment — and it made it all the more urgent and powerful. When Jerry sang these words, the crowd felt it and sent him a love that was undisguised and immediate. He responded with the music. They loved him and he loved them and this love expanded outward from all of them. These were the words and the feelings that had kept the scene alive for so long.

The first few notes of "China Cat Sunflower" flew out towards the crowd and the level of excitement went even higher. Everyone was dancing.

> *Look for a while at the China Cat Sunflower*
> *Proud-walking jingle in the midnight sun*

Minnie hadn't sat down since the show had started. He had his air guitar going. The girls were dancing in an innocent yet completely sensual way that warmed his heart.

> *Krazy Kat peeking through a lace bandana*
> *Like a one-eyed Cheshire*
> *Like a diamond-eyed Jack*

Minnie's burly self was moving in its own world. The band was cooking. Minnie, by definition, was taking up space. His dancing had escalated along with the music and those in the seats next to him gave way to his effort and to his controlled recklessness. Carried away, he turned it on and turned it loose. His eyes were closed and he shook and he shimmied, while his feet described the indescribable. His entire body became suggestive and ecstatic. Time stood still, but the dance continued.

The band moved flawlessly into "I Know You Rider" and to anyone who turned to watch him, it wasn't really Minnie they saw. He had become something else, bigger than just a big guy dancing. He had become love, sex, music, breath, movement and there it was, right in front of them, exulting in itself and in the fact that all of them were there together.

As the song came to an end, Minnie dipped once more and, in perfect time to the music, he reached upward and shot out of his body. He didn't need wings to propel him. The air became thinner, the stars popped out of the sky, which had turned a deeper blue, and, for a moment, everything was still. Then, slowly, he floated back down to Earth and to Susan and to those around him, who could only applaud and smile in wide admiration.

Meanwhile, the band played on.

Chapter Eight - One More Saturday Night

"St. Stephen," "Truckin'," "Franklin's Tower." The band kept going and time seemed to stretch out and take it a little easier than usual. At the break, Minnie went to find Bowman. He waited outside the bathrooms for half an hour. Bowman never showed. This was aggravating, but typical. To no one in particular, he said, "What an asshole," and returned to his seat. The break stretched on into the hot afternoon.

Minnie and the girls talked and shared sandwiches and beer and stared around at the wild bunch of people in the stands. There was long hair, tattoos, pierced body parts, and brightly colored clothes. Sunglasses and baseball caps were everywhere. Thousands of people were packed into the stadium and yet it was completely peaceful and relaxed. Everyone was having fun.

Minnie and Susan were talking and laughing. He suggested, suggestively, that after the show, she come back to his place to continue the party. Hearing this, she stiffened. Minnie sensed something was wrong.

"What do you think?" He was ready for excuses.

She glanced at her friends, who were talking to some guys with dreadlocks, and then, with a sad expression on her beautiful face, she confessed.

"Minnie," she said in a soft voice while looking down at the empty sunflower seed shells and paper cups beneath her feet, "I'm only 15."

Minnie drew back in shock, but recovered quickly and said, "That's the best 15 I've ever seen."

She smiled, relieved and grateful. "I like you. You're not like any old guy I've ever met."

"Old guy?" Minnie was shocked.

"You know what I mean."

He did, but he didn't want to. He gave her a tolerant smile and said nothing.

"Then it's okay? It doesn't make any difference to you?" She snuggled up to him.

Minnie felt a twinge of conscience and the twinge of something else.

He said, "You're sweet. And gorgeous..." But he hesitated.

It was like he was in a cartoon, with an angel on one shoulder saying, "Min, she's too young," and with a little devil on the other saying, "Go on. She's perfect." They struggled like this over Minnie's evening plans and before a winner emerged, the band came back and the music started up again.

"Johhny B. Goode" was blasting out at them and Susan was dancing wildly. Minnie looked at her. She could really move, 15 or not. He tried to clear his head and shift his focus. He shivered visibly and it must have dislodged his advisors, because soon he was lost again in the music. Or found again. Or something. He was into it.

After a couple more songs, Jerry and Bobby and the others lay down their instruments and left the stage to the two drummers, who took most of the crowd with them to a place where time was skewed and space expanded, the drums talking to each other and the crowd dancing.

After almost 20 minutes of pounding, noodling rhythm, the band returned and joined them in outer space. The guitars wailed in an eerie way, melody stumbled in one direction and then another and then, finally, miraculously, it all began to coalesce. The bass got in step with the notes of the guitars. The drums fell in behind them and suddenly the band was into the first bars of "The Other One" and they were off.

The afternoon continued and, mercifully, the clouds came up to cut the heat and throw a little shade on the audience. They needed it, because the band would not let up. The light had changed into that soft late afternoon glow and Minnie wondered how long the band could continue. When they broke into "One More Saturday Night," he knew that this would be the last song. It built and built, driving everyone crazy. Jerry threw out licks no one could believe, Phil's bass thumped, and Weir sang the words celebrating this and all Saturday nights in the past and in the future.

With one last refrain and the final chomp, chomp, chomp of the guitars, it was over and the crowd erupted with a roar. They weren't tired. As far as they were concerned, Saturday night could have gone on forever. But as the band waved and walked off stage, they knew that was it. They didn't expect an encore. What else could these guys do? They had played their asses off for hours and everyone wished them well. There would be another show tomorrow, but that didn't stop anyone from showing their appreciation. They continued to stomp, scream, and whistle for a long time until, at last, they looked at each other with ear to ear smiles and began to collect themselves and their stuff to leave.

Minnie and the girls gushed and hugged for a while.

Susan turned her huge brown eyes on Minnie, expectantly, and said, "Let's go."

Minnie couldn't look at her and, instead, he made plans with them to meet in the same spot for the show tomorrow. Then he took a deep breath, rolled his eyes, and drew Susan to him in a big hug. He whispered in her ear, "Let's not rush things, kiddo."

He tried to smile and tore himself away. His principles, such as they were, had held. Much to his dismay. He left the girls be-hind and slowly flowed up the aisle with the crowd and thought about what a fool he was. But then, after a minute or two, he caught up with the mood of the moment, which was way upbeat and still excited about the show that had just ended. He tried to remember the songs that had been played.

What a great day, he thought. They were too much. Greatest fucking band in the world.

As he walked down the long ramp to the parking lot, the sun was just past the horizon and the clouds were all lit up in colors no drug could improve. He could see the campground in the distance made up of brightly colored tents and buses and it was bustling with activity. Maybe he'd come back tonight, hang out, and take in the scene.

This thing with Susan was still on his mind. Fifteen? What was his problem? Maybe he should get glasses. Without a doubt, he began to feel old. It might have started to really get to him but, at that moment, he sensed a feminine presence nearby. He smelled perfume and felt the warmth of another body as a thin arm slipped beneath his own. And then he heard the soft words with the unmistakable message.

"Hey, big boy. You look like a guy who wants to be bad."

Chapter Nine - Baby, Baby, Baby

Of course, it was true. He did want to be bad. He always wanted to be bad. And he was bad every chance he got, with a few exceptions, like Susan.

He turned to see who had been reading his mind and found that he was staring at a long, thin, and lovely throat. Then he looked up. This girl, woman, babe (it was hard to tell) was at least a head taller than he was and she was beautiful. She was a goddess. Well, like a goddess.

She had green eyes, shaded by long, dark lashes beneath thin, arched brows. These eyes were looking into his in a most direct and disturbing manner, a hint of a challenge in them, a challenge Minnie was up for. He fell a long way into those eyes before someone bumped into him and he realized he was standing motionless in the way of people who were still on Earth and leaving the concert. He came to and he and the goddess stepped to the side of things.

He couldn't take his eyes off her. He couldn't speak. She had a straight nose, a wide, clear forehead, a red mouth with lips not too thin and all of this was framed by long, blond, big hair. The red lips were smiling at him and he found himself taken by desire. She was tall, long, and thin. She was wearing blue jeans and a loose white top that didn't hide much. The memory of the show melted like snow beside the heat of her.

She was standing quite close to him, waiting.

He finally blurted out, "Hellooo, baby."

This doesn't sound like much, but it had an eloquence all its own. She was listening carefully and she translated it correctly as "You took my breath away. You are the most gorgeous thing I have ever seen. Let's get out of here and lie down."

She turned up the wattage on her smile and Minnie had to move back a step. He could not summon his usual calm, ready-for-anything manner. It had been a long day, but she had suddenly brought him wide awake and totally alert. That wasn't all. His knees were weak, his mouth was dry, and his palms began to sweat.

She leaned closer and said, in a voice that was like warm syrup, "My name is Jasmine. Jasmine DeMenthe."

He swallowed hard. "Minnie, here." It was all he could manage. He couldn't believe his luck. He couldn't believe that this was happening to him, but he wasn't complaining.

Jasmine appreciated his stunned reaction and, squeezing his

arm gently, took control of the situation, as if she didn't have it already, and said, "Let's go to your place."

She then steered him through the crowd and down to the street.

They walked toward his car.

She said, "What a beautiful day. I'm glad it's not raining on all those people in the campground. I wonder what they do there."

She looked at him in a way that made her comment seem suggestive.

He stared at her, still in shock.

She kept talking. "Who are all these people? This town is packed. Cars everywhere. And weird ones, too."

She was a goddess who could discuss the traffic.

He was encouraged. He began to speak.

"Can you believe that concert? They were great. They blew me away. This was one of the great ones."

He raved about the concert and she listened, saying nothing, flashing her smile at him and laughing at his observations in a way that encouraged him to continue. His walk became a bit firmer. He began to feel less like he was complete putty in this woman's hands, though that was an image that struck his fancy, and more like he was in control of things. He stood straighter, he smiled confidently, and he wiggled his eyebrows at her.

When they approached the driveway to the Armory where Minnie had left his car, they saw that it was empty. Minnie had to check his memory. Had he parked somewhere else? The morning seemed like ages ago. They stopped and he looked up and down the street. There was no sign of his red bomb and no note lying on the ground where the car had once been. It had either been towed or stolen. Towed seemed more likely. No wonder he had been able to get a place right across from the stadium.

He burst out, "Fucking Army. Bunch of goddamn boy scouts."

He gave the finger to the now darkened, silent Armory. Then he remembered the goddess. He looked up at her sheepishly. She was smiling as if she knew that this was just another endearing part of his personality.

Without looking away, she raised her long, tanned, perfectly formed arm and, with an elegant whoosh, an immense black limousine drew up to the curb beside them. Almost before it came to a complete stop, a uniformed driver popped out and was around the side of the huge car, holding the door open for them.

This sobered him up a little. Minnie turned to look at her.

What was happening? Who was this woman? Whose car was it? For about two seconds the question, why me, flared in his mind. Then he said to himself, aw, fuck it. He looked closer. She was enjoying his confusion and let out a wonderful laugh.

"You don't want to walk, do you?" she said. "Walking can make you so tired."

Minnie had always believed in saving his strength and so shook his head no and then yes. He was losing his bearings.

Then he looked into those green eyes and said, "Baby, I'm with you."

She beamed at him, melting whatever resistance remained, and climbed in. Minnie followed her and it registered at some level, in his love-crazed mind that, as he got into the limo, he might just be entering a whole new ball game, in a whole new league.

Chapter Ten - Such a Night

Her intentions were clear and this was a game he was more than willing to play. He hadn't been with anyone for what seemed like forever and as much as he liked to think of himself as a wild man and as much as he was, he had also been protecting his heart for quite a while. He wouldn't admit it to anyone and only rarely to himself, but he had been hurt one too many times in the past. The last straw had been Gina giving him back the ring and saying she had a better offer. He had had enough of that shit, but life had to go on. His encounter at the show with Susan had only warmed his blood. He knew that with Jasmine he might get into trouble, but what the hell, he was on vacation.

For a brief moment, he thought of Susan and, in that moment, she appeared even more of a child beside this woman, this vision, this every man's dream named Jasmine DeMenthe. The wide seat of the limo seemed designed to make it difficult to sit upright and Minnie hung on tight when the dream pulled him closer and put her face against his cheek. She breathed hotly into his ear.

Had she asked him to take his clothes off or had she only inquired for the name of his hotel? Minnie found it difficult to think clearly.

"Eugene Holiday Inn," he said in a strangled voice.

She turned her head and spoke to the driver. "Sascha, did you get that?"

Evidently Sascha did, because the limo took off with a force that moved them back into the seat and even closer together. Minnie wasn't complaining.

It was a short trip to the hotel and when they arrived, the driver opened the door for them and then discreetly closed it until their embrace was finished. When Minnie and Jasmine emerged, they were smiling and though their clothes were disheveled, they were glowing like a million bucks. The desk clerk who had given Minnie so much trouble the night before now stood staring at them, actually at Jasmine, with his mouth hanging open as the two of them crossed the lobby.

She had her arm around Minnie's broad waist and though she was clinging to him in a way that should have made walking difficult, they virtually glided to the door of room 1009. He inserted the key and, as he did, she hugged him from behind and he realized he had nerves he had never known about. He couldn't believe this was happening to him. He again wondered why him. He considered this for all of three seconds this time and though many wonderful reasons presented themselves, he decided to let it be and go with the flow.

By the time room service arrived with the champagne and dinner, they were in the shower and the two bottles on ice and several plates full of food were left on the desk in the corner of the big room. Minnie needed a shower after his long day in the sun and from the way Jasmine was taking care of him, he suspected she must have had past experience as a nurse. At the least, she had an expert and imaginative way of washing.

With the light of the bathroom softened by the steam, Minnie thought she resembled a ripe, though tall, cherub floating on clouds. She was soft. She was wet. And she was with him. He asked her to pinch him to make sure he wasn't dreaming and he held her close beneath the warm water.

Even though the warmth of the water and the way it clung to her was endlessly fascinating to him, Minnie thought there might be advantages to lying down. As they both made use of the plump, soft towels, he sent a small prayer of thanks aloft, grateful that he wasn't sleeping in his car or staying on some friend's floor.

They made it safely to the bed and the evening became an endless stretch of alternating anticipation and fulfillment. He could read her response to his touch in the expression on her beautiful face, in the heightened color of her skin, and through wordless sighs full of specific meaning. She somehow knew things about him in a way that bordered on ESP. Things of which Minnie, up to this point, had been totally unaware.

As he poured another glass of champagne, he was amazed that he had found a girl who could teach <u>him</u> tricks.

"You are too much," he said.

"And you are just right," she responded. She shifted slightly and moaned, "Limbo lower now."

In a deep voice, he asked, "How low can you go?" and they broke up laughing.

The taste of her skin and the texture of it was something he was totally unprepared for. This was not the real world as he knew it. They had their own warm world that existed beneath the crisp sheets of the wide bed.

Personal communications had been perfected between them. When she inquired, he answered. What she requested, he provided. What he imagined, she made manifest. And when she beckoned, he was all too willing to come.

Fortunately, the night was young and there were long

moments, minutes, and hours when they each lay, propped on an arm, one admiring the other. It seemed too good to be true, but to Minnie, this was the way things were supposed to be. It had only required a vacation, a change of scene and perspective, to bring it about.

They recharged themselves with champagne and the now cold dinner from the tray. They smiled at each other like fools and he made the suggestion that they do this for at least a week, for starters. She didn't say no. She asked him questions and he was glad to tell her anything. He mentioned the bar and spoke of the islands and of his dreams and boats and bananas and those finicky offshore breezes and the feel of the white sand beneath his feet. He didn't know what he was saying.

He asked her about herself and she was evasive and vague, in a way that seemed odd to him, but it was a small thing, next to the warmth of her skin. She said things like, "It's better not to know," or "I want you to imagine me."

He was willing. He reached out to her. The line between imagination and reality had been erased long ago. She did say that she had once lived in Boulder, which surprised him. Why hadn't he met her?

She asked him other questions, which he found himself, in this pliable state, replying to almost against his will. And then she casually asked him if he had ever been to Guatemala and did he know a guy named Bowman. A red light flashing CAUTION began to blink on and off in his head. He thought immediately about the key. Had he put it in his shoe or his pocket? What was it with her strange questions? He shifted uneasily and it seemed that she had read his alarmed reaction. She moved closer, into the middle of these thoughts. She kissed him, the light stopped flashing, and suddenly all caution was forgotten.

They wrestled and giggled and laughed and made sounds like crazed animals. After more champagne, they regarded each other steadily and hungrily and things took on an even deeper tone of longing.

As the night went on, they grew closer together and farther away from the world outside. The air became thick with the darkness and all conversation ceased. Their sounds became whispers. They floated on the sea of sheets and swam toward each other. A rhythm began once again, though this time in darkness. Despite his vast experience, Minnie had never felt this way before. It seemed to him that there was no world, no bar, no worry, no time. Only their two bodies existed. That night, desire was their password and they passed it back and forth endlessly.

Chapter Eleven - The Wakeup Call

Minnie surfaced just before dawn. He was lying on his side and when he half-opened his eyes, he saw a faint light coming from behind the thick curtains. Even that was too bright. He closed his eyes again and mumbled "holy cow" as a way of expressing, even in sleep, his appreciation of and admiration for Jasmine.

She froze when she heard this. And not because she wanted to bask in its implications, but because she didn't want to be forced to complicate things. She was fully dressed and awake and, at that moment, going through what Minnie called his wallet. This was a wad of cards, bills, and notes, about two inches thick, held together by a wide rubber band. She had already gone through his bag, such as it was, and had found no useful information. Minnie muttered something she couldn't decipher and then settled into the pillow and began snoring softly.

She hadn't found what she wanted and decided that she would have to become more direct or more sneaky or try some unused trick to get what she needed. But for now, it was better to leave. If she stayed, there would be too many questions. Questions she didn't want to answer, especially in broad daylight. She wrote him a note.

Minnie—
Sleep on, sweet prince. I'll see you later. The night time is the right time to be with the one you love.

Jasmine

She placed it on the table by his bed and, as she did, she looked down at him without emotion. He was defenseless, at peace, and smiling. Her own face, so worshipped last night by Minnie, appeared in the cool light of morning as a mask that she carried with her. Though undoubtedly beautiful, it was as smooth and as brittle as glass. Minnie gave out a loud snort, which startled her, and she turned and walked quickly to the door. She let herself out silently as Minnie dreamed on.

Three hours later, Minnie still lay beneath the covers, deep in sleep.

What was it that woke him? Was it the car going by outside on the street below, or the birds singing in the glow of a new day, or was it the shiver of pleasure as his body remembered what had gone on the night before? It may have been the insistent knock on the door.

Minnie blinked a few times and with a groggy smile turned toward Jasmine and delight. He was surprised to find the space next to him empty and called toward the bathroom, but there was no answer. The racket at the door finally registered in his brain.

Deftly summing up the facts that Jasmine had gone, that he had a slight headache from the champagne, and that someone would not stop knocking, he growled, "Go away. I'm sleeping."

He thought vaguely that it might take two cups of Bowman's coffee to get him going today.

The knocking continued.

Minnie got out of bed, grumbled audibly as he pulled on his shorts, and stomped toward the door, ready to tear into whoever was so unwise as to do this to him.

He yanked the door open and the sunlight blinded him temporarily. He felt the heat and realized that the day was in full progress. Squinting, he saw a balding, paunchy guy with a pink complexion and tiny eyes. This odd figure, dressed in a suit, stood there, smiling patiently at him. Smiling in a way that might be trying to ingratiate or nauseate. It wasn't clear. Minnie noticed the big industrial/remedial shoes that held this blimp to the ground and immediately thought, cop.

"You've got the wrong room, man," Minnie said. He turned to go back inside.

A big, shiny toe blocked the door and the man said, "Mr. Minion, I'd like to speak with you for a minute."

"That's fine, but I need my sleep."

"It's rather important."

"So's my sleep."

The man reached into his jacket and pulled out a slim leather wallet and, holding it at arm's length, flipped it open in front of Minnie's face. Minnie inspected the card behind the plastic. There was a photograph, almost flattering, of the man before him and at the top of the card, in bold letters, it read INTERNAL REVENUE SERVICE. Minnie leaned closer and read the man's name — Edward Alan Kimberly.

"You can call me Ed."

It was too early in the morning for this kind of stuff.

"Ed, it's nice to meet you but I'm on vacation. Besides that, my extension is good until January. Just send me a letter."

"Mr. Minion, this is about another matter. One that won't wait." Ed made no move to leave. "I paid a visit to your bar, but you had already left."

"You should have waited for me." Minnie let out a groan. "Don't you guys understand vacation?"

Ed was impassive.

Minnie asked, "You don't have a warrant, do you?"

"We don't need warrants."

Minnie took a deep breath and nodded. It was obvious that he wasn't getting rid of this guy until he heard him out. "Okay, Ed. Come on in."

They talked. Or rather, Ed talked. He took out a small notebook, which he referred to from time to time. He had a long prepared speech. It started out as a polite expression of thanks from the IRS for Minnie's contributions through the years and then, regretfully, brought up what Ed called a misunderstanding about foreign income. This was a reference to Minnie's time in the islands when he had made a fortune selling mosquito-netting and had determined that he needn't pay the IRS what they considered their fair share.

"Ed, that was years ago."

Ed made a sick noise, which was his version of laughing, and said, "Mr. Minion, the IRS never forgets."

He continued and, as he did, his face took on an increasingly stern expression and gradually hardened, as much as its pudginess would allow. He got down to numbers.

"And so, Mr. Minion, you owe us," he looked down at his notebook, "$43,863.34. Payment in that amount is due December 31st. In full."

Minnie was in shock. This was a nightmare.

"Payment in full. And no extensions, partial payments, or excuses. Full payment," the big agent paused dramatically, "or jail."

"Jail?!"

Ed nodded solemnly. They stared at each other. Ed wasn't budging. Minnie couldn't believe this was happening.

Minnie finally said, "I've got a lawyer."

"So do we."

Minnie laughed nervously. "Couldn't we make a deal? Or something?"

Ed smiled for the first time since he entered the room. It turned Minnie's stomach.

"Well, Mr. Minion, there is something you could do for us."

Minnie couldn't imagine what that might be. He waited. Ed stared at him, but said nothing. It was awkward.

Minnie inclined his head toward Ed and said, slowly, as if he were speaking to a child, "And this thing is...?"

Ed kept staring stolidly at him and, after a moment, said, "I won't beat around the bush. We'd like you to get some information for us about the Grateful Dead. You seem to be on good terms with them."

Minnie laughed. He had been backstage and had even talked with Weir once, but that was it.

"We know they don't respect us."

Minnie laughed even harder at this. "Who does? You hassle us all year, you take all our money, and then you just piss it away."

For a moment, Ed said nothing. Then he patiently explained, as if it should have been obvious.

"Look, the Grateful Dead make a lot of money. They're not paying their fair share and we want it."

"It would only seem fair to you guys if they gave you everything. I've heard that the IRS has been hassli ng the Dead for years. Anything to try and screw up a good thing."

Ed ignored these comments. He continued, "Evasion is not a viable option. This is a lesson you could benefit from."

Minnie was tired of this conversation. He shook his head. "You guys are so fucked up." He couldn't believe this. "So what's the deal? You want me to spy on the Dead, like that's even possible, or pay you money I don't have, or go to jail."

Ed smiled again. "I'm glad we understand each other." He nodded and crossed the room.

Minnie just looked at him. This was absurd. It wasn't even noon yet.

"We'll be in touch," Ed said, as he turned and slipped out the door, leaving Minnie to think it over.

Chapter Twelve - Weasels Demanded My Flesh

"Goddamnit," Minnie said, as he pounded the arm of the chair. "Little weasels," he muttered. "And where's Jasmine? She could have at least said good-bye."

Then he saw the note on the dresser and read it. Okay, he thought, that's not so bad. He liked the "sweet prince" part.

He walked into the bathroom, turned on the water, and grabbed his toothbrush. He looked at himself in the mirror. Despite the visit of the IRS and Jasmine's departure, he softened at the thought of her. He was smiling, thinking of their wild night.

"What a woman."

He began to dance suggestively in front of the mirror and let out a soul shout. "Watch me now. Unnh!"

Then the reality of owing 43 grand to the IRS came back to him.

"Sons of bitches," he seethed. He stuck his tongue out at the mirror and began brushing his teeth. He continued his conversation through it all.

"Agggh du te fing they are? It's none da guwan bidness."

In the middle of this rant, he thought he heard someone at the door again. He turned off the water and listened. It was an unmistakable knocking. His heart jumped a little, thinking it might be Jasmine, but it seemed a bit too heavy. He listened some more. It definitely wasn't her. He took the toothbrush out of his mouth, made a face, and said to the mirror, "That asshole. He probably thinks I owe him money from the bar, too. Jesus."

He continued brushing as he walked to the door. He pulled it open with one hand and held the toothbrush in the other. There was a white foam on his mustache that only a dentist could love.

"Now what?" he bellowed.

But it wasn't Ed at all. Instead, he found a tall thin man in a blue military uniform, complete with brass buttons which were blinding in the bright sunlight.

Minnie shook his head. "Sorry, Sarge. Wrong room."

The man showed a smile as thin as the new moon and then, with a sharp, mechanical gesture, he saluted.

It caught Minnie by surprise.

"Mr. Minion," he said crisply. "I'm Colonel J. M. Able, U.S. Air Force, Andrews Air Force Base, temporarily on special assignment to Central Intelligence."

Minnie stared. Water from his toothbrush ran down his left hand.

Colonel Able's arm jerked suddenly and pulled from his pants pocket a piece of paper, which he held out toward Minnie.

"Documentation on your vehicle," he said simply.

"My vehicle?" Minnie examined the piece of paper.

"We took the liberty of washing it."

Minnie tried to think, but it was difficult.

Finally, he said, "You mean, you guys towed my car, washed it, and now are returning it to me?"

"That's right."

"I don't get it."

The Colonel cleared his throat. "Well," he paused. "May I?" he asked.

Minnie didn't know what he was agreeing to, but nodded with all the authority he could muster.

The Colonel shifted instantly from attention to at ease. His right leg moved sideways and his hands clasped each other behind his back. He began to elaborate.

"We requisitioned your vehicle at 1200 hours. It was about to be towed by order of the city PD. Glad to be able to do you a service."

Minnie didn't understand what all this meant, but he remembered that the towing of his car had occasioned the limo ride with Jasmine. He was about to thank the Colonel, when he was asked, "Mr. Minion, do you love your country?"

"Well, sure."

"And would you defend her against her enemies if the need arose?"

"What enemies?"

"Let's not be funny, Mr. Minion. They are everywhere."

Without thinking, Minnie looked around. He saw no one.

The Colonel asked, "Could we continue this conversation inside?"

This was the weirdest day Minnie could remember. "Uh, sure," he said. "Why not?" Then he put his finger to his lips and looked quickly in both directions for enemies. "Can't be too careful."

The Colonel nodded curtly in agreement and entered the hotel room.

There was something about the Colonel that made Minnie tolerate this bullshit. He reminded him of a math teacher from high school, Mr. Holstein, an ex-marine who always seemed a little slow and who had made Minnie's life miserable. He and Minnie fought all senior year until one time Minnie got in trouble for being a loud mouth. It wasn't the first time, but for a reason Minnie never quite understood, Mr. Holstein had defended him to the principal and saved him from being expelled. This Colonel seemed a lot like Mr. Holstein and had some of the same qualities — a complete lack of humor and an absurd but endearing earnestness.

Minnie returned his toothbrush to the bathroom, wiped his mouth, and, before going back into the room, shot himself an inquiring look in the mirror. He took a deep breath and went to see the Colonel.

Minnie said, "Have a seat." The Colonel sat, with military grace, placing his hat on his knees. He had a posture that seemed impossible to Minnie. The contrast between the two of them was ironic and Minnie was very aware of it. He wondered just what was going on.

"Mr. Minion, sir, I won't waste your time. Let me get right down to business. We, the intelligence branch of the government, are not as narrow-minded as you might think."

Minnie's eyes opened wider.

"We are aware of phenomena that occur for which we have no satisfactory explanation. Phenomena that, even though they are odd or weird, can be of service to the country: ESP, homeopathy, communication with plants, meditation, Voodoo. In the defense of the nation, nothing can be ruled out. For years, we have watched the rise of rock-and-roll — with interest and with some alarm."

He attempted to smile.

"Elvis was one of ours, you know. Served in Germany with honor. Mr. Jerry Garcia, on the other hand, resembles Karl Marx in a way that we think is more than coincidental. We've been using advanced genetic imaging techniques in investigating this and, also, our cryptonics agents have noted similarities in phrasing and general philosophical intent. I am personally disturbed by lyrics like 'Believe it if you need it, if you don't, just pass it on.'"

The Colonel was on a roll.

"Mr. Minion, the Agency, through its investigations, has learned that music, even rock-and-roll music, has special properties that go beyond mere entertainment and that may have application of a more strategic nature. Though we haven't confirmed this, we have long heard rumors to the effect that, at a certain concert of the Grateful Dead, the audience, through the influence of the music, achieved an independence of gravity. Levitation, in other words. Surely, Mr. Minion, you can imagine the value to us and to your country of such an ability."

Minnie tried.

"We want to study this. In secret, of course. We want to explore its possibilities and its feasibilities. We feel it has distinct military potential." He paused.

This was too much for Minnie. Was the Colonel high? Were they both high? Was he still dreaming? The clock on the desk said 12:05. He realized he hadn't eaten yet. What was all this? First, Jasmine, then the IRS, and now Colonel Able.

"Colonel, I don't know why you're telling me about this stuff. All I know is that the show starts at 2:30 and I've got to get going. So. . . ." He stood up.

The Colonel's voice was like a shot. "Mr. Minion, we want that tape."

"What tape?"

Minnie sat down. Able nodded.

"The bootleg of one of the last appearances of a singer called Pigpen. May 25th, 1972, to be precise. We've determined that you have the only copy. We need it. It would be a great service to your country. And your service would not go unrewarded." He smiled or tried to.

Minnie played along. He was thinking of his taxes.

"Rewarded?"

"A large sum of money and the gratitude of the President and the nation."

This was too weird.

"I can't believe I've got the only copy," he said, but he wanted to play along to find out just what this was about. "Hmm. Let me think about it. I'm not even sure I have that tape. Okay?"

The Colonel stood. "Fine. Think it over. We'll be in contact. In the meantime, you can rest assured we'll be watching out for you. But. . . ." His eyes narrowed. "We want that tape and mean to get it."

He didn't need to say any more, but he added, in a voice quite different, "Use the Armory parking lot today if you like. And don't worry about a thing. I'll fix it so you don't get towed."

He came to attention, saluted once more, and marched out of the room, closing the door behind him. Minnie was still sitting in the chair by the desk, shaking his head.

"What the fuck?"

Chapter Thirteen - Just One More Hit

The show started soon and Minnie had to get going. He also wanted to get out of his room before anything else happened. He locked the door and hopped into the shower.

After the events of the morning, the water hitting him in the face was a relief. All these weirdos — taxes, tapes — it was too much. And how did they know where to find him? He couldn't figure it out. Maybe, somehow, they'd all forget about him. He would go to the show, have a good time, get a good night's sleep, and be off in the red bomb the next morning to go fishing. That's what he really needed, not this unexplained and undeserved aggravation.

Maybe he should just take off now. He considered it, but then he flashed on the creamy texture of Jasmine's skin and on what had happened the night before. He couldn't leave her behind, or any other part of her. He laughed at his own joke. Even if she had slipped out early this morning and even if she didn't love him, which she probably didn't, she knew more about making love than anyone he had ever met. She was unbelievable, she was beautiful, she was an encyclopedia of love. He had to see her. Plus, he couldn't miss the show. It was as important as anything he did, even fishing. More than just a show, more than just rock-and-roll, The Dead always showed him something larger than himself, a possibility in which he had a part to play.

He heard it, as he was drying off. He acted as if he didn't, but it continued. He thought if he took his time it might stop. He dressed unhurriedly, but still he heard it. More knocking at the door. It flashed through Minnie's mind that hotel rooms, with their single entrance and exit, were of a flawed design. Even the fucking windows wouldn't open.

The knock, this time, was different than the ones before. It was not the patient, though insistent, knocking of the IRS or the no-nonsense rap of the military. This was a rhythmic, playful knocking and, once he figured this out, Minnie's heart skipped a couple of beats, thinking it might be Jasmine returning. He was at the door in two steps and pulled it open.

He was disappointed. It wasn't Jasmine. Instead, a young man stood before Minnie, smiling. He had on a bright tie-dyed t-shirt, black shorts, tie-dyed socks, and red tennis shoes. He was much younger than Minnie and had all his hair. In fact, he had more hair than Minnie ever had in his whole life. This kid had a ponytail that went halfway down his back and was about three inches thick and it sprouted out of a head of hair that should have had knitting needles stuck in it or robins nesting.

He had one immensely thick dark eyebrow that ran across his forehead and shaded his dark brown eyes — eyes that Minnie noted were quite dilated and bloodshot and appeared to be laughing and a little wild. The guy's beard ran off in every direction. This eyebrow and a mustache seemed to keep all the other hair at bay and allowed at least part of his face — his nose and eyes — to function freely. He had a big friendly smile and his teeth shone out of this cave of growth.

They contemplated each other for a moment. Then the kid with the hair said, "Hi. You must be Minnie. My name's Burger."

"You're the first normal person I've seen all morning." Minnie said. Then he held out his hands in apology. "You know, I don't have an extra ticket for the show today. I'm sorry." He started to close the door.

Burger shook the stuff on his head. "I'm not trying to score a ticket, but thanks. I need to talk with you. Can I come in?" He was still smiling.

Given recent events, Minnie was a little wary and said, "And who are you? You're not with the IRS or the Air Force or a narc or something are you?"

The kid laughed. "Man, you are too paranoid. I'm just a guy. I work for the Dead."

Minnie nodded. Another weirdo. "You don't have anything to prove that, do you? A card, a uniform, or something?"

Burger kept smiling. "No. Just me. Just what I'm telling you."

Minnie considered. This seemed like the first straight answer he had gotten all morning.

He said, "What the hell. It can't get any stranger than it's been. Come on in."

Minnie felt bad. This guy did seem pretty normal, whether he worked for the Dead or not. He could, at least, check him out. At the bar and in general, Minnie operated a lot on intuition. He wasn't always right, but it had served him well. He felt like he could trust this guy.

"I'm sorry. It's just been a tough morning."

Burger nodded. Minnie closed the door and they each took a chair.

Minnie said, "Burger? Like cheeseburger?"

The kid laughed. "No. I'm vegetarian. Burger is my name. Wendell Burger, but everyone calls me Burger."

All of a sudden, Minnie got a little uptight. "Hey, how did you know my name?"

"It's a long story. Let's see..." Burger got up and started to pace slowly back and forth. He said, "You want to smoke a joint or something?"

Minnie shook his head. "I don't think so. I want to find out what this is all about first. You guys don't want money or something, do you? You're not pissed about the bootlegs, are you?"

Burger smiled and waved this away. "No. You're cool. The truth is we need your help. The Dead do."

"They need my help? That's a good one."

The hair nodded.

"Well," Burger shrugged, "it's true." He went into his rap. "Here's the deal. You know that the Dead are interested in more than just music. You probably know about their environmental trip and the Rex Foundation. They keep their eyes open and they've got a lot of guys like me doing stuff for them. They've got all this dough and they're trying to do something good with it. So, we've got a lot of projects going. Being close to the street, we hear a lot of things. And lately, we've been hearing a lot about coffee."

"Coffee?"

This made Minnie sit up. This was a weird coincidence. First, the meeting with Bowman and the whole key business and now this guy with his talk about helping the Dead. What was going on? All these weirdos. He just wanted to get to the show and hear the music.

Burger's gestures became more emphatic as he continued. "Yeah. You know, there are tons of coffee places all over. Actually, there are like 5000 places in the U.S. alone. Gourmet stuff. Just think of all that caffeine. Just think what it could do to you."

Minnie laughed. "Man, I can see what it's done to you. You ought to cut down on that stuff."

Burger stopped for a moment and, with an bewildered look, said, "I don't even drink it."

He started up again. "But it seems like everybody is into it. The problem is that most of it is grown in Third World countries. The people there who do the work and the land that they grow the coffee on both get fucked by the guys making all the money. It's serious. And it's big money. There's like a 400 percent mark-up and that's just at retail. Think about the guys who deal the beans. That kind of money makes people crazy."

Burger's pacing accelerated. His frantic energy was calming

Minnie down, who sat back waiting for the next part of the story.

"One of the things we're working on is checking this stuff out. And the Dead want you to help us."

"Me?" Minnie laughed. "Why me? What's their problem? I'm just an old guy from Boulder who runs a bar."

Burger stopped and said, "You know Bowman."

Minnie was shocked and shaken. He said nothing. He thought again of the key he had. Where the fuck was Bowman? Things were beginning to get a little strange and he was beginning to get worried.

Burger said, "Well, we know him, too. As you can imagine, we know a lot of people. We know he's dealing a little coffee. He even gives us some. But he's in trouble now or thinks he is. He told us about you. We thought you could help him and us by finding out what's going on."

"Get him to find out for you. It's his trip." Minnie was on vacation, but Bowman was his friend and he was curious, so he asked, "How deep is he in?"

"Not deep at all, but it's weird. He says he's stirring up a lot of interest, even though he's not really involved. We like him and we don't want him to get hurt."

"What do you mean hurt?"

"Well, you never know when there's that much money involved. We want to find out more about the guys who are hassling him. Would you help us check it out?"

"Uh, sure, but really, aside from Bowman, why me? I don't know anything about it. You must have tons of people who could do this. I'm on vacation."

"Well, you know how it is." Burger looked away nervously and didn't speak for a moment.

After all the talk, this quiet seemed strange to Minnie. It didn't last long.

Burger said, "Well, you know, the guys have seen your face at the shows. They like you. And," he emphasized, "you know Bowman." Suddenly, he stopped his pacing and looked directly at Minnie. "You haven't talked with him lately, have you?"

This made Minnie nervous. Bowman's warning came back to him.

"Why?"

"Well, we're just trying to find him. You know, see how he is." He coughed and resumed walking back and forth. "Anyway, we just thought you might be in touch with him and could help us.

48

We thought you could help us with this other stuff too." He shrugged. "You know, it just feels right."

"Well, I'm flattered, but check this out. The IRS was here this morning and they want me to spy on the Dead about taxes. I owe them money and they say I have to get some info on the Dead's money trip for them or they'll put me in jail. Everyone seems to think I've got these connections. To you guys, to Bowman. It's weird."

Now Minnie stood up and started pacing back and forth. He thought about Bowman and his damn key and about Bowman's warnings. "It makes me nervous. I just came out here to see the shows. To relax. And now all this shit is happening."

Both of them pacing was too much. Burger stopped, sat in a chair, and tried to calm Minnie down. "Don't worry. Don't worry. Everything's cool. In fact, here's what we can do about the IRS."

"I don't want your money."

"It's not money."

Minnie was still walking back and forth.

Burger said, "Hey, you understand that there's no pressure to do this, right? Okay? But first, do you want to help us?"

Even though the thought occurred to him, Minnie knew he couldn't run out on either Bowman or the Dead. "Well, yeah. You guys, the band, have helped me for a long time. I'd be glad to try to do something for them."

"Okay." Burger thought for a moment. "The IRS wants the Dead's money. They think the band is making too much and paying too little. It's true that they've been on our back. I don't know why they came to you, but this can work for all of us. The coffee guys, the Coffee Cartel..."

"Coffee Cartel? You make it sound like they're moving cocaine or something."

"Well, that's what we call them. Hey, it's all money. They're not that different. The Cartel is all about money. And it's money the IRS never sees. You can imagine how they feel about that. Maybe, if you can get enough info about them, you could get the IRS off our backs and onto the coffee guys. Then the IRS would get the big money, which is what they want, and maybe they'd lay off you. It's worth trying."

Minnie began to see the possibilities.

"In the meantime, the show's going to start soon. I'll be backstage. You've got your ticket?"

Minnie said, "I've got a pass."

Burger nodded. "Okay, come and see me during the break and we'll figure out what's next. Don't worry. It's going to be great. It's great now, just hard to see it sometimes."

He stood up. He was smiling.

"I gotta go. Here's a little something for the show." He pulled a fat joint out of his pocket and handed it to Minnie.

Minnie took it. "Thanks." Then he raised his arms in frustration and said, "Burger, all this is too weird."

Burger nodded, shrugged, and then dismissed Minnie's worries by saying, "Yeah, but it might be fun. See you in a little while."

He walked out the door and Minnie took a closer look at the joint. It was rolled in a paper that had the Dead's skull and roses printed on it.

"Far out."

He straightened up the room, which meant throwing all his clothes on one chair. He put the phone back on the hook and collected his wallet and keys from the top of the dresser. His wallet looked odd. Even though it was a mess, it was a mess that he knew well. He was certain someone had been fooling with it. He had a sinking feeling it was Jasmine.

Just then the phone rang. It made him jump.

Chapter Fourteen - Fire Up The Disco Bus

He didn't know whether to answer the phone or not. He looked at his wallet again. What was going on?

Thinking it might be Jasmine, and that maybe she could explain, he picked it up.

"Yeah?"

"Minnie. This is Cowboy."

"How'd you get this number?"

"Minnie, we need you. This place is insanity. We can't figure out the orders. We can't keep up with stuff."

Minnie interrupted. "Cowboy, I'm on vacation. Okay? Don't bug me. I'll be back in a couple of days. I've got to take care of a few things here."

He hung up, grabbed his wallet and left before anything else could happen.

He drove straight to the Armory. He was going to take the Colonel at his word and make use of the parking spot. It was weird. Not only had they washed his car, they had filled the tank. Minnie thought the Colonel was delirious. Levitation? He had been high many times before and many strange and wonderful things had happened, but never levitation. The Colonel didn't get it. It wasn't your body you had to move, it was your mind.

Minnie thought that Bowman had better show up today. He wanted to get rid of the key. Everything was too weird. But it was another beautiful day, too beautiful to worry about all that had happened to him that morning. He was determined to enjoy the show. This was vacation, after all, and the Boys were going to play. He had a big joint in his pocket and there were girls in Section 153.

The scene was a repeat of the day before. Tons of people strolling to the show, having fun, hanging out. As he walked past the parked cars, he could hear bits of the Dead's music emerge from tape players and boom boxes.

He walked through the campground to check it out. There were tents and buses and people everywhere. Kids, really. They all seemed so young, like Susan, and this was their summer camp. A summer of traveling around following the Dead, going from show to show, looking for tickets or just hanging out enjoying the scene.

There were stands that sold organic food, drinks, and desserts. It was like an Indian bazaar or a camp of gypsies or the midway at the state fair. All kinds of things were laid out on blankets for sale — pipes, jewelry, windchimes, exotic clothing. People walked through the crowd with boxes of marijuana cookies and brownies or just selling it straight. They were discreet but not hiding anything. They didn't need to. Here was a gathering of what? Several thousand people? Kids. And no parents, no authority, no police.

Even though he had seen this before, it always amazed him. At night it would be in full swing with 300 people dancing to conga drums over there by the trucks and others dancing by the food booths and singing. There was even a disco bus that started up after dark. Here in the heart of Dead country, dancing was like breathing.

Everywhere you looked joints and beer were being consumed and shared. Campers lived side by side, closely packed on the fields around the stadium and even on the hard asphalt of the parking lot. All of this activity existed and there was no conflict, no fights. Everyone was peaceful and they got along. They helped each other. It was a wonderful and unlikely thing and had all grown out of the music.

Minnie grabbed a burrito and munched his way into the stadium. As he came out to where he could see it all, he thought it was like coming over the hill from Denver at night and seeing the lights of Boulder spread out below you, always surprising and exciting and tinged with a feeling of coming home.

The place was packed and they were playing Elvis over the sound system. He wondered, for a moment, if he would ever find the girls and the place they had all been just yesterday.

He needn't have worried. They were looking for him. He heard his name called by three young girls, the gorgeous Susan among them, and he lit up with pleasure. He adjusted his Moonbeam Tavern cap, and made his way over to them with a big smile on his face, like a sheik to his harem.

Susan put her arms around his neck and gave him a big kiss. Not feeling guilty, or parental, or whatever his confused feelings of the day before had been, he enjoyed the moment. The girls all talked at the same time and told him about their own wild night with the guys with the dreadlocks. Despite his adventure with Jasmine, Minnie felt jealous. Protective, too.

He looked at Susan. "Did you get home all right?"

She smiled and made a goofy face. "Yes, Dad. I was home by 12."

Though this was just friendly teasing, it pained him. They

were young. He was old. Well, older. He started to do the math. Fuck that, he thought. It's all relative. The hell with it. He determined to put these worries behind him and pulled out the joint from the Dead.

He didn't tell them the story behind it or about any of the other stuff, especially Jasmine. They all discovered just how good a joint could be. The show hadn't started, but they were dancing, music or no music.

A little later, Susan stood next to him while the other girls were talking with the dreadlocks. She said, "Minnie, you're a sweetie."

He liked to hear that.

She smiled at him in a way that didn't quite match the mostly innocent image he had of her and said, "I think we should make love."

He looked at her. He thought so too and said, "Right now?"

She laughed. "No, you goon. Later."

He nodded his head, but knew he had decided that one yesterday. He sighed, not quite believing he had such scruples.

There was a squeal of feedback and then the band walked up to the microphones and plugged in. Without speaking to the huge crowd and with barely a nod of the head, the band started off with "Here Comes Sunshine." Minnie forgot all about the visit of the three wise men that morning and got into the music. He and the girls climbed onto the seats and started shaking. Everywhere they looked, they saw wildness and dancing and people smiling. The tie-dyed flags waved in a gentle breeze and though summer was drawing to a close, it couldn't have been a more beautiful day.

As the set went on, however, and as Minnie came down a little from the joint, he began to think of his meeting with Burger backstage. He wondered what he was getting into and not for the last time either. The key in his pocket seemed to get heavier the longer he had it.

He could feel the set building toward the end and knew if he didn't start down to the stage soon, it would take him forever. Once the music stopped and the break started, everyone would be trying to get to the bathrooms or scoping out a better view or just trying to walk around. The aisles would be impassable.

He turned and gave Susan a kiss. It lasted longer than he intended, but he didn't regret it. He waved at the girls and said, "See you in a little bit."

He began his descent.

Chapter Fifteen - Who Put The Bop?

It took him a while to make it to the field and to the fence that separated the stage area from the crowd. As he approached, he saw that on the stage side there was a wide, open, calm space populated only by a few bouncers — big guys, all about six-eight and 400 pounds, in yellow shirts. He noticed their small ears or ears that in relation to everything else seemed small, like fortune cookies taped to the side of their heads. It was a sad thing, but these bruisers appeared to have no necks and no rhythm. From their places in front of the stage, they stared vacantly at the crowd, like Secret Service men.

On Minnie's side of the fence, it was all animated chaos. As he moved through the crowd, there hadn't been any empty spaces. Bodies moved in response to the music. Color everywhere. Looking from the calm to the storm, from one side of the fence to the other, was disorienting. Minnie saw guys dancing awkwardly and girls shaking everything they had. There were children on their parents' shoulders and most of them were smiling, enjoying the music. On his way down, he had passed by two women, blonde and bikinied. On their heads were nuns' wimples shielding their bare shoulders from the sun. They were posing for a photograph and they bent toward the camera, showing a lot of teeth and cleavage.

He had gone as far as was permitted. He squeezed through to a big guy in yellow, manning the entrance to the stage area, and flashed his pass. The bouncer's blank facade cracked with a smile, which revealed him to be a cream puff in a hulk's body, and Minnie was waved through.

As he walked by the side of the stage, on his way to the back, he could feel the intensity of the crowd behind him. All that attention focused in one direction was like a physical force. He passed the four or five privileged twirlers in the wide area between the stage and the stands. He watched as these beautiful (how could they all be beautiful?) girls in thin dresses and bare feet, spun around and around, like Sufis, arms extended and long hair swirling. They made him dizzy.

He passed through the shadow cast by the tower of speakers and found himself in back of the music. He thought there might be one or two songs left before the break. Looking around, it wasn't what you might call crowded, especially after being out front, but there were a fair number of people hanging around, many part of the crew, responsible for all this equipment. On stage there were a couple of guys working the monitors and tending to equipment. Most of the backstage people were off in a room in the stadium building, behind the stage, loading up on refreshments.

Minnie had been here before, but never with a purpose other than to use the bathroom and scarf some food. Everyone seemed uptight and always made him feel a little unwelcome. It seemed too much like work. He would rather be out in front where the show was really happening. The sound was better, too.

How the Dead thought he could be of help still seemed a valid question, but he knew he was here to get involved in something to do with coffee and the IRS and his old friend Bowman. Despite Bowman's trouble, he had to laugh. It was totally bizarre and hard to believe that a guy like himself could help the Dead.

It was all making him a little anxious. Where was Bowman? What was going on? Everything was getting weird, but he had to admit to the anticipation of an unlooked-for adventure. This wasn't the late-night stale beer grind of the bar, but a real adventure taking him, not to the inevitable closing time, but toward something unknown, something that might call on a larger part of himself than the one that kept things running smoothly and predictably.

He found a place where he could hear and see the band, but still be out of the way. He looked around for Burger, didn't see him, and decided to wait a little while. A few people were back there, digging the band, beer in hand, moving to the music. He looked across the big stage to the other side for Burger, but he didn't see him there, either. Perhaps Burger had been jiving him and didn't really work for the Dead. He was just another long-hair playing out some fantasy. Minnie had been softened up from the visits of Ed and Colonel Able and had accepted his whole act without any trouble. That would be a little disappointing but, what the hell, it was a warm, sunny day and this was a great show.

The band was doing "Playing In The Band" and Minnie was getting carried away.

> *I can tell your future*
> *Look what's in your hand*
> *But I can't stop for nothing*
> *I'm just playing in the band*

Minnie's eyes were shut and he was way into it when he felt a tap on his shoulder. With a big smile on his face, he turned and was surprised to find Burger and all his hair smiling back. Burger leaned close and said, above the music, "Glad you made it. Let's talk." He gestured offstage.

Minnie reluctantly pulled himself away and they walked to where it was quieter. There were small groups of people hanging out. The music was loud, but you didn't have to shout to be heard. They headed toward a place in the shade near two guys and a woman who were talking and laughing.

As Minnie and Burger approached, the woman ended her conversation and joined them. Minnie's eyes lit up, as they did for all women, but this woman was too much. When he looked at her, it was hard to catch his breath. Of course, she was good-looking, but lately it seemed that every woman was. She was something different.

She was about Minnie's height and, to his New Jersey eyes, foreign-looking and exotic. She had thick, shiny, black hair that hung straight to her shoulders, framing a face that glowed. It was a face he might have dreamed about, a blend of features, perfectly proportioned, that would make any guy weak. She had black eyebrows and lashes and a big smile. She was wearing a blue t-shirt and a short skirt with a flowered pattern. Below it were great legs, ending in sandals, but it was her eyes that really grabbed him. They looked straight at him with an unmistakable intelligence. She was checking him out. She was taking his measure. She wanted to know who he was beneath all his show. He saw her undisguised and unintimidated curiosity; it sparked his own.

Burger stretched out his arm and she moved into it, though never taking her eyes off Minnie. If shyness had been a bigger part of his makeup, he would have begun blushing.

Burger introduced her. "Minnie, I want you to meet Kiko Bahiana."

Minnie said, "That's beautiful. What kind of name is that?"

"Kiko?" she said.

"Well, that too, but Bahiana?"

"It's Brazilian."

He thought bossa nova, beaches, and babes. He envied Burger this wonderful girlfriend, but was glad to meet her and said so.

Burger said, "Kiko is going to be working with you on this coffee thing. She's been investigating it for months and is up to date on Bowman and all that."

Minnie couldn't believe it. He was going to be working with her? She would be working with him? And what did up to date on Bowman mean? He reached into his pocket and felt the key.

Burger said, "Let's go somewhere where we can really talk."

Kiko and Burger turned and even though Minnie was eager to find out about everything and get to know Kiko, he held up a finger and said, "I've got to hear just one more tune."

Chapter Sixteen - Baby, What You Want Me To Do?

It turned out that one more tune was all there was. The band got to the end and, amid the cheers of the crowd, walked off the stage for their break. They walked right past Minnie, who had been leaning on some speaker cases. As he passed, Jerry gave what Minnie interpreted as a particularly significant look. Minnie was all smiles, rendered a little goofy by everything that had happened to him on this vacation so far.

Burger and Kiko were waiting for him. He walked over to them and gave Burger a high five, saying, "That was too fucking much." Burger agreed. Though Kiko didn't state her opinion in similar terms, it was obvious that she had enjoyed the set.

The three of them strolled toward the stadium and the refreshments inside. Minnie, always hungry, loaded a plate with carrot sticks and cheese and grabbed a beer. They went down a hallway and through a door which opened into a deserted locker room. Minnie sat down on a bench facing Kiko and went to work on the carrot sticks. Burger sprawled on the floor. Minnie watched Kiko watch him. He lifted his beer in a salute to her South American beauty. She acknowledged his toast with a nod of her head.

Burger spoke first. "Okay. I guess Kiko better fill you in. It's really her project."

She smiled at both of them. Burger took it in stride, but when Minnie saw it, he had to breathe deeply and grip the bench a little tighter.

"Minnie," she began.

He loved the way she said his name. She had a delicate accent that reminded him of water and waves coming to the beach, and it filled his head with a white noise that calmed him. He could almost feel the warmth of the sun baking his bald dome and the gentle breeze moving off shore. Graceful sea birds flew overhead.

"Minnie? Are you okay?" Her eyes searched his.

Minnie started at the sound of her voice. He was suddenly back in the locker room. He put on an attentive face and spoke seriously. "Yeah. I'm okay. Fine. Really."

"Well..." she began. "To put it simply, these coffee guys are killing the rainforest with the way they plant their coffee. That's the main thing. They're clear-cutting huge areas and planting a crop that after a few years leaves the soil worthless. They're also a bunch of thugs.

"From what I can gather, it's not just coffee, though that's their main business. They're pressuring and threatening the people who live there in order to gain control of their land. They give them drugs, they blackmail them, they use violence. It's awful. And then," she looked away for a moment, but kept talking, "this whole thing gets personal for me. This is where I come from."

"But you have an American accent." He thought of his vision of the beach. "Well, sort of."

She gave him a patient look and said, "My father brought me and my brother to America. I've lived here practically my whole life, but that's where we come from and I still have relatives there. I've worked for the Dead for a long time doing all kinds of things. About six months ago, I got a letter from my cousin, Mariana, who still lives in Ipamari, a small village near Rio.

"She told me about some men who had come and offered everyone in the village a lot of money for their land. Some of the people sold, but most didn't. The company these men represented was called Terra Gorda. They said they were going to build a resort. Everyone thought they were crazy because it's back in the jungle. No beaches or anything like that. It didn't make any sense.

"I looked into it. Using my computer, I could get into public records and insurance company files in Brazil, but I couldn't find out much. The records were unclear, but I did figure out that this company, despite it's name, had huge coffee holdings, both as traders and planters. This was really why they wanted the land.

"Mariana and I kept corresponding. I wanted to help her as much as I could. Over time, things kept getting more intense down there. I was talking about it one day at work and the guys from The Rex Foundation decided to fund me so I could keep researching. There had been other instances like this that they knew about. They're concerned about the rainforest and wanted to find out if there was a connection.

"I looked at all the research and information about the area. There was plenty. Everything pointed to exploitation for profit by these guys and no concern for the environment whatsoever. The trend was obvious, but we didn't know who was really behind it. That's my main focus, to find out exactly who is responsible so we can possibly do something about it. Organize, or make the information public, that kind of thing."

She looked at Minnie, whose expression was fixed, glazed almost.

"I'm not boring you, am I?" she asked.

He blinked a few times. "No, I'm fascinated." And he was, though it was difficult for him to keep his mind on what she was saying.

She looked skeptical, but decided to take this as an encouraging sign and continued.

"I'm trying to trace the ownership of this company. I've found out some names, but unraveling the organization or the corporate structure of this thing and who's really doing what is taking some time. Meanwhile, we can see that more and more of the rainforest is being destroyed and people like Mariana and her neighbors are being pressured to sell their land and move. Since I got into this, I've made contact with several people like Mariana who are there in the villages resisting. It's getting ugly.

"Basically, it's the big money people paying off the government and the big money making bigger money. They don't care about the environment or the villagers. I'm focusing on the coffee guys, but there are plenty of others doing the same kind of thing — timber interests, oil companies, agriculture. Like everything, it's the money that controls how things are."

She described the work she had been doing. She told him of the files full of information she had compiled, the many contacts she had made all over the States and also down in Central and South America, especially Brazil, where the company was based. From these contacts, she had learned that they were growing more powerful every day and that they were expanding their market in the U.S. at an alarming rate.

Her information came from all over. From conversations with scattered Deadheads, old school friends, Bowman, a Brazilian samba master, a shipping agent in El Paso, Amazonian Indians, a woman named Melba who ran a truck stop in Cucamonga, assorted sources who wanted to remain anonymous, her younger brother in the Air Force, from environmental reports, Greenpeace, even information that was compiled by the government. Everything she found out disturbed her, but nothing so much as the reports from the Indians and villagers that vast tracts of land were being cleared deep in the rainforest for planting.

Burger interrupted. "It's one thing to speed up America with caffeine, but this rainforest thing is too much. There's a lot of information, but we need to get specific names. A way to really get them. That's your job."

"My job?" Minnie was amazed. All he needed was another job.

"Man, I'm on vacation."

Kiko kept her gaze on Minnie, who was riveted, both by her and the wild nature of her story. She told him that she had been working out of her house down in California, in Bolinas, where she had sophisticated computers and everything they would need for their work.

She looked down for a moment and then, with a tone of voice that seemed to come straight from her heart, she asked Minnie, "Will you come to Bolinas and help me, help us to uncover the truth about all this? It's a big project." She paused. "I want to warn you up front that it could prove dangerous. I know you have a whole life back in Colorado and that you're on vacation. You're probably wondering why we're asking you to get involved."

Minnie was wondering.

"The main reason is that you know Bowman. He told us about you."

Minnie thought, this is just like Jasmine. Well, almost. Were these guys after Bowman's key too? Did they also want whatever it was Bowman was hiding?

"Bowman said you could be trusted. He said you were okay."

Minnie wondered if Bowman had said anything about the key. He remembered his old partner's words of warning. He wasn't about to mention it, even to these guys, until he met with Bowman. It was his deal.

He stared at her as if to say Bowman would trust anyone.

She ignored this. "I just think you can help me. Will you?"

She looked at him, her face displaying no emotion, only a clear interest in this process of decision, waiting for his answer.

Minnie returned her look. He thought again of Bowman. Where was he? This was all too weird. He decided to play along until he talked with him. His answer couldn't commit him to too much. He was on vacation, but he felt he owed Bowman something, though he couldn't imagine why. Bowman had always gotten him into trouble.

It was easy to forget about Bowman and trouble when he looked at Kiko and, anyway, he'd see him soon. He thought she looked radiant. She waited patiently. He had gone on this vacation because he was bored and burnt out and he realized that the idea of danger or whatever this was actually appealed to him. Kiko was Burger's girlfriend, but he felt something for her that he couldn't pin down. Probably lust. He decided that was as good a reason as any to play along.

Everything lately had been weird and there had been all these women. That, in itself, was unusual. First Susan, then Jasmine, and now Kiko. It crossed his mind that maybe he was getting a little out of touch with reality. That things were getting out of hand. Too much loud music, too many odd things happening. Maybe all those drugs were catching up with him. And now the Dead. The Dead were asking him for something. How could he refuse and ever listen to the music again? A notion flashed through his mind that he really might be able to help out, to make a difference of some sort.

He shook his head. It was all too unbelievable. Then he smiled. Kiko smiled back.

"Okay," he said. "When do we start and what do we do?"

They made plans for Minnie to drive down to Bolinas and meet her. She would fly down ahead of him and get things ready. She drew him a map to her house and wrote her phone number on it.

Just then they heard the muffled thump of the bass coming through the walls. Burger stood up and grabbed Minnie's hand and shook it. "That's great, Minnie. Really great. Thanks." Minnie had forgotten all about him and was surprised to see him there.

Minnie and Kiko looked at each other for a long moment. Something was happening between them. They were smiling like kids who were about to get into trouble. He stuck his hand out to her.

"See you in Bolinas," he said.

"Be careful," she said.

They shook and Minnie walked out of the locker room and back to the show. The band was playing "Truckin'." As he passed the twirlers, he took a couple of turns himself. He felt oddly elated. When he got to the fence, he reached up and slapped the bouncer on the back.

He shouted 'Keep on rockin' and plunged back into the crowd.

Chapter Seventeen - We Bid You Goodnight

The show was going full tilt. Shimmering guitar riffs floated past the crowd and sailed out of the stadium into the lazy afternoon. The notes drifted down into the city, entering driveways, visiting backyards, settling on front porches. As they did, Minnie slowly made his way through dazed and ecstatic characters and up the crowded aisle to where he had left Susan and the girls. He wanted to check in with them and then try to find Bowman. He wanted to check out this whole coffee story with him and get rid of the damn key, though the idea of working with Kiko was tempting.

He stopped and leaned on a railing that separated two sections of seats. He caught his breath and looked out over the crowd. There were so many people. He checked his position again and was certain this was close to where they had all been sitting just one hour before and yet, for all his looking, he could not find them.

No one called his name, though he should have been obvious if they were looking for him. He was hard to overlook at the most confused of times and, even though this might have been one of those times, here he was, going against the current, big as life, bigger maybe, facing into a sea of faces. But the more he looked and the more he scanned each row for the girls, the more sure he became that he was not going to find them.

Had they just up and left him? Had they gone to find better seats? Was he all fucked up and mistaking up for down and left for right? Or had something happened to them? Something that had to do with the other weird events that had begun to collect around him? He was getting paranoid, he knew, but he thought not without provocation. Things had definitely taken a turn for the weird since he had arrived in Eugene, and this might just be another instance of it.

The band had gone into the drum section of the set. Usually he got off on this trippy interlude, but right now he found it irritating. He was worried about the girls. "Stupid fucking drums," he muttered.

He slowly continued his climb up the aisle. Yes, it was the right one. Yes, they had been sitting right about there. In fact, there were the guys with the dreadlocks. Minnie waded in and shouted over the music to them. The dreadlocks turned their stoned eyes toward him and, recognizing him, maybe, they held out a medium-sized bong.

"Hey, go ahead, man."

Minnie tried to make himself clear, but it was useless. He made his way back to the aisle and kept going up until he came out at the top where there was room to breathe and think. First Jasmine had left him and now the girls. What did he expect? It happened every time. He was with some babe and then, without explanation, she leaves. What was the fucking problem?

He went to find Bowman. He waited by the bathrooms for half an hour and then roamed the wide aisle behind the stands looking for him. There was plenty to look at — guys with elaborate squirt guns strapped to their backs, girls in sexy over-alls, hair everywhere you looked. He cursed Bowman for being a spaced-out moron who had never learned to tell time. Where the hell was he?

He leaned on the low wall behind the last row of seats and watched as the band finally and mercifully, he thought, came out of the drums and space and went into the next tune.

Forty-seven thousand people were jammed into the stadium and he knew it would only be luck if he found the girls. But they could take care of themselves and it was a friendly and peaceful crowd. C'est la vie, Daddy-O. It had promised to be a difficult situation anyway. That Susan was too cute. And now there was all this other stuff to worry about. Bowman. And Kiko.

He listened to the music and it not only lifted him out of his worries, it brought him back down to Earth. It was one of those shows. It was all working. The audience was tuned in. The weather couldn't have been better and, as the show went on, everything went to a higher level. Everyone, band and audience, was expansive, embodying all kinds of what might, in a different light, be considered clichés, but at this moment seemed and actually were the most important truths.

The crowd went wild.

By the end, Jerry had blown everyone away and Weir had screamed himself hoarse. The last verse was sung, but Jerry would not let go of the song. His guitar kept pouring out a string of notes and the drums and the bass backed him up until he had done all he could and then he finally resolved the chord and released them all. There was a final crash of cymbals and the band said, "Goodnight everyone," and was gone.

After a while things calmed down. There was no sign of Bowman and Minnie let himself be carried by the crowd out through the gates and once again down the long ramp toward the parking lot. No sign either of Susan and the girls. He was thinking that, despite all the strange occurrences of the last day or so, these had been two of the best shows ever. Not quite as good as that time at the Fillmore East in '71 with the bikers and two hits of sunshine, but right up there. Of course there was that New Year's show out in San Francisco. Hmm, hard to beat that. And Red Rocks. . . .

He might have gone on in these fascinating comparisons for quite a while except that a hand grabbed and pulled him to the side of the crowd. The lips that went with this hand planted a big kiss on his. It was all familiar and he wasn't complaining. His head was bent back slightly and he was looking up at Jasmine.

At last she let him go and, in her bad-girl voice, said, "How ya doing, big boy?"

He gave her a squeeze and wiggled those eyebrows at her. Neither mentioned the night before, but neither had to. As they walked towards the cars, Minnie asked her how she had liked the show.

"I was waiting out here for you. I didn't see it. I don't really like that music anyway."

That stopped Minnie in his tracks and he turned to look at her. He then remembered his suspicions about the wallet and her questions about Bowman and the coffee. He shivered in spite of the heat. There was something wrong here.

"Not that they're not great." She shrugged.

She was beautiful and he knew she drove him crazy, but this information was alarming. Not everyone had to like the same things, but there was something about the way she said it that put him on his guard and confirmed his growing feelings of distrust. What was it she wanted? Who was she working for? What the hell was going on here?

Chapter Eighteen - Sidestep

They continued on their way toward the Armory, where Minnie had left his car. He wondered what they had done to it this time. A new paint job? Re-upholstering? Jasmine held him closely as they walked. Her perfume and the sweet smell of her skin were intoxicating and, though they stimulated memories of last night and promises of the one to come, Minnie could not ignore his intuitions.

He was intuiting trouble. He couldn't figure it out, but he could feel it. There was an awkward silence between them which Jasmine tried to cover up by holding him even tighter and caressing him as they walked. From time to time, Minnie gave her a close look and what he hoped was an encouraging smile, but mostly he was staring ahead trying to sort things out.

He realized that she really had gone through his wallet. It hadn't been his imagination. It hurt him. Her questions of the night before were not as innocent as she wanted him to believe and he was pretty sure she was one more element in this odd combination of things, somehow connected to the coffee guys Kiko had talked about.

She said, "Let's go to your place. I want to show you something."

Minnie smiled as he tried to imagine what that might be, but then he remembered Kiko's parting words of caution. He looked into Jasmine's blue eyes and the deeper he looked, the less he saw. That scared him and he found himself saying, "I thought I saw it all last night."

She stopped, pulled him to her, and gave him a kiss that almost made him faint. His lips tingled, his ears turned crimson, and steam rose in small, vaporous clouds from the top of his head. He floated two inches off the pavement but she held on tight and pressed closer to him.

"I was just getting warmed up," she said.

He believed her. It went against all his principles, except that of self-preservation, but he made the decision to stall for time.

"I've got to meet someone for about an hour," he lied. "Let's get together at my place for dinner and you can show me what you've got."

He took her in his arms and kissed her, really turning it on. As he did, the clocks in all the cars and houses within a hundred yards lost nearly 60 seconds, Eugene Water and Electric registered a significant drop in power, and an intense static took over the phone lines.

He let her go, hoping she hadn't noticed his deception. She was flushed and she staggered slightly. She signaled, as she had the night before, and the limousine appeared. The driver jumped out.

She gave Minnie another kiss and said, "See you at dinner." She added significantly, "I'm starving," and then entered the car. Sascha closed the door and turned to look at Minnie, who had his eyes shut and was swaying from side to side. Minnie heard Sascha's door and opened his eyes. He blew Jasmine a kiss but, because of the smoky windows, couldn't tell if she got it. The car sped off and Minnie was left on the sidewalk.

He watched until it was out of sight and then he slapped his forehead.

"Fuck," he yelled.

This was typical. He thought he had something good going and then... The girls at the bar were too young, his cleaning lady was married, Susan was 15, for Christ's sake, and now Jasmine was some kind of agent. She didn't want him, she wanted information from him. He knew he didn't trust her. She might make him delirious, but then what? Hit him with a champagne bottle? Smother him in his sleep? Have Sascha run him over with the limo? She was, without a doubt, the sexiest woman he had ever known, but she scared him. This was a disappointment to his romantic heart. He was such a sucker. This was nothing new, but it hurt all the same.

He got his car, returned to the hotel, and quickly threw his stuff together. He wasn't going to make it for dinner. Or dessert. The shows were over and it was just too weird in Eugene. He had no idea of how to contact Bowman and he wanted out of all this mess. Then he thought about Kiko and their agreement to meet in Bolinas. He didn't feel right just running out on her. He did want to give the key back to Bowman and get rid of it and he didn't want to hang around and have things get complicated with Jasmine. Or with Ed or the Colonel for that matter. He decided he'd go to California and see Kiko. Maybe Bowman would call. Anyway, he could leave all this craziness behind.

As he checked out, his friend the desk clerk raised his eyebrows and said, in a leering way, "That was some babe you were with last night. I hope you had a restful stay and that you'll visit us again the next time you're in town."

"Fat chance, asshole."

The light was getting dim as Minnie threw his bag and his

pack into the Chevy. He wanted to get far enough away from Jasmine that his temperature might return to normal, then maybe he would be able to figure out what was going on. Things were complex enough without her lies. He didn't need that kind of excitement. He made a quick check to make sure he had everything and then got into the car and started it up. He put a tape, Fillmore West 2/26/69, into the player and shifted into reverse.

Before he made it out of town, Minnie wanted to stop for gas and fill the tank. He went inside and got a cup of coffee, two Butterfingers, and a pack of gum. He waited in line to pay. The pimply cashier was ringing someone up when the phone rang. He made change and said something into it. As he took Minnie's money, he looked up. He scanned the store and then considered Minnie with tired eyes. Into the phone, he said, "Just a sec," and held the receiver out to him.

"It's for you."

"What do you mean?"

"Big bald guy with a red beard. That's you."

Minnie took the phone.

"Yeah?"

"Minnie, this is Cowboy. We've got a problem here."

He couldn't believe it.

"What do you mean you've got a problem? How'd you get this number? Every time I turn around you're calling me. I'm on vacation, remember? I'll be back soon. Now, fuck off."

He slammed the phone down on the counter and walked out. Outside, he had a moment of sympathy for Cowboy. He had been there many times himself. Hell, that was why he was on vacation.

Chapter Nineteen - A Simple American Life

The drive down the coast from Eugene to Bolinas was just what Minnie needed. The scenery calmed him, the music on the tape player kept his foot to the floor, and he wasn't plagued by phone calls from the bar, visits from weirdos, or the perils of romance. It was a simple American life. A man and his automobile, a long winding highway, and a wallet full of credit cards.

He had plenty of time to relax after all that had happened in Eugene and he needed it. The stuff with the IRS and that weird Colonel was trouble enough, but the thing with Jasmine was really bad. He had fallen for her, like he did for everyone, and she had betrayed him. When was he going to learn? And Bowman? Where the hell was he?

He decided to stop to fish. He found himself a place beside the Coquille River, south of Coos Bay. That was French, wasn't it? And coquille, a kind of sandwich? Or perhaps it meant feather? His French was rudimentary. Or was it rudimentrois?

Two hours later, with the help of a fly named Jackson's Flea and a fair measure of luck, he finally caught a fish. The air was still and all around and above him the spruce trees gave off a tangy scent. Sunlight filtered lazily through limbs and the peace of the place was audible in a way that bypassed the ever-present rock-and-roll ringing of Minnie's ears. While he breathed in this idyllic scene and serenity, he was able to forget about the strange turn his life had recently taken.

He considered the fish, with its scales glistening in the afternoon light, a fellow creature with whom he had much in common. Perhaps he would have quoted a line or two of Whitman, Garcia, or Weir, except that the fish had the bad manners to bite him, which made him decide that that was enough fishing for one day. He returned the unpoetic squirmer to the river.

He was tempted to throw the key into the river too and be done with the whole mess, but he knew it meant something to Bowman, and then there was the fact that Kiko was waiting for him in Bolinas. He could stand it a little longer.

Once safely back on the road, he bombed through towns with colorful names like Pistol River, Crescent City, and Orick, past landmarks like the Seven Devils Wayside, Humbug Mountain, and Lake Earl, and down Highway 101 toward Bolinas and Kiko.

It took him three days, including the fishing. The scenery was so unbelievable to him that it required an effort to stay on the road. This, he thought, was vacation. There were green trees on his left, blue sky above, and the nearer, more tangible plane of the ocean on his right. The water changed appearance with the light. One moment it was a glittering steel blue, all surface, and where it met the shore it exploded into a spectacular white foam. In another light, it was black, endless and unrelenting, and conveyed a sense of limitless depth. And yet, through these changes, Minnie's mood was a steady one of acceptance, peace, and relief.

He was glad to have left everything behind in Eugene — the demands of Ed and the IRS, the paranoia of Colonel Able, and the complications of Jasmine and Susan. But what about Bowman? When would he see him? It was true that up ahead there was this coffee business, whatever that was, but there was also Kiko and the possibility of doing something that mattered. Or mattered in a bigger way, it seemed, than his normal daily acts. His everyday routine operation. A routine that would have required closer scrutiny than he was willing to give it before it yielded up its treasures.

It was a bright morning when he and his red convertible breezed into Bolinas. He had taken a right at Petaluma and driven past Point Reyes, south to the lagoon, outside of town. There the egrets were out getting breakfast and a few sea lions lay beached on a sand bar, sleeping off a hard night of tuneless carousing. The sun had poked over Mt. Tamalpais and was bouncing off the still surface of the water right into his eyes. The seagulls wheeled and cried in the blue sky. There was the hint of fog just dispersed. He couldn't get over it. The beauty of the place was almost overwhelming, but he tried to ignore it and concentrate on the map he had pinned to the seat with his leg.

Turn right at the huge eucalyptus. That was a big help. Go 1.3 miles and take a left at a long row of mailboxes. Watch out for the bumps. Veer left at the wind chimes. Wind chimes? He shook his head and thought of how California was more than a little like Boulder.

There was a tall fence and he saw the old blue Toyota she had mentioned in a parking area next to a big pile of dirt. He pulled in and turned the tape and the car off. The car was quiet now, but his body was still vibrating from the three hours of driving that morning and the double espresso he had gotten in Olema.

It was peaceful here. Kiko's house was out of town, if you could call Bolinas a town. Bolinas appeared to Minnie to be a bunch of old houses and turn-of-the-century storefronts down by the water. It was quaint and seemed undecided about its next move. Dogs reluctantly got up from the middle of the main street and made room for traffic. Longhairs and idlers sat on the curb or on benches or in the back of old pickups and watched the day go by. Philosophers, he thought.

Kiko's house was on the outskirts and sat near the end of a dirt lane. It was a neighborhood of quiet and mostly modest homes, all much concerned with privacy, hidden behind rough fences or impenetrable vegetation. To show they had no hard feelings and to make it easier for the mailman, some of them had hand-scrawled signs with names figured in weathered paint.

Kiko's had no such sign. You had to be in the know. Minnie heard the cry of a seagull and could feel both the calm of the warming day and the presence of the ocean at the end of the lane. He couldn't see and he could barely hear the water from where he was, but he knew it was there. To him it was both reassuring and alarming. The ocean had a power and attraction for him, but it also, to his mind, made the ground unstable. As if erosion was not a gradual process, but one which might wake you up in the middle of the night. It being California, there was always the possibility of earthquakes and this could mean extra trouble with the ocean only a few hundred yards away. Minnie remembered all the jokes about California falling into the sea. He had even told a couple of them.

As he sat there feeling all this, he sent a small prayer down the lane in hopes of appeasing both land and water for the length of his stay. This reverential mood was interrupted by a clear voice which warmly called his name. He looked up and then she was there, leaning on the door next to him.

She straightened up, waiting, in shorts and a t-shirt. She was dazzling him with her smile. He forgot all about erosion and earthquakes.

"Hi," he said, trying to be cool.

She said, "Welcome to Bolinas. You made it."

He smiled back, feeling a little foolish, not knowing what to say, and still feeling the effects of the coffee.

Eyeing the empty paper cup on the seat beside him, she said, "I can't believe you're still drinking that stuff."

He looked at the cup and the others like it on the floor. "Oh, that. I don't really drink it. It's research."

Chapter Twenty - Get Down To It

Kiko's house had a yard full of plants and trees that were to remain a mystery to Minnie forever. During their time together there, she repeatedly told him what they were, but the information never really registered. These plants, like all natural things, fascinated Kiko. They had the same effect on Minnie, but the details never seemed to take root in his brain. He was amazed by their color and odd shape and the fact that you could eat either the fruit or the leaves or both of most of them, but the names went right by him. This California landscape was green, complex, and unbelievably varied, and it seemed to complement the simple and elegant design of her house.

Inside, the house consisted of one large room, with lots of windows, looking out at the vegetation and kept private by the high fence. Everything was made of wood - the floors, walls, and ceiling. This warm space had a wood stove, a high ceiling fan, and huge stuffed chairs which looked inviting. Off three of the corners of the room were alcoves, one containing a kitchen, one a bathroom, and one a bedroom. Books lined an entire wall and there was a table to one side for meals. The house was simple, efficient, and cozy.

Kiko's workplace consisted of a long counter which stretched along the side of the room. It was covered with stacks of papers and magazines and a phone with buttons indicating different lines. Computer equipment dominated the central part of the long desk. Newspapers were piled at one end on the floor. The wall above all this was covered in dark cork with notes and newspaper clippings and pictures pinned to it. The computer's fan provided a steady sound that suggested unceasing work.

She gestured, indicating the room. "This is it. Command Central."

Minnie, impressed, nodded his approval. He looked around and wondered where he was going to sleep, but then let it go as he heard Kiko speak.

"I'm a little worried about Bowman. I haven't talked to him in a while."

Minnie thought about his meeting at the motel in Nevada and restrained an urge to check the key in his pocket.

He did say, "I saw him last week, before the concert. I was supposed to meet him there but he never showed."

Her face registered concern. She ran a hand through hair that looked like black silk.

She said, "You know he's dealing coffee?" She shrugged. "A little bit, anyway."

"He said he was giving it to the Dead."

Kiko laughed. "He is. They felt guilty about drinking it. I think that's why they're bankrolling this project."

Minnie nodded.

Kiko said, "The last time we talked, he told me his connections were getting pressure from some people to cut them in on the business. We think they are connected to the guys in Brazil. They're everywhere. He didn't tell you anything, did he?"

Minnie wondered if she knew about the key. He wondered if he should tell her.

Kiko continued. "Bowman didn't say much, but I could tell from his voice that he was worried. He told me someone was following him. You know how he is. I usually don't pay too much attention to that kind of thing, but I could tell that this time he wasn't exaggerating. He said he kept seeing the same Ford van off and on since he left Mexico." She paused to let this sink in. "He was in Flagstaff when he called and he was freaking out."

Minnie said, "I don't get it. You think it's the Brazilian guys? Why would they want to hassle him? He just imports this stuff to finance his vacations and to pay rent on a teepee he has up in the hills."

"Yeah, but it seems he's upset somebody somewhere. These coffee guys are intense. I've been getting reports from my friends in Brazil that they'll use any means to get what they want. It's terrible. The other thing I learned is that with the recent frost and the higher prices, they're moving huge quantities across the border."

Minnie nodded and asked, "What about the legal dealers?"

"I'm in touch with most of them. Their volume has dropped and the entire distribution set-up in the States is getting really complicated. It's hard to tell who's legitimate and who has connections that aren't. It's big money now. It always was, but the explosion of gourmet coffee and gourmet coffee places and the big mark-up on it has changed everything. It seems people are obsessed."

Minnie laughed. "No shit. I just had a double espresso this morning. In Boulder, it's like a health drink. They've torn down gas stations and replaced them with coffee joints. You can get a refill every 20 feet. They're hurting our bar business. It used to be just "Cup de Yup" and a couple of places where you could buy beans, but now it's everywhere. It's a wonder anyone sleeps."

Minnie thought about how much sleep he had gotten lately and decided it wasn't enough.

Then Kiko said, "It's definitely a trend and an addictive one. Coffee is the world's most widely used mind-altering drug." She made a melodramatic face and, shaking her finger at him, said, "Just dare to keep your mind off drugs."

They both laughed.

Minnie said, "Well, it does make people edgy. They go through red lights because they just can't slow down. Everyone is in a big fucking hurry. They're uptight. It can't be good for them and it probably makes them vote Republican." He leaned toward her. "Just between you and me, I heard that they vote that way because they had diaper rash as babies."

Kiko ignored this important information. "Well, those people can do what they want to, but this is too much. In Brazil, some of the villagers decided to take the easy money and sell out, but a lot of people didn't want to be bullied. They don't want to move. It's their home, but these guys don't care about that. They don't care about the rainforest. They do whatever they have to to make money."

Minnie shrugged and, in an effort to calm her down, said reasonably, "Well, Kiko, there are plenty of guys doing that. And always have been. This kind of stuff is happening all over. To everything."

She gave him a look that was at once fierce, tender, and outraged.

"Oh, that's fine," she said. "So what do you propose? Just to let them do whatever they want, with no opposition whatsoever? Just to forget the whole thing, as long as they stay out of your way? As long as they don't dig up your lawn?" She turned away.

Her words stung him. It was true that he had mostly ignored issues like this, but he couldn't help but be moved by her anger. He admired her passion and commitment.

If only Bowman would call. This was getting too complicated. It wasn't really his scene. This was supposed to be vacation. He decided that until he talked with him, he would try to help. He had told Kiko and Burger he would and he felt that he owed at least that much to the Dead for everything they had done. If he and Kiko could actually accomplish something in the meantime, it would be great. He was beginning to see that this was important and in the face of her obvious concern, he felt ashamed.

He smiled and with a seriousness that surprised him, he said simply, "Kiko, I'm on your side. Tell me what I can do."

She thanked him and looked around the room as if in search of an answer.

"We can keep trying to track down the people in Brazil. We need to get some specific names and details before we can really do anything and I want to help my cousin Mariana. She's so incredible. She's the one down there dealing with this stuff everyday. She's really fighting this battle. We need to help her any way we can. I only wish I could do more."

"What about Bowman?"

All this talk about the guys in Brazil and the way they did business was making Minnie worry. Bowman should have met him or at the very least called Kiko. They were obviously in touch.

"If we can help him, we will. But he's a symptom of this bigger situation. Plus, he can take care of himself. He always has. And he hasn't asked for our help. He's just keeping us informed. He cares about these people too."

"Do you think he'll call?"

"Don't worry. He'll call and you guys can figure everything out. He'll be surprised to find out you're working with us."

No kidding, thought Minnie. The idea that Bowman would call soon reassured him slightly and he said, "Okay, what's our next step?"

"How about lunch?"

It sounded like a good idea.

Chapter Twenty-one -
You Can Say That Again

Over the next few days, Kiko showed Minnie what she had learned. It figured, he thought. Double-dealing and crooks were to be expected anywhere the money was big. Nothing new about that. It was just one more of those things that screwed up the world. A big frustration. Injustice caused by guys who were greedy, who were stupid, who were uptight. Too much caffeine probably. He just wanted to hang out, to be mellow. What was wrong with everyone else?

As they talked and as she showed him the data, he began to understand the scope of the rainforest problem. The data wasn't sketchy or unsubstantiated. It seemed that everyone, except him, was well aware of the facts. The information was public knowledge, but even with all of the evidence, nothing was being done. He had never paid much attention to this stuff. Sure, he knew that something like it was happening, but he had always thought that there was nothing he could do about it. Maybe that's what everybody thought. But now, maybe this was his chance.

The pictures from the Amazon that Kiko showed him were obvious enough and the statistics seemed clear. What was worse was that Minnie knew this was most likely only a part of the full story. This wasn't just paranoia. Minnie had enough experience to know that, in matters political, financial, and environmental, what seemed like paranoia was eventually confirmed as fact and usually was an understatement of some sort. At first he couldn't begin to understand what destruction on a scale of hundreds of thousands of acres really meant, but it was becoming clearer.

Kiko was giving him an education. It wasn't just the coffee guys but also the cattle ranchers, the oil conglomerates, and the lumber companies. Maybe they were all the same company. What difference was there really between them? They were tearing into this vital and necessary place in order to feed their insatiable greed, to fulfill their twisted and self-serving economics.

Minnie thought it was as if these guys saw the Earth as their private farm or factory or warehouse and didn't care about anything or anyone else. The Amazon, like a lot of other places, was distant enough that no one could make the connection between what they were using or consuming and how it had got there. The consumers couldn't see the trees falling or what happened to the people who had lived there forever.

They had what they wanted and didn't care or couldn't imagine the effect their actions might have. Everything now was thrown away, without a second thought. For the businesses, cynicism and self-delusion ran high. Talk of need and opportunity and growth were twisted around until it was difficult to know what was true and what was not. They created markets where none had existed and none were really needed.

Minnie was looking at an article with pictures taken before and after the change from forest to farmland. He said, "This is fucked," and threw the magazine into the corner. He started pacing. Kiko watched him as he began to rant out loud.

"The published reports alone are enough to drive you nuts. It's easy to turn away and to be diverted by TV or by your own shit or by the stuff happening down the block. I'm as guilty of this as anyone else. The big stuff is left alone and gets completely out of control. It's all on the other side of the world."

He looked at Kiko and knew he was preaching to the converted, but he couldn't stop.

"We won't own up to any of this. Every asshole thinks, just let me take care of what's on my list or make it to the next vacation or until Junior gets to college. Then I'll think about it. Then I'll try to do something."

"Amen." She was smiling at him.

He stopped and faced her. He was a mess. "These bozos don't care about anyone. How much fucking money do they need? Do they think they're immortal or just that they'll be outta here before the shit hits the fan? In the meantime, they think it's okay to swim around in the champagne and screw everybody else." It was all getting to him. "And what about Bowman? Where the fuck is he?"

Just then the phone rang. Minnie was still fuming. He grabbed the receiver and snarled into it. "Yeah? Who's this?"

"Minnie, this is Cowboy."

He was stunned for a moment. Then he said, "Can't you see I'm busy? How the hell did you get this number?"

"Minnie, we got a real problem here."

"Don't talk to me about real problems. Having the same soup du jour for seven years is not a problem, it's a convenience."

"But Minnie..."

"But nothing. I'm on vacation. Get Beaver to fix your problem. I'll talk to you later."

He slammed the receiver down and gave Kiko an exasperated

look.

"Maybe you should have helped him," she said.

Minnie snorted. "These guys call me all the time. They need a goddamn babysitter." He looked at the phone as if it had just told a bad joke. He turned to Kiko and said, "I thought you said this phone was secure?"

"It is. It's unlisted and I had the Dead's tech guys wire it in some way that makes it untraceable."

"Right." Minnie nodded but thought that if the bar could call him, who else would? Susan? His mother?

The phone rang again and they both jumped. Minnie gave Kiko a look and said, "If this is my mother, we're pulling the phone right out of the wall."

He grabbed the receiver. "Who's this?" he snarled. He listened for a moment. "Oh sure," he said with a disgusted sarcasm. He hung up and shook his head again and looked out the window.

Curious, Kiko said, "Well, Mr. Operator, who was it? How's everything at home?"

"The guy said he was Jerry Garcia." Minnie laughed.

Kiko said, "It probably was. We're working for him, remember?"

Minnie closed his eyes, made a face, and said, "What an idiot."

Chapter Twenty-two - That's The Touch I Like

They talked and worked through the afternoon and past dinner. Kiko decided to call it a day. "I can't do this anymore." She looked over at Minnie and saw that he was staring at her. His expression had a soulfulness that struck her as pathetic. It was fixed in a way that would have frightened a weaker woman.

"Minnie, you look like you just swallowed a chili. Are you okay?"

He continued to look at her, saying nothing. She made a face which registered compassion and impatience and then she got up to prepare for bed.

He put a hand on hers and glanced up at her, attempting to change her mind. She hesitated.

"Kiko, you are really some kind of babe."

She smiled ironically. "Minnie, you have a way with words."

"What I'd really like is to have my way with you." He turned up the wattage on his leer, as if the sheer intensity of his desire would melt any resistance. It had always worked in the past, at least in the beginning.

Kiko was laughing and sat back down.

"Okay," she said, "let me have it."

Minnie leaned forward, searching for her lips. His eyes were slightly glazed and half-closed. A semi-audible murmur issued from between his teeth.

Kiko watched all of this and, even as she leaned back away from him, she remained unmoved. It could have been her scientific training, her vast romantic experience, or just common sense, but whatever it was, she was able to resist his advances.

"Minnie, take a break. It's not working."

He blinked rapidly for a minute.

She continued. "I asked Bowman all about you."

Minnie laughed. "Like he'd know. Hey, when did you talk with him? What did he tell you?"

Maybe she knew more about the key than she was letting on. He was fully awake now. He straightened up, his paranoia at full force.

"He told me you had lots of girlfriends."

He slumped back and said, sadly, "Oh, sure." He looked at her without illusions, without hope.

"He said one of them told him you had the Touch."

"The what?"

"The Touch. That you drove all of those girls wild with the Touch.

"Uh huh."

Minnie saw that although she was interested in this Touch, whatever it was, and possibly even in him, it was interest of a theoretical nature. This was a disappointment, to be sure, but it did nothing to blunt his fascination with her and with her beauty, which was so incredible to him it almost hurt to look at her. He looked at her now. He decided he could bear it. He saw that she was smiling at him and that, even though she was not falling for him, she was at least smiling and in a not unfriendly way.

Kiko said, "Well? What about it?"

He gave her his biggest smile and wiggled his eyebrows at her. Then he gave a little shrug and, looking away, confessed. "The Touch? I love women. That's all." He didn't know what was wrong with him. He had never been this shy before.

"That's all? That's a lot." She was thoughtful for a moment. "Why don't you show me the Touch?" She extended her arm toward him.

Her arm was gorgeous and so was the rest of her. Shyness proved to be a fleeting thing with him. He took her arm and, with one hand, began to caress it. Her skin was soft and, sitting so close to her, he could feel her warmth.

Her eyes closed involuntarily. Her face relaxed, though her breathing increased in intensity. Then she gave a slight shudder and stood up suddenly. She walked to the desk and straightened a few papers.

Minnie realized that the Touch was working. He said, "What about your boyfriend?"

She turned and said, surprised, "What boyfriend?"

"You and Burger."

Kiko laughed.

Minnie said, "You two looked pretty close at the concert."

"We are. Not that it's any of your business. He's a friend. I don't have a boyfriend right now. I'm busy or haven't you noticed? Besides, I've known him forever. He's like a brother."

"A brother?" he said skeptically.

Kiko nodded and shot him a look.

Minnie could see she had a temper hidden somewhere.

She walked back to the couch and stared down at him. She was a little intimidating even if she was gorgeous.

She asked, "What about you? What about all your girlfriends?"

Not that it was any of her business, but Minnie knew that lewd thoughts about your cleaning lady did not constitute a girlfriend. Neither did a come-on from a 15-year old. And Jasmine? She wasn't a girlfriend. She was like a bad sunburn. It felt good at first, but then. . . . He was again uncomfortable, aware of her betrayal, her calculated behavior, her manipulation of him. He tried to convince himself that it hadn't been so bad. And in one sense it hadn't. He wanted to talk about what had happened to him in Eugene and he felt, somehow, that Kiko might understand.

Minnie told her the whole story, including the fact that Susan was 15 and that Jasmine had played him for a fool and then gone through his wallet. He told her that Jasmine had asked about Bowman and the coffee. He felt he should tell her about the key, but he remembered Bowman's warning not to tell anyone, not to give it to anyone. Until he heard from Bowman, he would keep quiet. He told her that he couldn't quite figure it out, but that he thought Jasmine was involved, in some scary way, with the people in Brazil.

He laughed as he suggested, "Maybe I could subdue her with the Touch."

Kiko also laughed. "It sounds like you did."

The lights were dim and the house was quiet.

She said, "I hope you've seen the last of her."

"Me too."

He reached over and took her arm and began to caress it again. She softened visibly. He gazed at her in a dreamy way and said, "Isn't it time for bed?"

"Oh no you don't." She pulled her arm back. "Look, Minnie, I like you. You are. . . ." She hesitated. "You're an unusual guy." As she said this, she laughed and then continued, "But we've got work to do here. Important work." Their faces were close together. "I have a past. You have a past. Life is complicated. I don't know you very well. You better stick to the futon."

Minnie hadn't realized until this moment just how infatuated he was with her. Maybe he had gotten nowhere with her, but she fascinated him. And she was fun. He looked out the window at the black night, thinking. It didn't register when she stood up and walked toward her part of the house. He barely heard her when she said, softly, "Goodnight, Minnie."

Chapter Twenty-three - The Letter

Kiko was really a wizard on the computer. She was a master of the hard drive. She operated at a high transmission speed. With fingers like little dancers, she bounced between programs. She tapped into different databases all over the world. She downloaded files, she created code, she really understood this stuff.

Minnie was fascinated by the difference between them. He considered himself a more natural, simpler kind of man who relied on his instincts and reflexes rather than on megabytes of data. He liked his cabin in the mountains. He preferred a harmonica to a synthesizer. He used a calculator when he had to, but that was about it. The only thing about him that was technologically up to date was his music system. He maintained that at the cutting edge. To him, it was essential.

All the rest of it, computers, networks, and such, just overloaded him with too much detached and detailed information and got in the way of the vibes. He liked his dealings one-on-one. This was how he remained fairly calm, content, and, in his own eyes, sane.

But he did admire Kiko's ability and affinity for things more abstract. Or were they more precise? He couldn't decide. He watched her graceful fingers blur over the keyboard and guide the mouse, clicking furiously, while she pulled some obscure bit of information out of the air and made it appear on the monitor.

From time to time, he took a break from the simple, more mundane, and less demanding tasks that Kiko gave him, such as the exciting job of checking license numbers against a list of names and searching public tax records. At these moments, he gazed over at her and fantasized about applying the Touch. He wanted to really check this out. As he contemplated this, she sensed his attention and, without taking her eyes from the screen, said, "Don't even think about it. We're working." But she smiled slightly.

Minnie thought this girl had a fierce work ethic and he admired her for it. He had one himself, but his gave way to higher priorities like smooching. He had never before thought of this attribute, this essential part of his nature, as the Touch, but he liked the way it sounded. In his mind, he kept repeating the phrase and considered all its possibilities and potential, turning them over and over.

He stopped searching the computer printout for a moment and a far-away look appeared on his face. He was lost in contemplation of something that had nothing to do with coffee or evil profiteers. He was contemplating the Touch and its implications. It was something he intended to pay more attention to in the future.

He didn't notice that Kiko had paused in what she was doing and was staring at him with a mixture of amusement and tenderness.

"Minnie, stop it right now." It was as if she could read his mind. "It's an asset," she said, "but it's not a raison d'etre."

Minnie returned from his thoughts, turned to her, and said, defensively, "No French, okay?"

She laughed. "Min, your Touch is a wonderful thing, but don't let it go to your head."

He smiled and started to reach out to her.

She gave him a scolding look. "Work," she said and turned back to the computer.

He sighed and went back to his job, for a moment. Then he decided it was getting close to lunch time and he pushed his chair back, got up, and stretched. He walked out through the yard toward the fence and the mailbox beyond. As he did, he took a deep breath of the sea air and marveled at the vegetation in the yard. He knew the pink ones were roses, but the white blossoms by the fence, the ones edged with purple, were something Kiko had repeatedly pointed out to him. He tried to remember... Aspartame, arugula, Augustus something? He gave it up. He knew Kiko would know and he loved to hear those long names spoken by her.

He was halfway back to the house and halfway through the mail and thinking again that, no matter what, he just liked being with her. He tried to convince himself that even if they weren't smooching, even if they never did, and it seemed as if they might not, he was glad he was there. He thought she was the greatest babe he had ever met and he had finally left all of his bar craziness and most of the weird stuff in Eugene behind him. These days seemed to flow in and out, like the waves he could hear faintly on the nearby beach. He realized that she was the reason that he was here.

There was plenty of mail. An REI catalog, L.L. Bean, and one from a place called Daniel Smith. An envelope that declared "Lowest Terms Possible. No Annual Fee." A bill from the phone company and two smaller envelopes addressed in the handwriting of an actual person.

Then he came upon a letter with his name on it. He couldn't believe it. At first he thought it was from Cowboy. Maybe Cowboy thought he could be more convincing in writing. But he looked closer and came to a complete halt when he read the name on the return address: Internal Revenue Service.

He began to sweat, even though the late morning air was still cool. He walked to the house and sat on the front steps, looking out at the peaceful yard. It seemed like his troubles had followed his path down the coast and had finally found him. He thought maybe it was a mistake, but as he opened the letter, he knew that wasn't possible. His eyes went directly to the signature — Edward A. Kimberly, Western District Assistant Manager — and his worst fears were confirmed.

He heard the door open and Kiko, sensing that something unusual had happened, sat next to him.

They read the letter together:

September 6, 1994

Dear Mr. Minion,

Everything just seems to get more complicated these days, doesn't it? Take tax collection, for instance. In most cases, it is a routine matter. We send you the forms, you fill them out and return them with a check. What could be simpler? But sometimes a disagreement arises about the amount or there is an error in calculation, a misreading of the tables, or an unconscious oversight.

The letter went on like this for a while and then continued.

Fortunately, in our business, there is a simple solution. The world and the world of taxes gets more complicated, but you can keep it simple. Just send us a single payment of the balance you owe.

Mr. Minion, your balance due, with interest, as of September 1, 1994, is $43,863.34. Prompt and complete payment will be appreciated. As an incentive to pay now, we are pleased to inform you that, upon receipt of the above balance, all charges, penalties, and planned prosecution will be dropped. The prospect of a jail term will be forgotten entirely.

84

So send us your payment today and continue to stay current with one of your most important commitments as a citizen of this great country.

Sincerely,

Edward A. Kimberly

Edward A. Kimberly
IRS Western District
Assistant Manager

P.S. For your convenience, Direct Electronic Transfer of funds from your checking account can be arranged today. Please call us at 1-800-342-6115.

At the bottom, in a primitive bureaucratic hand was a more personal note, which read:

IF This isn't possible or if you are still interested in The Arrangement we discussed earlier, meet me AT The McDonald's in Mill Valley on September 9Th AT 11 A.M. Tell No one about This meeting. You see? I haven't forgotten you.

Ed.

Chapter Twenty-four -
Be Good For Goodness Sake

Minnie had a distracted expression on his face. It could have been interpreted, accurately, as shock. Not only was he reminded by this letter of the reality of the large amount, the gross amount of money that he owed the IRS, but he also understood that he had nowhere to hide.

Kiko read the letter again and asked, "Is this guy serious?"

Minnie said, "It's hard to tell. Or would be, except that I've actually talked to him and he is."

Over lunch, Minnie told Kiko the story of his meeting with Ed. "I call him Ed." He explained the mosquito-netting enterprise which had been so successful for him down in the islands.

She said, "Minnie, just think. You, a mogul."

"Not a mogul. I was just trying to bankroll my time on the beach. And it worked." He said this as if he still couldn't believe it. He took his attention from the salad and turned it on her. "And, the most important thing was no mosquitoes. No see um the no see ums."

He lowered his head a little. "It was after my dealing days with Bowman. I needed to do something and this seemed to make amends in a way. You know, a public service."

"And you were on TV?"

"My face was all over the place. I couldn't walk down the street without people calling out my name. I never paid for a cab. People bought me drinks. It was incredible. Whenever they had extra time, they threw on my commercial. It was filler. I was on all the time. Early in the morning, late at night, Sundays."

"Minnie, I had no idea you were so enterprising."

"There's a lot about me you don't know."

Kiko gave him a look that said, so tell me more. He was more than willing to comply.

"I was a folk hero. Like Soupy Sales or something. People would give me this goofy look and then slap their arms, trying to kill the bugs, just like I did in the commercial. It was too much."

"And you didn't pay taxes on any of this?"

He was indignant. "I'm the one who made the money. I was in another country. That's the way I saw it." Then he made a helpless gesture. "The IRS saw it differently. And now they want to nail me. The assholes. As if they didn't already have enough money to waste."

He told her about how the IRS wanted him to spy on the

Dead and to get tax information about them.

Kiko was incensed. "Spy on the Dead? That's typical and awful. The band pays plenty and the government hassles them all the time. DEA agents at the concerts, plainclothes guys trying to disrupt the shows. You wouldn't believe it. So what are you going to do?"

He admitted that he could have been mistaken about his ideas of foreign investment and, regardless, it was impossible to get rid of these guys once they were on your trail.

He said, "They want to put me in jail."

"They can't."

He gave a nervous laugh. "Oh yes, they can."

He told her of the plan he and Burger had thought up to divert the IRS from the Dead to the Cartel.

"That's a great idea, but what are you going to tell him? The IRS is going to want names, dates, specifics," she said.

"Right. I'll meet with him and string him along until we find out."

"Why McDonald's?"

"You got me."

Later that afternoon, Minnie was totaling the information they had about shipments made by the Cartel. Thirty-two tons of Colombian to Seattle. Bales of Brazilian beans up through Mexico. All those numbers were getting to him and he pushed the calculator away and put the pencil behind one ear. Kiko was engrossed in the computer and the clicking of her keyboard had distracted him. Not that it took much to do so.

He stared at her gorgeous profile. Her black hair fell all over her gorgeous shoulders. He noticed her gorgeous breathing. He couldn't help it. He was moved beyond words and toward action.

He eased his chair over next to her and hoped she would ignore the squeaking of its wheels. He reached over and began to work the Touch on her gorgeous left shoulder. This slowed her down a little, until she realized what was happening. She turned in her chair and faced Minnie, who had a dreamy, but determined expression on his face.

"Min, forget it," she said.

He sighed and continued smiling in a wistful way.

"You're not such a tough guy, are you?" It was as if she just figured this out. "You're really a romantic."

Minnie made a slight motion with his head and shrugged. "Maybe."

Kiko examined him as if he were a new kind of flower that

had popped up in the garden after a long spell of rain. She said, gently, "How'd you get that way?"

Minnie wasn't bothered by her rejection. It was about what he expected. He was just glad to be around her. He relaxed in his chair, looked at her and, at the same time, listened to the birds chirp and squawk outside in the yard.

With a sigh, he answered, "It was wicked Felina, the girl that I loved."

Kiko scrunched her eyes. "What?"

"Out in the west Texas town of El Paso, I fell in love with a Mexican girl."

Kiko said, "Marty Robbins."

Minnie smiled and nodded and told her, "I used to have a radio by my bed as a kid. Rock-and-Roll, Venus in Blue Jeans, Poetry in Motion, Primrose Lane, El Paso. It did something to me."

He sighed again and thought about the Touch and Kiko and this led him to Jasmine. He found he still hadn't gotten her out of his mind. She had been bad to him, but she had also been the latest occasion for what he now thought of as the Touch and that part of it was something a guy could not ignore or easily forget.

He thought of his time with Jasmine, which, bad as it was, at this moment seemed not that awful. But then his imagination shifted back to Kiko. She was different. So different from Jasmine.

Where Jasmine was a flood, Kiko, he was sure, would be a long hot bath. Where Jasmine had been a 100 watts, okay, 300 watts, that flicked off and on, Kiko would be an endless smoldering fire. The thought of kissing her made his mind mush and melted his heart. It felt so good to be with her it scared him. His experience with Jasmine hadn't helped. All this was getting out of control. Everything lately was making him a little nervous. But he decided that wouldn't stop him, it would just make him more cautious. He filed these thoughts away and brought his attention back to the delicious matter at hand.

He looked up and saw that Kiko was staring at him with concern.

"I wasn't sure if you were going to come back," she said.

Minnie cleared his throat. "I was just thinking."

She nodded and prompted him, "Thinking about what?"

He started to speak, but was interrupted by the phone. The sound of it made him jump.

"You get it. It's always for me," he said.

Minnie marveled as he watched Kiko move gracefully to the

phone. She gave him an irresistible smile and picked it up.

"Hello." Her voice was sweet.

Minnie continued to watch. He couldn't help but think how beautiful she was. It was amazing to him. Then he saw her body stiffen. She was listening closely, not saying anything beyond yes and nodding from time to time. Something terrible had happened.

Finally she said, "Let me know if you find out anything else."

She replaced the receiver and looked over at Minnie. All the color had gone from her face.

"That was Burger. It's Bowman. They found his car outside of Eugene a few days ago, all smashed up. There was lots of blood and Bowman was slumped over the wheel, dead." It took her a second before she could go on. "It must have happened last week, before the shows. The police aren't sure what happened. They say it was an accident, but they found him way out in the sticks on a back road."

Minnie couldn't believe it. He said, "Bowman hasn't had an accident since he was sixteen. He's been driving the roads between Colorado and Guatemala every winter for 15 years. He's a driving machine. That's crazy."

Minnie walked over to one of the big chairs and fell into it. He closed his eyes and tried to take in what he had just learned. He had just seen him. He had know Bowman for 25 years. In their way, they were like brothers.

Kiko came over and sat on the arm of the chair and put her arm around him.

"They're sure it's him?"

She nodded.

In shock, Minnie stared into space. Tears rolled down his cheeks. He looked up at her and a sob shook him. It was the first of many. She leaned over and held him close. They didn't speak. Minutes passed. Minnie didn't believe that this was an accident and he was beginning to realize that this adventure of theirs was no game. Bowman was really dead. Gone. The finality of it began to sink in and Minnie was just beginning to feel the loss.

Later that night, they talked about it and Minnie still didn't say anything about the key. With Bowman gone, murdered probably, he decided it would be safer if he didn't. He would wait and see what developed.

Chapter Twenty-five - And Check The Oil

The next morning, Kiko walked with Minnie out to the car. He was almost looking forward to his meeting with Ed. The day before, he and Kiko had discussed various strategies to placate the IRS while they found out more about the Cartel, but they hadn't settled on any of them. Minnie was just going to wing it, which was the way he liked it.

Minnie climbed into the red Chevy and thanked God he wasn't paying normal rates. He didn't know when he was going to get home.

Kiko had her hand on the door and was looking at him in a strange way.

"You feel okay?" Minnie asked.

She said, "Yeah. I just want you to be careful."

They were both thinking of Bowman.

Minnie was quiet for a moment, but then said, "Don't worry. Ed is a pussycat. This is just about money."

"So's the other stuff."

"Yeah, you're right. But I'll be fine." He waved it all away.

He turned the key and the car coughed a few times as if it were choking on something and then all was quiet. He hadn't driven it for days. Minnie and Kiko looked at each other. He tried it again and got the same results. He cleared his own throat and got out and lifted the hood.

"I can handle this," he said in a manly way. He looked over the cold and recalcitrant engine and then wiggled a few wires. He tapped on the battery cables and thumped what he thought were the valve covers.

"That ought to do it."

As he climbed back in, he noticed that Kiko was regarding him in a peculiar way. He took it as a kind of awe at his mechanical abilities. He turned the key and was met with the same coughing and lack of response. He sat motionless for a moment, trying to deduce the problem and its solution.

Kiko asked him to open the hood again. She bent over the engine as he got out to join her. She was fiddling with a screw somewhere.

She smiled at him and said, "Try it now."

He gave her a doubtful look and tried it again. It started right up. With the hood raised, he couldn't see her, but she obviously had made another adjustment because the engine began purring like it never had before. She lowered the hood and it banged closed.

"Kiko, you are a constant source of revelation."

She bent her head, accepting his praise.

He was wondering how she did it but he said, "Yeah, well. Gotta go. I'll be back soon. Hi yo Silver, away."

Kiko returned his wave and watched as he motored smoothly down the lane and out of sight.

The sun was breaking up the fog and the air was crisp. As he drove up Mt. Tamalpais, the ocean shone with a clear metallic brightness. He was thinking about Bowman and their history together. He was sad and mad. Outraged. He shouted something at the slow car ahead of him. He also thought about Kiko. He couldn't help it. She was so great, yet so untouchable. These very different thoughts occupied him until, negotiating the tight curves on the fringe of Mill Valley, he turned his attention to his meeting with Ed.

When he entered the McDonald's, he saw that Ed was already there, sitting in the corner next to the Lego tables. He looked up at Minnie but made no sign of recognition. Minnie waited in line to order and watched as those behind the counter, in uniform, bustled back and forth, carrying brightly colored packets of food. At times, these hard-working souls clutched their heads as if they were going crazy. Minnie sympathized. When it was his turn, he ordered two Big Macs, Supersize Fries, and a chocolate shake.

He made his way around a couple of the many children running between the tables and didn't spill a thing. He slid deftly into the seat opposite Ed.

"Got your letter. Quite a style you've got."

Ed nodded. His cheeks were bulging even more than usual and he said something that sounded polite.

Minnie watched Ed, fascinated. Ed had on a white short-sleeved shirt with a pocket protector full of pens. His face was red and fleshy and his eyes, which had initially reminded him of a pig's, small but intelligent, still looked too small for such a face. It was as if the face had expanded at some point and taken on weight and substance while the eyes had remained behind, left in a trail of candy wrappers and empty take-out cartons. For all that, they had a sharp edge to them and they were now focused on Minnie.

"Ed, this stuff can't be good for you."

Ed motioned towards Minnie's own tray, which was loaded.

"Yeah, but Ed, this is like a food vacation for me, whereas for you, it appears this is home base."

There was a handy McDonald's Nutrition Facts chart on the wall next to their table. Minnie hooted at the very idea of nutrition in a place like this. He got up and examined Ed's tray and then sought out the items on the chart.

"Okay. Two QuarterPounders with cheese. Large fries. Chef salad. That's a healthy touch, Ed. Vanilla shake. Baked apple pie and some Chocolaty Chip cookies for later. Let's see," he calculated, "that's about 125 grams of fat. I guess you won't have to worry about keeping warm this winter."

He sat back down, easing himself into the chair which was fixed immovably to the floor. He unwrapped one of his Big Macs. He looked at the wimpy bun and the carton of skinny fries and then looked over at Ed.

"It's amazing that big guys, like ourselves, can even fit into these chairs. Or get out of them once we've eaten. But then I'm not on a diet."

Ed had finished a mouthful and, assuming a more professional manner, said, "Cut the crap. We've got things to talk about."

Chapter Twenty-six
You Turned The Tables On Me

"Ed, lighten up. I only owe you guys $43,000. I know you're after bigger fish than me."

"43,863.34. It's not chicken feed, Mr. Minion." Ed seemed to soften a little. "I guess I am under a lot of pressure. I've got a boss and he wants action."

Minnie wondered if Ed was apologizing or being unnaturally clever.

Ed took another bite of his QuarterPounder and wiped the ketchup from a corner of his mouth with a delicate gesture. Minnie asked him why here, why McDonald's? And Ed replied that it was close to lunch time. What could be more natural? And besides that, he explained, it was a safe, anonymous place.

Minnie laughed. "What an understatement. Everyone looks like everyone else — dazed by the lights and the high fat content."

Through his mouthful, Ed said, "Well, are you going to pay us or cooperate?"

Was this hardball?

"Ed, paying you would be cooperating. But I think I've got something for you that will make your boss happy."

Ed smiled for the first time and Minnie tried not to look at the sesame seed stuck between the big accountant's teeth. Ed leaned over the table and said in a conspiratorial whisper, "You mean you've got the goods on the Dead?"

Between the general din of the place and the insipid toy-piano music playing in the background, Minnie couldn't hear him. He cupped his hand behind an ear and said, "What?"

Ed repeated himself, but this time a little louder.

Minnie leaned forward and said in a clear voice, "Ed, you don't have to whisper. For one thing, no one could possibly hear you over this shit." He gestured vaguely at the air. "And for another, none of these people even know who they are."

He meant the Dead, but he wondered about the general implications of what he had just said.

"Ed," he continued, "the Dead are small potatoes." To illustrate his point, he grabbed a handful of fries. He held them up in front of the IRS man. "What you really want is to make the big score. You don't want to waste your time on a bunch of hippies. You want to go for the big dough. The whole enchilada. You want the Big Mac."

This was a metaphor Ed could understand and he agreed wholeheartedly. The more money he could bring in for his bosses, the better off he was. He was eager to hear more and, as he took another bite, he indicated that Minnie should keep going.

Minnie thought it was time to seriously negotiate and he asked, "What do I have to do to get you guys to forget about my bill and get you off my back?"

Ed assumed a blank and mysterious bureaucratic expression and said, "We will evaluate your information and make the appropriate deductions."

"Oh, you mean we're going to have to itemize?" Minnie was amused, in spite of his position.

"That's correct."

"Well then, how much is it worth to you to know who we're talking about?"

Ed thought for a moment. He played with his fries. "How about $250?"

Minnie was outraged. "$250? Two hundred and fifty measly dollars? That's it? That means I still owe you $43-something thousand."

Ed nodded. "$43,613.34. It's going to take a lot more than your bullshit to get us to forget that much money." He was playing hardball. "I don't care who it is, the Grateful Dead or somebody else, but we need details, names, a way in, and, ultimately, we want their money. Our duty is to be efficient in our collection. If the amount is big enough, we'll expense off what you owe us."

Minnie thought about it and said, "Fair enough. How long do I have to get the information together?"

"You've got until the end of the year. About three and a half months. If we haven't worked anything out by then, either with the Dead or whoever or with a payment from you, then we'll have to take further action."

"You mean jail?"

Ed nodded, but not maliciously. He then said, "Mr. Minion..."

"Call me Minnie."

"Uh, Minnie, I don't want to put you in jail. I really don't. I'd rather have the money. That would make everyone happy. The IRS will make deals, but they don't fool around, understand? If you know of some bigger money, tell me about it and perhaps we can work something out."

Minnie paused dramatically and then leaned over the remains

of his lunch and asked, "Ed, do you drink coffee?"

Ed cupped his hand behind a rather large ear and said, "What?" exactly like Minnie had. Then he smiled and said, "Just kidding."

Minnie shook his head in disbelief. "Ed, that's like a sense of humor. Now I know we can do business."

He went on to explain to Ed the general idea of the Cartel. He drew a picture of haughty businessmen laughing behind the back of an ignorant IRS, growing richer with every transaction. Unreported profits from illegal sales. He sketched the huge numbers involved. He described tax evasion on a hemispheric level.

"Ed, this will be the biggest thing for you guys since Al Capone. Think of what this will do for your career."

Ed sipped thoughtfully on his shake.

"So what do you think? $250? $400? How about $475?"

Ed took out a small black book and pulled a pen from his shirt pocket. He opened the book and made a note.

He said, "$315. That's by the tables."

"You've got tables for this kind of stuff?"

Ed gave Minnie a meaningful look. "You don't understand, Mr. Minion."

"Minnie."

"Minnie." He drew himself up as straight as possible in the tight seat. "The IRS is an institution of great logic, efficiency, and probity. That means elimination of error, minimization of risk, and standardization of procedure. It works. It's a model others would be wise to adopt." He looked at Minnie and saw the long hair or what was left of it, a straggly beard, a t-shirt, jeans and a person who now owed $43,548.34. "You could benefit from our example."

"I do," said Minnie. "I do. I am. Ed, this whole conversation is an inspiration to me."

Ed wasn't buying it.

Minnie said, "Look, I need to find out a bit more before I can turn these coffee guys over to you." Now that was an understatement. He knew where they were, but not who they were. "Let me do some work and let's meet again in a week."

"Day after tomorrow."

"Ed, this is a big job."

"Day after tomorrow." Ed was unmoved and unmoving.

Minnie hoped he might be able to come up with something. Otherwise he'd have to stall for more time.

"Okay. Where should we meet?"

"Let's meet here. Same time."

"Here?"

Ed explained, "I've got to eat."

Minnie looked at him and couldn't argue with that. "Okay. It's a deal. I'll see you then." He stuck out his hand.

Ed looked at it as if he might be considering it for dessert, but he finally extended his own and they shook. A new partnership had been formed, though to Ed, forever the skeptic, the outcome seemed less than promising.

Minnie unloaded his tray and walked out the door with a heavier stomach, but with a lighter heart. He owed $315 less to the guys who never forgot.

Chapter Twenty-seven - Taken For A Ride

Minnie left McDonald's and crossed the street, heading toward his car. He was relieved to be out of that place and also relieved to know he could make a deal with Ed and his bosses. The question was how was he going to carry it out. All he knew was that there was a Cartel of coffee maniacs and it seemed like they were everywhere — Brazil, Guatemala, Arizona, Seattle, Boulder. Turning them over to the IRS was a good plan in theory, but now he had to come up with something concrete, some actual names and numbers.

He was lost in these thoughts and he failed to notice, until almost the last moment, that there was a man leaning against his car. Worse, this man was in uniform. At first Minnie thought he was getting a parking ticket, but then he recognized the features of Colonel Able. It was difficult, though, because the Colonel had his cap pulled to his nose and his head was bent low, as if he were trying hard not to be noticed.

It was a shock. What was he doing here? First Ed and now Able. He couldn't get rid of these guys. The Colonel was looking around furtively and muttering, always the paranoid. Minnie didn't take Colonel Able seriously. How could he?

"Colonel, you old goat. What's shakin'?"

"Now get this straight, Mister. I am a Colonel in the United States Air Force, not the barnyard brigade."

"Oh Colonel, you're so uptight." Minnie flashed on Mr. Holstein.

"Mr. Minion, we need to talk."

Minnie leaned against the car. "Okay, shoot." Maybe he shouldn't have said shoot. This was, after all, a representative of the Armed Forces.

Colonel Able quickly scanned the street and then gave Minnie a withering look. "You civilian. Are you crazy? We can't talk here."

He made a motion for Minnie to follow him as he walked towards a nondescript blue Chrysler sedan with government plates.

"Let's go for a ride."

"Colonel, you know I'd like to, but I really have other things to do."

"Mr. Minion, your country calls. Failure to answer could bring severe penalties."

"How severe are we talking?"

The Colonel just stared at him in a way that would have frozen water.

Minnie considered things. "Okay. What the hell? Let's go."

They got into the sedan and the Colonel pulled out of the parking space with a squeal of tires and without regard to traffic. The Colonel drove at an alarming rate of speed. His white knuckles clenched the wheel. His eyes shot toward the rear view mirror every couple of seconds. The acceleration and braking were making Minnie a little nauseous after his big lunch. Minnie had his seatbelt on, but it wasn't very reassuring. He had one hand on the dash and the other gripped the armrest.

"Jesus, Colonel. Slow the fuck down."

"Minion, this is evasive action. We need to elude our pursuers."

"Pursuers?" Minnie almost threw his neck out by looking backwards at the same time that Colonel Able stomped on the brakes and swerved to avoid hitting a woman who was crossing the street with a little girl.

"Minion, this is dangerous business."

"What is?"

"Government work."

"Sure," Minnie said, humoring him.

"We're talking national security. Defense of liberty. Protection of our freedoms, rights, and way of life."

Minnie had to laugh. "Oh, it's that, is it? And who's after us?"

The Colonel took his eyes off both the road and the mirror and stared at Minnie for a dangerous amount of time.

"This is no laughing matter, Minion. There are plenty of people who would like to see us stumble."

Minnie wasn't worried about stumbling, but he was worried about having an accident. So he said, "You're right Colonel." He stabbed his finger in the direction of the road in front of them. "You're so right. I'll do my part. I promise. Just watch the road, okay?"

The Colonel's eyes pierced Minnie for a second longer before returning to the street.

They were crossing the Golden Gate Bridge.

Minnie took notice of this and said, "Uh, Colonel? Just where the fuck are we going?"

"I can't tell you that."

"Oh, that's great. Come on, tell me."

"I'm not at liberty to say."

"Isn't this like kidnapping?"

"We call it conscription."

Minnie shook his head. In honor of his old teacher, Mr.
Holstein, and his past associations, Minnie wanted to cut the
Colonel some slack. He resigned himself to this craziness. "Okay.
Then let's talk."

"Not here."

"Why not?"

"It's not secure."

Minnie looked around. "Colonel, it's just the two of us. We're
in a car on the highway. The windows are rolled up. The air
conditioner is on and we're going 65 mile an hour. Who's going
to hear us?"

This didn't fool the Colonel. "Minion, you've got a lot to learn.
We'll talk when I tell you."

Minnie was losing his patience.

"Look, asshole,"

"That's Able, mister."

"Whatever. If we weren't going so fast, I'd get out right now
and you could talk to yourself."

"And leave your country in the lurch? That's so typical. How
old are you?"

"Forty-two."

"Did you serve?"

Minnie flashed on the bar. "That's all I do," he muttered.

"I meant the Service." The Colonel looked Minnie over as if he
were a lower form of life. "Obviously you're not a veteran. No
respect for your appearance.   Mr. Minion, Americans, true
Americans have a certain level of self-respect which you seem to
fall below."

Minnie was angry now. "Colonel, assholes, true assholes are out
of touch with reality."

Neither of them said anything for the next few miles. Minnie
thought of Kiko. He wondered what she would think of this
insanity. Hell, even Ed was easier to take than this guy. At least
they got to eat. Colonel Able was after the tape for reasons and
delusions all his own. It had been laughable to Minnie before
and it still was, but now he had better things to do than drive
around with a military lunatic.

"Colonel, just where the hell are you taking me?"

"I can't tell you."

"Top secret, huh?"

"Minion, this entire mission is top secret. Our country's defense may rest on you know what."

"You know what?"

"No, you know what."

"I know what?"

"Yes, you. Now shut up. We're almost there."

They were driving down a long deserted road. Tall wire fences lined either side. There were no other cars. Eventually, after what seemed like miles, they came to a gate. There was a guard, complete with rifle, and beside him, on the fence, was a sign — HRC AFB. No Admittance Without Authorization.

The Colonel flipped open his wallet which contained his ID. The guard inspected it carefully. The guard looked at Minnie and then at the Colonel. Colonel Able nodded, in an unspoken agreement that didn't reflect favorably on Minnie, and said, "I'll be responsible for him."

The guard stared hard at Minnie but waved them through.

They drove past some buildings and out onto a huge set of runways. There were hangars and warlike planes scattered across an endless stretch of concrete. The Colonel pulled up next to a particularly nasty looking plane.

"This is it."

"What's the deal, Colonel?"

"We're going for a ride."

This was getting out of hand.

"In that?"

"That's right, mister."

"Cool."

Chapter Twenty-eight - Contact

There were a couple of mechanics servicing the plane. One of them came over and saluted the Colonel and then turned to Minnie with a look of wonder, disgust, and disbelief.

"What are you looking at, mister?" barked the Colonel.

The mechanic snapped back to attention. "Nothing, sir."

"Is everything ready?"

"Yes, sir."

Minnie wondered why these military guys had to shout all the time.

The other mechanic brought them flight suits and Minnie struggled to put his on.

"One leg at a time," suggested the Colonel.

The suits were a dark iridescent blue and covered with pockets and zippers. Minnie was zipping and unzipping all over himself.

"Stop that," the Colonel ordered.

They were handed helmets with large tinted faceplates. Minnie imitated the Colonel and put his under his arm.

The Colonel turned and mounted the steps to the cockpit. Minnie saluted the mechanics but they only laughed at him in an unfriendly way. They evidently thought Minnie had fallen below that level below which no true American should fall.

Minnie looked at the plane. It was small and sleek. Next to the big commercial airliners he had flown in, this was like a go-cart. It was painted black and the designation 153-88F was on the side in white next to an Air Force insignia. Its wings swept backwards at a sharp angle and it had a long narrow nose with a pointed spike at the tip. The black tires of the landing gear came up to Minnie's chest and resembled bloated, but elegant sneakers. The metal gleamed in the sun.

"Get in. We're scheduled for takeoff."

Minnie climbed in behind the Colonel. One of the mechanics had followed him and helped him strap in and connect his radio and oxygen. The mechanic saluted the Colonel once more, ignored Minnie, and then pulled the Plexiglas top of the cockpit forward, where it locked with military precision.

"Can you hear me?" the Colonel asked.

"Ten four, Elinor."

The Colonel said, "Stow it, Minion, while I get us off the ground."

The Colonel then had a conversation with the control tower that, to Minnie, was incomprehensible and seemed to consist almost entirely of numbers. They slowly rolled to the end of a runway that didn't seem long enough. They waited until they got the go-ahead and then the plane leapt forward with an incredible roar. Minnie was pushed back into his seat. They only needed half of the runway because, by that point, the nose was lifting and the Colonel and Minnie shot up into the air.

"Holy shit," yelled Minnie, who strained at the seatbelt to get a better look at things.

This was a rush unlike any Minnie had ever experienced, with or without drugs. He checked the dials in front of him. Needles were moving, digital readouts were flashing, and various screens were displaying data. None of it made sense to him.

There was something that resembled a steering wheel in front of him. Minnie grabbed it and said, "Colonel, let me try to fly this thing."

He heard the Colonel's voice over the radio as if it were inside his own head. "Minion, I wouldn't let you use my toaster, let alone property of the United States Air Force worth 30 million dollars. Now shut up and listen. I brought you up here because it's the only secure place we could meet. Our enemies are every-where."

"That's right, Colonel. And they'll stop at nothing." Minnie smiled at his confirmation of the Colonel's paranoia.

"I'm glad you finally understand the seriousness of this. Have you thought about our previous conversation concerning the tape?"

"Yes, sir," Minnie shouted.

"You realize its importance to the nation, don't you?"

"Yes, sir. And I bet there are other things about it that you aren't even aware of."

"Other than the levitation properties? Like what?"

"A 23-minute Dark Star."

"Dark Star? Is that a code name?"

"Colonel, you do know about it."

The Colonel was cagey. "Dark Star...Tell me more."

"Are you sure we're alone?"

"Of course, you idiot. Now tell me about this Dark Star."

"Well...." Minnie wanted to make this good. He couldn't believe what was happening to him. Here he was, miles above the Earth. Hell, miles above the clouds, hurtling through the air at about 500 miles an hour in a plane not much larger than his Chevy. All they needed was a tape player. He wanted to give the Colonel his money's worth.

"Well, Colonel, Dark Star, to the uninitiated, seems like just another song by the Grateful Dead, but in fact, it's a way to contact beings from another planet. It works on a vibrational level using certain harmonies and rhythms." He let the Colonel think about this one.

"Another planet?" said the Colonel in a horrified tone. "What planet?"

"How should I know? I only know they call it the Dark Star."

"I see. This is better than I thought." And he continued to think about it while Minnie enjoyed the ride.

Finally he asked, "Are you prepared to give me the tape?"

"I have to find it first."

"Find it?" the Colonel shrieked.

Minnie tried to cover his ears, but there was no getting away from this.

"Colonel, I'm not as organized as you."

"Minion, don't play games with me. I know you have that tape and, believe me, I can make your life a living hell. I'd rather that you cooperate, as any real American would and should, but my patience is limited. Do you understand me?"

"You bet." Somehow Minnie wasn't worried about these threats. The whole situation was too absurd.

"You are not under my command, unfortunately, and I'm not ready to use force or violence. That's not the American way."

"It isn't?" Minnie was incredulous.

"Minion, it's a last resort. I'm counting on your sense of patriotism."

Suddenly there was a crackling on the headsets and a gruff, authoritative, military voice broke in, "Go ahead, Colonel, use violence, threaten his ass with a jail term. We want that tape."

Minnie saw the Colonel jump in his seat, despite the belts.

"Who the hell is that?" the Colonel yelled. "This meeting is top secret. Who's there? Answer me."

But the voice never returned. The Colonel was having a fit. In his frustration, he slammed the controls, which sent the plane into a spin that demanded all of the Colonel's attention to set right. To Minnie, it was just part of the ride.

The Colonel brought both the plane and himself under control.

"Minion, you're dealing with me and me alone." His voice was shaking. "Get me that tape. And if you don't..." He paused for effect. "The responsibility for the consequences is yours alone. Do you understand me?"

"Okay, boss. Whatever you say."

Chapter Twenty-nine - Talk To Me

They landed with a bump and taxied back to the hangar. The Colonel was still fuming about their interrupted conversation. He snapped at the mechanics and immediately went to a phone inside the hangar and made a call. Minnie could see him hit the wall with his fist and dance around in anger. The sound of his voice traveled all the way out to where Minnie was standing.

Minnie was trying to adjust to being back on the ground. He swayed, still a little unstable. He was so worked up that he went up to one of the mechanics, slapped him on the back, and excitedly began to tell him about the ride.

"It was so fast. Way too cool. Have you ever done that? Five hundred miles an hour! In-fucking-credible!" And on and on.

The mechanic just looked at him and shook his head, pitying the civilian. This didn't stop Minnie. He kept talking even though no one was listening.

The Colonel walked up to him and Minnie burst out, "Colonel, let's do that again. That was unbelievable. I can't wait to get back in the air. To soar like a bird. To loop the loop. To roar like crazy." He was flapping his arms about.

"Goddamn it, Minion, shut up. And get in the car."

Minnie tried to talk with him, but as they drove out through the gate and down the long road to civilization, the Colonel was still furious and only muttered to himself. Minnie gave up and watched the scenery as it flashed by and thought about being able to tell Kiko all about it when he got back.

The Colonel's driving hadn't improved and Minnie's thoughts soon turned toward prayer. Somehow they made it back to McDonald's without an accident and the car screeched to a halt.

The Colonel's hands still clenched the wheel, but he looked at Minnie and said, "I want that tape. Your country needs that tape. And you better have it the next time I see you." He turned and stared out the window for a moment. "If I didn't have to deal with an old hippie like you, believe me, I wouldn't, but at least you're an American, though only by a technicality."

Minnie smiled at him. "Don't worry, Colonel. I'll find that tape, even if I have to clean the house." It was hard to take him seriously. He got out and leaned in the window. "It's my duty and, by God, I'm going to do it."

The Colonel snapped, "See that you do. Or else." Then he stomped on the accelerator and peeled out, leaving Minnie in the middle of the street.

It was beginning to get dark but Minnie could tell something had happened to his car. It was still in the same parking place and there was no ticket, but it gleamed unnaturally in the streetlights. It had been washed since he left it that morning and he had an idea of who had done it. He opened the door and it was obvious that someone had searched his car. It was unbelievably clean. Definitely the work of a military sensibility.

His tapes were stacked neatly in the glove compartment. The gum wrappers and receipts and other bits of debris had disappeared. He knew this was the work of the Colonel and his boys and he appreciated it. He was glad the Pigpen tape was at Kiko's. He was hoping to stretch out this farce to include another ride.

When he got back to the house, he hurried in, excited to tell Kiko of his adventures. She was working at the computer. He said, "Kiko, you won't believe it."

Her eyes were glued to the screen and she raised her hand to stop him, but he kept going.

He pointed toward the sky and, in a strangled voice, said, "The plane. The plane." He started laughing.

She shot him a look that silenced him. It was obvious she didn't want to talk. That he was interrupting.

Disappointed, he went into the kitchen and began to fix himself a cup of coffee. He made a lot of noise and muttered something about the "fucking computer" and he thought about how the future was going to be completely silent except for the hum of those damn machines and the clicking of mouse and keyboard. Communication would be limited to e-mail and fax and everyone would be silently banging away in their lonely cubicles. No conversation, no hanging out, no Touch.

He noticed that he was using the last of the beans Bowman had given him. That calmed him down a little. He thought about his final meeting with him in Nevada. It seemed like years ago and now Bowman was gone. Dead.

He wondered exactly what he thought he was doing and considered forgetting the whole thing and going back to Boulder and the bar. He wasn't equipped for this. He wasn't a spy or a cop or whatever was needed to deal with these guys. He was just a guy who liked to get high and listen to music. He was just trying to get by and stay away from this kind of trouble. He just wanted to live his life in peace and safety and chase after his cleaning lady. That was as dangerous as he wanted things.

He looked at the empty bag and then over at the cup of

steaming coffee and thought, this is the cause of it all. This stupid coffee, and now Bowman is dead. Why am I drinking this shit?

He decided that this would be his last cup. No more. Zip. It would be a way to honor Bowman.

As he drank the rich, intense coffee, he thought about his old pal, and the more he thought, the more he felt he had to go forward with this thing. Even though he might be an old hippie, like the Colonel said, and even though he didn't know what was going to happen and even though he felt like he was getting in way over his head, maybe there was a way to pay these Cartel guys back for Bowman.

Out loud, he said, "Greedy assholes."

He banged his cup down on the counter and looked up to see Kiko leaning against the door watching him.

"How'd it go?" she asked.

He was still mad at her. "Didn't you notice that it was kind of a long lunch for McDonald's? Aren't you glad to see me?"

Now she got it. She walked over to him and touched his arm. She looked into his eyes. "Of course I am." Then she said quietly, "I was busy." She nodded her head in the direction of the computer. "Maybe we should get rid of that box before it takes over. Come on," she smiled, "tell me all about it. What happened?"

She pulled him into the other room and down onto the couch. His irritation vanished when he saw her smile. He wondered if maybe she really could like an old guy like him.

"Okay." she said. "Tell me everything. Every little morsel."

He tried to look upset, but it wasn't working.

Finally, he smiled and said, "Okay, but you're not going to believe it." And then he launched into the details about lunch.

Chapter Thirty - The End Of Salads

"And you, of your own free will, ate that junk?" Kiko asked. Minnie rubbed his ample belly. "Sweet stuff, it was an experience."

"No kidding. But you shouldn't make a habit of it. It's not good for you. Also, it's part of a plot to pacify the populace."

"Very funny. You sound just like the Colonel."

"Who's he?"

"Another guy who's after me."

"Another guy?" She was incredulous.

"I'll tell you about him next. But the good thing is that Ed and I seemed to be able to come to an agreement. The bad thing is I have to tell him something. I'm supposed to meet him in two days."

"And what are you going to tell him?"

"Well, that's the problem. I don't know. I need to give him names and numbers. Details. What do we know?"

"Not enough. I've been talking with my cousin Mariana. I told her about you." She laughed. "She calls you 'Meanie'."

"That's endearing."

"Isn't it? Anyway, she and I have been talking and it's made me think that what we really need to do is to get off the computer and go down there and check it out ourselves."

"Down where?"

"Brazil."

"Oh sure, that'll be easy. We'll just hop in the car."

"I mean it. Mariana is down there doing everything. I admire her. She's really doing something. Fighting the battle. All I'm doing is pushing buttons."

"Don't you think it might be safer fighting the battle from here?"

"That's just it. We can't see these guys. Can't really get at them."

Then Minnie considered it for a second. "There would be advantages. It would almost be like vacation. The beach, the ocean breeze, Samba..." He was up and singing, dancing suavely before her. "The girl from Ipanema goes walking and when she passes, he smiles, but she doesn't see. No, she just doesn't see. Woo, woo, woooo."

She pulled him back down to earth. "We're talking work. And no girls from Ipanema."

"Right."

She was laughing. He wondered if she could be jealous?

"Look," he said, "we can't go. I have this meeting with Ed. I've got to be there. He can put me in jail."

"He wouldn't."

"Yeah he would and we should stick around in case we hear anything about Bowman."

The mention of Bowman sobered them both up.

"You're right," she said. "But let's keep it as an option. I feel guilty about Mariana. Everyone is taking risks except me. If things had been different it would be me down there."

"I'm glad it's not."

Minnie reached out to her. She changed the subject.

"Now who's this Colonel? We're not talking about Colonel Sanders, are we?"

"You are such a wit. No, gorgeous, we're talking about Colonel—I don't know what his first name is—Able. These military guys don't have first names, only a rank. They aren't like the rest of us."

He told her the story of his first meeting with Able and then of his wild flight that afternoon.

"And you really have this tape?" she asked.

"Of course. It's killer, too. The Colonel is out of his mind, but it is a great tape. And I'm feeding his fantasies. He thinks it's going to save the country from somebody."

"How can it be the only copy?"

"I don't know. It can't be. It just shows you how nuts this guy is."

She changed the subject. "What kind of plane was it?"

"It was black and small and incredibly fast."

"No, I meant the model."

"Like a Ford or a Chevy?"

"Well, just describe it in detail."

He did. He told her its approximate length, that it held two people and he described the dials and everything else he could remember.

"It sounds like a McDonnell Douglas HF-37. It's been around for a few years, but it's a great plane."

"How do you know about this stuff?"

"My brother. He's in the Air Force. I've been up in that plane."

"Come on," he said.

"I've even flown it."

"No." He looked at her with increased admiration.

She shrugged. "I'm licensed for all kinds of planes. My father was a great flyer. World War II. Before he died, he taught me and my brother. I've always loved flying. I still do a lot of it."

"That's incredible. Why aren't you in the Air Force or something?"

"Are you kidding?"

The phone rang. He got up, spread his wings, and flew over to it. He began to samba again, but was stopped in his tracks when he heard, "Minnie? Cowboy here. I've tried not to bug you, but this is serious."

"Cowboy, again? Don't you ever go home?"

"Well, you're gone and I don't trust these other guys. I can't believe we let them use knives."

"Me neither. And I have second thoughts about you." He looked over at Kiko and shook his head.

They talked for a while and Minnie got the lowdown and then, in response to Cowboy's question, he recited the recipe for a kind of salad dressing called Caesar's Death. He tried to reassure Cowboy.

"Don't worry. The place hasn't burned down yet, has it? Okay. So don't sweat it. Keep those burgers turning. No, I will not be back tomorrow. This is vacation, remember? Yes, I will be soon. Vacations don't last forever. Now stop calling me, okay?"

He hung up. "Jeez, that place. It's not like we have a fancy menu. It's burgers and sandwiches, for Christ's sake. Soup, chili, and pizza. It's a bar. I don't know why we even bother to have food. What's wrong with pretzels?"

The phone rang again. He grabbed it.

"Cowboy, get off my case." He listened for a moment. "Okay. Sorry. Yeah, just a minute."

He held the phone out to Kiko. She came over and took a seat.

"Hello?" She listened and as she did, she stretched and got a pen and began writing. "Boy, am I glad to hear from you. What's happening?"

Respecting her privacy, Minnie went over and put on a disc. He turned it loud enough to hear, but low enough so that it wouldn't bother Kiko.

> *I've been ballin' a shiny black steel jackhammer*
> *Been chippin' up rocks for the great highway*
> *Live five years if I take my time*
> *Ballin' that jack and drinking my wine*

He thought about his wild day. How did he get into all this? Bowman was dead. He still couldn't believe it. He'd go along, doing his thing, forgetting all about it, and then it would come back to him. The reality of it. That would take a long time to get over. If he ever did. What had started out as a vacation had become something else entirely. Bowman was gone, that damn key was in his pocket, and everyone was after him. The voice in his head kept repeating danger, danger.

Maybe so, but he had to admit that it was much better than hanging at the bar. At least for now. He began to speculate on just how dangerous it might be. This was not a good activity and luckily Kiko came over and interrupted him, although what she had to say did anything but calm these fears.

In fact, it showed him that he was underestimating.

Kiko's face was ashen and her eyes were red. Tears streamed down her cheeks. Minnie instinctively put his arms around her and simply held her as her body shook with emotion. He waited, saying nothing. The sobbing subsided and Kiko spoke. Her voice was hoarse and low and quiet.

"Oh Minnie, it's my uncle Luiz, Mariana's father. He's dead."

Minnie turned his head and stared out the window.

"What happened?"

She looked up at him, her face wet with tears.

"He was coming home from a meeting in a neighboring village. Mariana says they had been talking about how to stop the coffee guys. It was late at night. His car ran off the road and hit a tree. He was killed instantly."

Minnie flashed on Bowman.

She put her head back on his shoulder and cried some more. Minnie tried to comfort her.

"Minnie, I feel so sorry for her."

"What about the police?" It seemed a reasonable question.

She tried to bring herself under control. Minnie saw her gather her strength and could hear the anger in her voice when she said, "There are no police out there. Well, there are, but they've all been bought off. They said he had been drinking, but Mariana told me he never drinks. This is the same thing as Bowman."

Minnie nodded.

"Mariana doesn't know what to believe. I've tried to tell her before that this is bigger than just her village, that these guys will stop at nothing, and she knows that, but it's been hard for her to really understand. She just sees her village. It's different down there. When stuff like this happens, the police look the other way or paperwork disappears or witnesses do. There's no difference between them and the thugs. It's the money. That's all that matters to them.

"This was no accident," said Kiko. "I need to be with Mariana. I can help her. I can warn her. We need to go down there and find out for sure what happened. Find the connection between this and Bowman. We've got to go."

Minnie nodded, but this news scared him more than anything had.

"We've got to go," she repeated. And then shaking herself, "I'll make the reservations."

She looked into his eyes and his heart went out to her. Her grief and sense of outrage was overwhelming her and yet she was so beautiful. And brave. He had serious doubts about his own courage.

She asked him, "Are you ready for this? I don't know what will happen down there. You shouldn't be involved in this anyway. You don't have to go. I'll understand."

He shook his head. "No way. We're in this together. I'm not leaving you now. Okay?"

She nodded. Minnie continued to hold her and, though he was decided and determined, the thought of what might lay ahead scared him.

Chapter Thirty-one - Not My Usual Self

It was two days later, the day Minnie was supposed to meet Ed at McDonald's. He was scheduled for a Big Mac, but instead he and Kiko were at the San Francisco airport taking off for Brazil. They were seated halfway back on the right side, the plane was in the air, and Minnie was looking out the window and singing in a voice surprisingly soft and gentle, considering. He was trying to swing some lyrics from the thirties.

Kiko was making a lot of noise and fussing impatiently, trying to straighten out the newspaper without hitting him. Finally, she smashed the pages so she could do the crossword; it was a mess.

Minnie leaned over and asked, "Did you ever see "Flying Down to Rio?"

"A movie?"

"Yeah. Fred Astaire, Ginger Rogers. That's kind of like you and me," he said. "See, there's this pilot, who's really a playboy, and lots of babes..."

Kiko had stopped listening and was trying to figure out a five-letter word for "bogged down." From time to time, she said things like "uh huh" and "yeah", but her eyes never left the paper.

She was really thinking about her uncle and Mariana. Still in a kind of shock, she stared out the window. Minnie tried to cheer her up with a few jokes.

"Okay. A horse goes into a bar. The bartender comes up to him and says, 'Why the long face?'"

She continued to look out the window.

"Hmm. Cheeseburger goes into a bar. Bartender says, 'Sorry, we don't serve food here.'"

It wasn't working.

"Minnie, I appreciate the effort, but these jokes just aren't funny. And even if they were, I don't think I could laugh at them."

Minnie nodded. "I don't even think they're funny. Well, the one about the cheeseburger."

"I can't believe all this is happening." She turned back toward the window. Minnie looked up the aisle as the plane droned on.

There was a layover in Dallas for an hour and they left the plane and bought some frozen yogurt from a cart near the gift shop.

As they walked around in circles, Minnie gushed, "There's so

much food in this airport. Pizza, pasta, ice cream, burgers, breakfast, alcohol. We could live here."

Kiko looked at him and said, "Oh yeah. That'd be a lot of fun.
We could settle down and make our home on that nice bench
over by the water fountain."

They were glad to stretch their legs because this was no short
hop. They had 10 hours ahead of them. As they were
reboarding, Minnie nudged Kiko and pointed out a tall woman
in sunglasses. "Check her out."

Kiko turned to him and said, "We're not in Ipanema yet, big
guy."

"No. She looks familiar. I think she's following us."

"Sure." She shook her head at him. "In your dreams."

Back in the air, they played cards for a while, using the meal
tray as a table. Minnie was on his third scotch.

"Gotcha," he said as he won another hand of gin rummy. He
leaned back and tried to stretch his legs. "I suppose you've flown
one of these babies too?"

She smiled. If she couldn't win at cards, she could at least have
the satisfaction of blowing his mind. "As a matter of fact, I have.
My dad used to fly commercially. He'd take me along to the
training sessions, let me work the simulator, and I used to ride in
the cockpit."

"So you've never really flown one?"

"Well, that's a technicality and, without certification, it's illegal
and dangerous. But the simulator is the same thing. It's like
flying with your eyes closed."

"Oh great. That's the way I always fly too."

He got up and went to the bathroom. On his way back, he
casually glanced at the woman he had seen boarding in Dallas.
Her head was bent over a magazine and he couldn't get a good
look at her. It bothered him. When he got back to his seat, he
mentioned this to Kiko, who told him he was just paranoid like
Colonel Able.

As the trip continued, they lapsed into a state somewhere between sleeping and stupid. The drone of the engines sounded
continuously in the background and created a quiet acceptance
and resigned patience in them, but after a while, Minnie had his
head in his hands and was moaning in a low voice.

"Min, what's wrong with you? Ever since we decided to go,
you've been odd. Odder than usual. You're kind of grouchy, you
don't look good, and you keep moaning. What's going on?

You're not getting cold feet are you?"

"I'm not grouchy and thanks for all the compliments. I think it's the coffee."

She gave him a blank look and he realized that she was not as attuned to his every action and fluctuation of mood as she should have been.

"Haven't you noticed anything different about me?" he asked.

"Well, yeah. You're grouchy, you look pale, and you moan all the time."

"Not that. I haven't had any coffee for two days. No, three days. Shit, what day is it? I feel awful. I'm depressed. I just want to lay down and die, but these seats won't let me."

Just then, the phone in the back of the seat in front of them rang. It startled them. Minnie pulled it out of its place and then immediately replaced it. They waited and, after a few moments of silence, were reassured.

She said that it was probably a wrong number and then resumed the conversation. "No coffee? You?"

He told her the story of Bowman's last beans and his decision to stop drinking. She pulled him closer to her, though the cord to the headphones was an awkward restraint, and kissed his cheek. His state of mind improved immediately.

She said, "That feeling will pass in a day or two. You see? It's more of a drug than you thought. Your body's so used to that artificial buzz, it never gets to make use of its own."

"I kind of like that buzz, but..." He fiddled with his glass and shook the ice.

"I know," she said, quietly. "First Bowman and now my uncle. And they're just the people we know. But you're here and we're going down there to find out who's done this."

"Aren't you scared?" he asked.

"Of course I am, but what else can we do? We can't go back to sleep now that we know all this. And, besides, we probably won't get killed. They don't know who we are."

"Uh huh. Probably won't get killed. That's great. Now I feel better."

He turned his head toward the window and began moaning again.

Several hours, three meals, and two snacks later they began their descent. Kiko reached over and took Minnie's hand. She smiled at him in a way that gave him courage. But, by this time, he was so sick of being in the air and not really moving that it wouldn't have mattered if they were met by 30 guys carrying guns and machetes who looked like Juan Valdez. Minnie would have charged out of the plane and been glad to see them.

His head still hurt, he was still depressed and still scared, but he thought anything would be better than the fact that his feet barely fit into his shoes, his throat hurt from the cold, processed air, and that the food had been lousy. His ears hurt too.

All this began to dissipate when he saw the coastline and the blue of the ocean. With each minute, he and Kiko both grew more excited and they had almost convinced themselves that they were like any other tourists who wanted to feel the sun and hang onto their wallets.

The door of the plane opened and they made their way down the aisle toward it. As they got closer, they began to feel the heat and the humidity of the foreign country. After being cooped up in that tin can for 10 hours and in spite of everything, it was intoxicating. They drank it in and stumbled off into the next phase of their adventures.

Chapter Thirty-two - A Samba Beat

They waited with a small crowd for their bags in a stunned kind of relief at being out in fresh air again. Well, relatively fresh. Fresher than that of the plane. Minnie looked expectantly at the unmoving baggage carousel. He thought about that word, carousel. So appropriate for a town that was always in celebration. A town of romance, in Minnie's mind, that mostly lived for sun, music, and love. A town possessed by spring, powered by wine, and wild beyond the fantasies of even a sensual, balding North American like himself.

He looked around at his fellow revelers from the plane and was disappointed. What did they have to do with romance? He saw mostly older Americans: white hair, pale skin, a big people, and most of them wearing glasses. Surrounded by them, he began to feel old too. Did he look older? He needed a mirror and was thinking of finding one when he saw the woman from Dallas with the sunglasses. This mercifully distracted him.

Kiko was standing beside him looking for their bags. He directed her attention toward the woman. "See? What do you think? Is that a wig or what? And she hasn't taken those glasses off yet."

He examined the woman closely, out there in the light.

Kiko was saying, "Minnie, stop it. She's just someone on vacation. Has she talked to us? No. Has she even looked twice at us? I don't think so." She leaned closer to him. "Don't worry," Kiko said as she studied her a little more. "She's oblivious to us. You know, you need to relax a little."

He wiggled his eyebrows, hoping she might help him relax, but she had her attention elsewhere and then suddenly a terrible feeling came over him.

Minnie took Kiko's arm for support and, in a hushed voice, said, "It's Jasmine."

Kiko shook her head. "Now I know you're paranoid. Just like your friend the Colonel."

"It's her. I mean it."

"Okay. Well, go talk to her." Kiko was losing interest.

"Uh uh, not me. I don't ever want to see her again. You talk to her."

Just then, the woman, Jasmine, whoever she was, swung her head in Minnie's direction, sunglasses still in place. He turned away quickly.

"This is weird, Kiko. This is trouble."

"Take it easy. You don't know it's her. And you won't go and find out. So forget it. Maybe all your girlfriends are down here."

That didn't make him feel any better either.

The bags tumbled out of the chute and moved around the carousel. Minnie and Kiko grabbed theirs and started the long walk toward the outside world. Through the windows of the airport they could see the ocean and the green and blue mountains that surrounded them. Color was an integral component of this place, another element like the heat and the water. And it was not just in the landscape, it was part of the people too.

In direct contrast to the pallid Americans who had flown with them, they now saw a range of skin color that was beyond imagining: warm tans, a velvet chocolate, the deepest darkest bluest black. Descendants of Indians, Portuguese explorers and traders, African slaves, immigrants from all over the world. Humanity seemed to expand before Kiko and Minnie in a way inclusive of all, tolerant toward one another, and allowing of every possibility.

This was the first blush. Later they would come to understand the distinctions that existed. The contrast in Rio between rich and poor was stark and ever-present. The streets were lined with homeless people, while the rich flashed by numb and unmoved. The poor clustered together in the favelas on the hills above the city and looked down on the lights and the life that seemed forever beyond their reach.

But for now, after their long flight, Minnie and Kiko were only interested in getting a cab, finding their hotel, and taking a bath. They appreciated the exotic and the foreign, but they were tired Americans.

The taxi situation was chaotic. Lots of people were elbowing their way into cabs, yelling at each other. And the cabdrivers themselves were either asleep, peeling out from the curb, or flying past at a dangerous speed. No matter what Minnie tried, whether politely raising his index finger to hail the next vehicle or shouting in a language known the world over and presenting a more meaningful finger, nothing worked.

A distinguished dark-haired man with round glasses and a little mustache was watching them with amusement. He was wearing a light linen suit and a bow tie. Lean, tan, a local newspaper under his arm, he approached Kiko and Minnie and, taking Minnie's arm, he said in a clear, midwestern American accent, "Perhaps I can be of some assistance?"

He gave a short, high-pitched whistle and a cab immediately pulled up before them. He said a few words in Portuguese to the driver and then turned back to their grateful faces.

"I hope your stay is a pleasant one."

Minnie thought the man's eyes narrowed for a moment and appeared menacing, but it may have just been his own fatigue.

Then the man continued, "Watch out for the heat. It can be dangerous." He emphasized the word, dangerous, in a way that disturbed Minnie. Having said that, the man turned and walked away without looking back. As they watched his retreating figure, Kiko asked, "Who was that masked man?"

The driver took their bags and closed the door behind them. He spoke the equivalent of "Where to?" and after an endless ride, one spent torn between the urge to sleep and curiosity about their surroundings, they arrived at the Sol Ipanema, a tall bank of windows that looked out at the ocean over the infamous beach.

Several hours later and after a much needed nap, Kiko was on the phone with Mariana and Minnie was on the balcony looking out at the ocean. Below him and extending off in either direction was a wide strip of sand. Small white breakers rolled in without ceasing. The mountains stood high in the distance. Minnie had never seen anything so beautiful. From a radio somewhere, he heard a rhythmic music that made him want to dance. It sounded like "Truckin'" with a samba beat, but he could have been mistaken.

The beach below was dotted with tiny figures. He knew that approximately half of these would be women, gorgeous and exotic. He had seen the travel pictures of the beach girls with their skimpy suits, their fabulous tans, their unmatched beauty. He was in a state of growing excitement and impatience.

Hearing Kiko enter the room, he called her name. He continued to gaze at the scene that was making him forget all his apprehensions. "Let's get going. Just look at that beach."

She answered from inside the room. "This may be as close as you get. We've got work to do."

"Yeah, yeah. But the beach. Kiko, we've got to get our bearings. You know, get acclimated. Besides, I keep thinking about Bowman. I need to do something that doesn't have anything to do with coffee or weirdos."

"Okay. Okay."

The beach was just what he needed. It was so long it seemed

endless. The waves never stopped and the air was thick with the heat, even though there was a slight breeze. The smell of the water revived Minnie and just as he had imagined, there were gorgeous and exotic women everywhere.

"This is more like it," Minnie gushed.

He looked over at Kiko and she fit right in. It was as if he were in heaven and when he saw his first topless female Brazilian, he knew it was true. As soon as he saw one, it seemed that all the women he saw were tall, tan, and topless.

Kiko said, "Easy, big guy. Don't have a heart attack."

It was obvious that she, herself, was heart attack material, but she hadn't fallen for the Touch and it was beginning to drive him crazy.

He said casually, "What about you? Wouldn't you feel more comfortable...?" He gestured at a babe walking by who had on a bright fluorescent pink piece of fabric that barely covered anything.

Kiko knocked him off balance with her shoulder and said, "Get a grip."

"That's just what I was thinking." He leered at her.

"Oh Minnie, you're such a sensitive guy."

Minnie laughed. "I know. Well, what about us?"

"Us?"

"Yeah."

She smiled. "I think you being topless is enough for both of us."

Chapter Thirty-three - All Shook Up

The next morning they were driving along roads that deteriorated in proportion to the distance they were from Rio. What started out as a wide freeway became a two-lane highway as soon as they got beyond the suburbs, and then eventually became a dirt road with ruts, bordered on each side by a narrow shoulder and what appeared to Minnie to be a jungle.

Mariana was driving. She was a round, friendly woman with wild hair and wild driving habits. Minnie was in the back seat trying to decide whether it was better to keep his eyes open or closed. Kiko and Mariana were in front talking mostly in English, as Kiko's Portuguese was minimal. Mariana was filling Kiko in on all the news from the village. Tears appeared as she spoke of her father. Kiko reached over and put her hand on Mariana's shoulder. Mariana took a hand off the wheel, which made Minnie frantic, and covered Kiko's.

She brought a smile back to her face as she glanced in the rear view mirror and said in her low, almost hoarse sounding voice, "Don't worry, Meanie. I'm a good driver."

Minnie covered his eyes again and muttered something incoherent.

The funeral was to be that afternoon and even though Kiko had only met her uncle once, she knew that Mariana was devastated and it was an emotional time. Minnie tried to listen to the conversation in the front seat, but everything he heard alarmed him. Mariana told how the pressure had been stepped up and that since her father's death, the people who hadn't sold out were torn between resisting and caving in.

It was hot and Minnie was sweating like crazy. His t-shirt stuck to his body like another layer of skin. The breeze coming through the window as they drove didn't help at all.

Minnie had sympathy for Mariana, but he felt for Kiko. Her uncle's death and the situation in what was more or less her village had given an awful immediacy to their work. He knew Kiko was more determined than ever.

As they got closer to the village, the scenery alternated between a lush jungle, thick and impenetrable, and wide fields under cultivation. Minnie felt relieved when he saw these wide open spaces, which were not as claustrophobic to him as the normal, natural state of the land.

He was thinking how admirable this pursuit of agriculture

was and about how hungry he was when Mariana pointed and said, "This used to be Corinto, a village like ours, only bigger. Now look at it."

There was nothing to see. Minnie's eyes were opened.

She said, "Meanie, this is what happens. The jungle is destroyed along with all the people. Everything is replaced with this." She spat the words out. "And what is left? Nothing. Only this coffee. No life, really. Everything is gone."

Minnie was quiet and more subdued as these wide green spaces became more common. He thought that back in the States, the landscape had also changed. It was happening everywhere, but to different degrees. This realization made him feel like a pessimist.

After a couple of hours of bouncing, swerving, stopping, and starting through the thick and often towering vegetation, the village suddenly appeared around a tight curve and off to the side of the little road. It was a magical place. Huge trees towered above them with wide leaves letting the sunlight fall gently over the whole scene. The size of the village was in harmony with the jungle around it and a sense of peacefulness greeted Minnie. .

Now that the car's engine had stopped its droning, there was a quiet that he had never experienced before. And as Minnie stood looking around and as his ears adjusted to it, sounds came out of this silence — a breeze ruffled the big leaves, birdsong floated toward him like music, insects buzzed and hummed, and other sounds, ones he couldn't identify, made themselves known. They all combined to create this place.

It was an ocean, he decided, without the water. This forest that he saw and felt all around him was huge and mysterious, with currents below the surface and a power he could only partially sense. The intense green, the heat, the density were almost more than he could bear. He put his hand on Kiko's shoulder both to steady himself and to connect with someone, with something he could understand.

The village consisted of a clearing with a few rough houses extending off and away from this obvious gathering place. The people of the village were there, as if awaiting their arrival. But when the three of them walked over, they saw that the villagers weren't interested in them. Instead, they were focused on a bare and simple coffin. A couple of people came over to them and embraced Mariana. One of the big women with tears on her cheeks put her arms around Kiko. This was Mariana's mother. There was a moment of silence and then the villagers began singing in a quiet, melodious tone.

Four men lifted the coffin and the entire group, maybe 25 people total, began to walk at a solemn pace behind it. They moved out of the clearing and onto a pathway that led deeper into the forest, singing all the time. Minnie was at the end of the procession. Kiko was up toward the front with Mariana and her mother.

They came to a cemetery, a clearing really, with wooden head-stones, dark and overgrown with moss, which marked the graves. They placed the coffin in a shallow hole and all gathered closely around it in an attempt to comfort both the deceased and them-selves. A man talked in a low voice for several minutes and every now and then the mourners responded with a word or a short phrase, punctuating the man's sentences and adding to his senti-ments.

Then suddenly it was over and they filed back down the path, leaving two men to cover the grave. They walked slowly, singing once more and as they walked, people began to leave the proces-sion at intervals, going down paths Minnie hadn't noticed on the way there. Soon they were back at the clearing, Kiko, Minnie, Mariana, her mother, and a couple others. Everyone embraced and the ceremony was over.

Kiko and Minnie spent the afternoon as guests of the village. A meal was served and conversation arose. There was talk of the troubles they all faced, but it was subdued and the day passed quite sadly. Eventually it was time to go. Goodbyes were offered and then the three of them walked to the car.

Minnie was the first to see it and he let out a cry of surprise. All the windows, the windshield, and all of the lights were bro-ken. Glass littered the ground and reflected the afternoon light. They stopped and looked around worriedly and then looked at each other. Everything was as still and peaceful as before, but in the midst of it was this wreck, this act of violence, to remind them of what they were really dealing with.

Mariana broke the spell by screaming something in Portu-guese, an anguished cry of anger and frustration. She turned to them and said, "Let's get out of here."

They drove back without conversation and as Minnie looked out through the hole where the window should have been, he saw big earth-moving equipment near the road. He didn't un-derstand how he could have missed this on the way there. He felt the air on his face and was listening to the whine of the small car's engine when suddenly a big pickup pulled alongside.

There had been few cars on the road since they left the village and no one had seen this coming. They weren't going very fast.

The man on the passenger side of the truck was wearing a baseball cap and dark glasses. He smiled down at Mariana and then, without warning, the truck swerved into them, its fender hitting their car with a jolt. Kiko screamed as Mariana somehow kept the car on the road and sped up.

Minnie leaned out the window and shouted, "Get the fuck over, asshole!"

As an answer, the truck hit them again. There was a horrible sound of metal against metal. Everything happened as if in slow motion, but before they could really react, their car was going into the ditch.

It was only Mariana's wild driving experience that saved them. The pickup honked its horn and roared off while Mariana cranked the wheel and stomped the brakes, bringing them to a stop just in front of a huge tree. Minnie crashed into the seat in front of him, but Mariana and Kiko somehow held on.

Just as suddenly as it had begun, everything was suddenly still. Their motor idled, dust was settling, and off in the distance they could hear the pickup fading away.

They looked at each other in shock. Mariana asked if they were hurt. No one was. They sat there for several minutes stunned. Minnie could feel the warm breeze of the jungle and hear the life within it. He was at a loss for words. Then Mariana backed the car, drove up the low embankment onto the road, and headed for the city.

Chapter Thirty-four - This Latté's For You

After this incident, they decided to lay low for a while and try to figure out their next move. Kiko and Minnie stayed mostly in their hotel rooms and Mariana stayed with friends in the city. They made an appointment to get together three days later.

They met at a place called the Polar Bear Club, a small bar, a few blocks in from the beach. It was dark inside, but it opened onto the street and had a small patio that held a couple of tables.

After their experience on the day of the funeral, this was like a reunion. They all embraced and were glad to see each other. Mariana had a friend with her named Ze, a huge, dark-skinned guy with short curly hair, who, amazingly, was wearing a Grateful Dead t-shirt. Ze, it turned out, was from a nearby village and spoke little English, only a dialect of Portuguese. Mariana said that he wanted to speak to them. She and Ze had been working together for the past few months trying to organize their neighbors and find out what they could about the people who wanted their land. She translated for Ze. When he wasn't talking, he smiled gravely and nodded.

He looked over at Kiko and said in halting English, "I am sorry about your uncle."

She nodded. He turned back to Mariana and reached out for her hand. His smile was full of compassion. They were all quiet for a moment and then he began his story.

"I come from a village near Mariana's. Our families are friends and when the trouble started we both wanted to do something."

Mariana translated between his pauses.

"Well, first, these smooth operators from a company called Terra Gorda came and offered us money, wanting to buy our land. They came with cash and talked of all that was waiting for everyone here in the city. All the good things. Some people thought this was great. Crazy people offering lots of money. They took it and ran, but others of us are not as naive as we once were. It seemed like a lot of money there in the village, but in the city it is different. We know that life can be hard away from the village and friends."

He leaned toward them. "I can tell you from personal experience." He gave a short laugh. "Money is easy to lose, land is more difficult. Our life in the village is simple and we know it and trust it. We have a rhythm. It is slow and the land has been in our families for generations. We don't do much with it, but we all get by somehow or we help each other.

"Life has been much the same there for a very long time. It is sweet mostly and peaceful. Or it was until these men came and changed everything. Our life is not as fast or as hard as this..." He gestured at the narrow and busy street before them and at the buildings all around.

"So most of us refused their offers. These men were not happy when they went away. But they came back and though they offered more money this time, they were not as polite. The people began to get afraid, and strange and awful things began happening."

Minnie and Kiko were listening closely.

"What kind of strange things?" Kiko asked.

"Official-looking letters arrived, though they turned out to be false, saying that the government was taking our land. Then a fire burned down the house of a man who had refused to sell. There were mysterious threats. Dead animals were left on doorsteps. Some more people sold their land, but still most refused." He smiled briefly. "We are simple, but stubborn."

Kiko asked, "And these were people from Terra Gorda who were applying the pressure?"

Ze and Mariana conferred for a moment. He then nodded and said, "It had happened in other villages. Everything had been taken and their land cleared for planting. I've been doing some checking and, as I told Mariana on the way over here, the men from the company were Brazilian, but they represented Americans."

Minnie broke in. "Americans? What do you mean?" All this time he had been imagining this to be the doing of some kind of Brazilian Mafia.

Ze spoke with Mariana again and she asked him a couple of questions.

Mariana then continued to translate. "I've spent the last two weeks going through the records that are public and have tried to find out as much as possible. What I uncovered is that the people behind this are Americans who have lived in Brazil since World War II. They left America because they were sympathetic to the Germans during the war."

"American Nazis?" Minnie asked. He was dumbfounded. This was getting weirder every minute. "Nazis?" he said again. It was hard to believe. "And they're still alive? That was a long time ago, you know."

Ze shrugged. "All I know is what I've heard and what I've been able to turn up. They are old and very rich, very powerful. It appears the government is involved too, which means trouble. The corruption is on a large scale. Everybody has been bribed and bought off.

"What tipped me off was a visit I had from a representative of the company. He was apparently a powerful person, high up in the organization, who came to pressure me. He was smooth and persuasive. And although he spoke fluent Portuguese, he was white and when I continued to refuse to sell, he lost his temper and yelled at me in English— with an American accent. I didn't understand it, but it was enough. That got me to do more checking."

Minnie and Kiko just stared.

Ze continued. "Then my cousins, Joao and Paulinho, were found dead. Their car had gone off the road. The police said it was an accident, but no one believed them. That's when everyone really began to sell out, but now the prices weren't so good. That was last month. I was there two days ago and most of my village and at least half the land around it has been flattened and there are armed guards in jeeps patrolling these new fields. All are planted in coffee. And ours is not the only village this has happened to. This is going on everywhere. It seems like the whole jungle is being flattened and everyone driven off."

All this time he had been telling the story with a kind of hard anger, but now his voice was choked and he looked away. Minnie saw a tear on his dark cheek. There was nothing they could say. Kiko and Mariana ordered fruit drinks and Minnie and Ze each a beer. City life continued around them.

Then Kiko brought out a big envelope filled with papers and spread them out on the table. Ze had his own folder. The four of them discussed what they knew and put their information together. It was fairly thorough and consisted of names and addresses, bank-account numbers, and distribution routes.

Kiko was very excited. "This is it. This is great. We'll be able to at the least complicate things for them."

She looked over at Minnie. He was excited too.

He was smiling at the Brazilians and saying to Ze, who, though he didn't speak the language, understood the sentiment, "We'll nail those bastards and shut 'em down."

Ze handed Mariana a piece of paper. He said something to her which made her mouth drop open. She looked at the paper. Minnie could see that there was a name written on it. Then she and Ze had a rapid conversation. Mariana was almost shouting and was gesturing wildly.

Mariana grabbed the newspaper she had brought with her and tore through it until she found what she was looking for. She shoved the paper at Ze, pointing. He grabbed it and his eyes widened. As soon as he saw it, he began shaking his head affirmatively.

Mariana turned to Kiko and Minnie and waving the small piece of paper said, "This is the name of the man who yelled at Ze. I remembered reading it in the newspaper this morning."

She took the newspaper from Ze, who was still reading it, and smoothed it out before them. Minnie and Kiko saw a whole page obviously devoted to society happenings. There were pictures of well-dressed partygoers with wine glasses, one of a large mansion, and several more of small groups of people, men with dark eyebrows and women with lots of jewelry. Toward the bottom of the page was a photograph of a couple posing next to a yacht.

Pointing to it, Mariana said, "This is the man Ze met with."

Kiko looked at Minnie, grabbed his arm, and said, "The guy at the airport. With the taxis."

Minnie had paled considerably. "That's Jasmine with him."

Kiko couldn't believe it. "Your Jasmine?"

Minnie threw up his hands.

"This is too wild," Kiko said excitedly to Mariana. "This guy's an American and Minnie knows the woman who's with him."

Mariana looked at Minnie questioningly.

"It's a long story," he said.

After this revelation, they discussed the situation and decided that Kiko and Minnie would pursue the leads they had in light of this American connection and that Mariana and Ze would do some digging on their own. They would meet again in two days — same place, same time.

Minnie took one last look at the photo and at Jasmine and was thinking quite personal thoughts when Kiko pulled him away and the four of them waved goodbye.

Walking back to the hotel, Minnie and Kiko had a lot to talk about as they made their way through the sea of people. While waiting in the crowd at a corner, a voice — an American voice — close to Minnie said, "Go home while you're still in one piece. This isn't any of your business."

Minnie turned, but no one was there. He looked down the sidewalk and saw a thin man in a linen suit walking away quickly, losing himself in the crowd.

"Did you hear that?" he asked.

Kiko nodded, but said nothing.

Chapter Thirty-five -
Put That Wig Hat On Your Head

Minnie said, "We need to talk with these guys even if they are Nazis. I've got to get names and information for Ed." He looked at her and then made a decision. "I'm going after that guy. I'll meet you back at the hotel."

And before she had a chance to say anything, he rushed off down the busy sidewalk in what appeared to be a futile pursuit. He took off after that threatening voice and at first feared he had decided too late and had lost the man in the crowd. But toward the end of the block, he saw the thin man in the linen suit turn back and scan the sidewalk apprehensively. The man saw Minnie and began to run.

At one time Minnie had been, without question, Livingston High School's number-one Nose Tackle. He liked to think of himself as a player so big, so fierce, and so fast that sometimes the opposing teams would forfeit rather than face him. Admittedly, that was some time ago, but time for Minnie was a relative thing, very relative, and inspired by past deeds of glory, he turned on the speed. Minnie felt he was gaining on his quarry when he saw the man turn the corner.

In accordance with some immutable law of physics, Minnie was huffing and puffing and had slowed considerably by the time he reached the same corner. He looked down the block and the man had vanished. Minnie stopped to consider his options and, incidentally, to catch his breath.

"Damn," he managed, in a voice loud enough that several innocent passersby looked over at the Nose Tackle.

Minnie thought that either this guy he was following was incredibly fast or he had ducked into one of the buildings lining the street. At this very moment he might be flattened against a doorway, one eyeball peeking around the side of the building, his gun drawn, ready to fire. Or he could be crouched in a narrow alleyway, prepared to spring upon Minnie as he passed by. Or he had simply vanished mysteriously, the way foreigners do. Except that Minnie suspected that this man was an American.

No matter what the real story was, Minnie wasn't taking any more chances. He waited. Finally, he regained his equilibrium and his breath. Seeing no sign of the man, Minnie began to walk down the street cautiously.

His head was turning from side to side to prevent being taken by surprise and his body was in a half-crouch of defensive readiness that had the natives commenting on the irrational fear of Yankee tourists. After a while, Minnie began to admit that the chase was over. Somehow the man had eluded him and it seemed that now all his caution was unnecessary. He straightened up and was wondering what to do next when a long black limousine drew up to the curb beside him.

He took a step or two backwards and considered it. This was too weird. He smiled, because he thought he knew what was coming. The back door opened and a voice called out, "Minnie?" It sounded familiar. Then a hand, a female hand with bright red nails became visible and, with a long, sensuous finger, it beckoned him toward the dark cavern of the limo.

He took a step closer and tried to see who was doing the beckoning. Running a hand over his dome, he reached back to straighten his remaining curls. He cleared his throat.

"Oh, no," he said. "I may be a romantic. I may be a fool for love. I may be reckless in matters of the heart." This is sounding good, he thought. "But I'm not falling for that. You come out here where I can see you."

There was a moment's pause and then he heard the sound of silk on leather as the rest of what was attached to the hand slid to the open door. A long leg in skin-tight silver hose extended itself out toward the street. At its end was a red leather cowboy boot. Minnie considered the possibilities.

He calmly waited and when she emerged, she was wearing sunglasses and what was obviously a wig.

"I know it's you," he said.

The woman laughed in a way that wasn't funny, in a way that had only the barest acquaintance with amusement. She then pulled off the wig, gave her own hair a shake, and removed her glasses.

Minnie flashed on some buried knowledge of Shakespeare. Something about the fury of a woman scorned.

He couldn't resist asking, "Jasmine, you're not still mad at me for standing you up, are you?"

"Oh Minnie, you old fool."

He was sensitive on this point. He bristled, "Just how old do you think I am?"

At this point in the conversation, she pulled out a small, elegant, but completely believable revolver and pointed it at Minnie. The encounter was taking a nasty turn.

"Oh, Jasmine," he said. "What about our love?" Despite the

seriousness of his situation, Minnie had to laugh at that one and he broke into a loud cackle.

"Love," she said with disdain. "We're not talking about love, we're talking about coffee. We're talking about you and that girl getting in the way of progress."

"Progress?"

She laughed for real at this and smiled at him. "Okay, money. I like you, Minnie, but that's in the past. This is the end of the line for you."

Just then Minnie heard a high-pitched ringing. Jasmine picked up the cellular phone next to her, never taking her eyes or her gun off Minnie. Jasmine paused, answered, and then handed it to him.

"It's for you," she said in an astonished voice.

Minnie took the phone. He listened for a second. "Yeah? Cowboy, not now. I'm busy."

He handed it back to her while she examined him, questioningly. He wasn't explaining.

After a moment, she said, "I think it's time we went for a ride."

He looked at her. This had gone too far and he was getting mad. "I think you've already taken me for one. I'm sorry, but I've got other plans."

Just then, Sascha got out from the driver's seat and began to walk around toward Minnie. Jasmine raised the gun and said, "I'm afraid that whatever these plans are, you'll have to cancel them."

Chapter Thirty-six -
Reach Out And Touch Someone

Sascha clamped a big paw on Minnie and smiled down on him.

Minnie wasn't having fun anymore and asked, "What are you smiling at, shithead?"

The big Russian gave Minnie a short but devastating punch in the ribs and Minnie felt a sharp snap somewhere inside.

Jasmine said, "Enough, Sascha. I still need to talk with him."

Minnie recovered a bit and acted innocent. "Talk to me about what?"

"Don't play games with me. I need to know everything you've learned about our business dealings."

He thought about the envelope of information in his pack and the key in his pocket.

"What? Like I know anything? I'm here on vacation. And by the way, that was a nice picture of you in the paper."

She was getting impatient and, in a voice like a knife, ordered, "Tell me."

To buy time, Minnie found himself saying, "I'd rather tell it to your boss."

After he said it, he wondered what was wrong with him. Was this an expression of courage or had he simply spent too much time in the sun? Sure, he wanted information on the Nazis to feed to Ed, but this verged on being truly stupid.

"Okay," said Jasmine. "But you're not going to like him."

She picked up the phone and punched in some numbers to call and make arrangements. Minnie was holding his side, wheezing. Sascha still had him in his powerful grip. The street, inexplicably, was almost empty and the few who were there paid no attention to this odd gathering at the curb.

Jasmine was conferring with her evil cronies, arguing. Minnie looked up and Sascha was sneering at him.

"I know, I know," Minnie heard her say. "But the plan's changed. That's not my fault. You can't do that!"

Minnie was wondering just how he was going to get out of this mess, when a strange noise erupted from the phone. It was a sharp and surprisingly loud burst of static. Both Minnie and Sascha could hear it. At the same time, Minnie distinctly saw a flash of bright blue sparks pass between the phone and Jasmine's ear. She gave a cry of pain and jerked violently in her seat. The next thing Minnie knew, she tumbled out of the limo and hit the pavement with a sickening thud.

She lay looking up at them, her eyes open, staring at nothing. Her mouth was slack and a small stream of blood ran out of the corner of it into the dirty street. She didn't look like she was breathing.

Sascha let go of Minnie and went to her aid. It was Minnie's only chance and he took it. Holding his side, he ran in the direction of the hotel. He looked back as he was about to turn the corner. Sascha was still bent over Jasmine's lifeless form. The way to the hotel was clear.

He forced himself to be calm and he walked, more slowly now, toward the hotel. As he did, he tried to flag a cab, but with no success. He had to walk the entire way, stopping every now and then to get his breath.

The pain had let up a little by the time he got to the hotel, although he was soaked in sweat. The doorman held the door politely, but he gave Minnie an inquisitive look.

"Too much jogging," Minnie told him. He glanced back at the sidewalk and then quickly stepped into the sleepy lobby and made his way to the elevator.

As he knocked at Kiko's door, he felt just how tired and hurting he was and hoped she was there. It opened a cautious crack and then the chain rattled and Kiko popped out. She was beaming.

"Oh, I'm so glad to see you," she said and threw her arms around him.

He cried out and Kiko drew back and examined him.

"You look awful. What happened?"

He tried, "Too much jogging?"

She laughed and pulled him into the room and motioned for him to wait. She stuck her head out into the hall and then pulled the door shut behind them and locked it.

Minnie lay himself carefully down on the bed. Any kind of sudden movement hurt him. Kiko propped up the pillows behind his head and as they sat there looking at one another, the noise of the street below came through the open door of the balcony. It was the same as it had been the day of their arrival — droning steadily and punctuated only by the honk of a horn or a particularly loud truck. Kiko and Minnie, however, had both been changed by their time in Rio.

She leaned close to him and kissed him. It was a quick but warm kiss that went a long way toward reviving him. She drew back.

Minnie was beaming. "Let's try that again. I feel better already."

She shook her head and said, "Minnie, tell me what happened. Where does it hurt?"

She hadn't seen any blood and she thought that was encouraging.

Minnie pointed to his left side. "I think I broke a rib or something. No big deal." He smiled weakly.

She demanded, "Who did it?"

"It was her," he said.

"Who her? Her who?"

Minnie smiled. "Her who?" he repeated. "You are too much." He began to laugh until it hurt. When he could go on, he explained, "The woman on the plane. With the wig. Jasmine."

"She broke your ribs?"

"No, gorgeous. Her goon, Sascha. He caught me when I wasn't looking. And I was right. She was following us."

He went on to tell her the details of the chase and about the ghastly aftermath.

"Electrocuted by her own cellular phone," he said. "It's got to be some kind of instant karma. I hate those phones. Maybe her bosses got rid of her. It's too technical for me. Anyway, that's when I made a break for it."

He paused. "Kiko, these guys scare me. They're not fooling around."

"No kidding. While you were out there, I had a little adventure of my own."

Minnie sat up with a jerk, but the pain forced him back into the pillows. "What happened?"

"Well, after you ran off like a maniac, I walked back toward the hotel and, while I did, I began to get this feeling that someone was following me. All the things that have happened, the Nazi talk, my uncle, it was getting to me. I thought maybe I was just overreacting, but I looked behind me and there really was a guy staring at me."

"That's not weird. Who wouldn't?" Minnie said.

"Thanks for the compliment, but he was weird. Not smiling. So I walked a little quicker and didn't look back until the end of the block. At the light, I looked over my shoulder and didn't see him. Well, that was fine, I thought, but then I spotted him about 20 feet away. He was with another guy and they were both staring at me. One of them said something to the other. The other guy nodded and they started walking toward me.

"The light hadn't changed, but I wasn't waiting around to find out what they wanted. I ran out into the traffic, dodging between cars. I looked back and they were chasing after me. I was really scared then. Once I got across the street, I ran as fast as I could. I could hear them behind me and they were shouting something in Portuguese. I was bumping into people and I couldn't figure out where the hotel was."

"Jesus, Kiko. This is incredible." He reached out to her.

"It gets worse. I crossed another street and almost got hit by a delivery van. They were still after me."

"What did they look like?"

"They didn't look like Nazis, but they weren't very friendly. I was just about ready to collapse when I saw a guy ahead of me on the sidewalk. For a moment I thought he might help me, but then I saw that it was him. The guy from the airport. The guy in the paper. It got me going again. I tore down an alley and, when I came out, a truck turned in almost hitting me, and cut them off. I could see the hotel. It was a miracle. I ran like crazy and I've been here with the door locked ever since."

Kiko was out of breath, just like in her story.

They were quiet for a moment and then Minnie said softly, "I'm glad you're safe."

She asked, "What about your ribs? We should take you to see a doctor."

Minnie said, "Oh no you don't. It's too dangerous. This is a foreign country and I'm not going to any of their hospitals. Anyway, I'll be fine tomorrow."

She looked doubtfully at him. Just then the phone rang.

Minnie stared at the phone wide-eyed, in fearful anticipation of another accident, but Kiko picked it up, put it to her ear, and listened.

She put her hand over the receiver and said, "It's Mariana."

They lay on the bed against the pillows with the phone between them, listening. Kiko gave Mariana a brief rundown of both their encounters, while Minnie felt the heat of her body so close to his. He shifted his position as if to hear better. Kiko couldn't help smiling, though she had other things on her mind.

The first thing Mariana said after hearing her story was that they should leave Brazil immediately.

Kiko protested. "Not now, not after all this has happened."

Mariana insisted, saying, "It is too dangerous for you. You don't know your way around here. Too many people have been hurt. Killed. You can be more effective back home alive than dead here in Rio."

This was an observation Minnie could agree with wholeheartedly.

"I don't want to be responsible for anything happening to you."

Kiko broke in. "You wouldn't be."

"This is no time to argue. Both of you must go home. I know you want to help. You want to take care of me but, really, I can do that myself. And I know it's hard for you, Kiko. At the bottom of it all, you feel like a stranger in both countries.

"But you can do more good for all of us when you're back in the States where you can find things out and where you can contact people and give them the information we've gotten. In Brazil, that's impossible. I know this is bigger than just my village, my story. Something's got to be done. Here you'll just be in the way and at risk."

Kiko tried to argue, but it was no good. She knew Mariana was right. They spoke a little longer, stretching out the goodbye and agreeing to talk soon once Kiko was back in California.

Minnie said, "Goodbye. Don't worry."

Kiko hung up the phone. They were still close together on the bed, looking at each other in silence. It was dangerous for them. Both in Rio and there on the bed. Kiko leaned over and gave Minnie a kiss. A real one. He kept his eyes open.

Then she got up and said, "We better get out of here while we can."

Minnie attempted a deep breath and nodded.

Chapter Thirty-seven - A Bright Idea

An hour later they were at the airport checking their bags and making their way to the gate. Outside, through the windows, the scene was as it had been on their arrival, lush and green and exotic, but it didn't seem as warm and had none of the exciting invitation it had had just a few days before. Minnie thought it now seemed menacing to both of them. Not a place of fun and music and beaches, but one of fear and danger and death.

Even though they were leaving, Minnie was nervous and he kept looking around at the crowd. He didn't know what to expect, but at one point, as they stood in line for their tickets, he saw a woman in sunglasses and what seemed to be a wig. His heart began racing, but he looked closer and saw that he was mistaken. His mind flashed back to the picture of Jasmine lying on the pavement and he remembered that he had witnessed something awful and final.

At last their flight was called and they were boarding. As they shuffled in the line to the gate, the few remaining hairs on the back of Minnie's head went up and he turned to check out his fellow passengers. It was probably nothing, he thought, just this place and all that had happened. But then he saw, standing on the fringe of the now empty seats of the waiting area, the man who had helped them with the cab, the man he had chased after.

At that distance, Minnie couldn't read the expression on his face. He was about to go after him when the flight attendant at the door asked for his boarding pass. Minnie saw the man turn and disappear into the crowd.

"Sir? Your ticket please," she asked again.

Minnie was distracted and growled, "Don't call me sir."

Once aboard, Minnie told Kiko what he had seen. He was kicking himself for not running after the guy and breaking his neck, but Kiko just rolled her eyes. After a while, he forgot about the airport and began to focus on her lips. She had a thoughtful, but not encouraging look on her face.

"Thank God we're out of there," she said.

They were silent for the first part of the trip, both thinking about what had happened. Minnie, in particular, went over the week's events and thought that he should have done more. He should have caught the guy he had chased. He should have been more observant.

The situation was terrible and he was worried about Mariana

and Ze. It was important that he and Kiko had gotten all of that information from them. With it they should be able to do something. When he thought of Jasmine's awful end and the possibility of something similar happening to himself or Kiko, he knew they had made the right decision. It wasn't such a bad idea to leave.

Ze's information appeared to be true that the coffee guys, alias Terra Gorda, alias the Coffee Cartel, were Americans. Everyone who had threatened them had been American. Even the guy in the truck had been wearing a White Sox cap. He and Kiko had the information from Mariana and Ze, but it would have to check out first.

He hoped it was accurate and complete enough to convince Ed to take some action. Being an accountant, he would be hard to convince, but they now had the names, pictures, and numbers they needed to connect these people and he wanted to turn them over to Ed. Besides this, there was all the information publicly available about the rainforest — pictures, statistics, scientific reports. They just needed to get someone to do something. Kiko and Minnie were no match for all the money and the guns of this Cartel, but Ed and the IRS might be able to hassle them. They were, after all, the ultimate hasslers.

During the long hours of the flight, they talked it all over. There was cause for hope, but they both agreed that the situation made them feel disappointed and defeated. The information on the rainforest had been available for years and no one had done anything yet. It was depressing.

Maybe nothing would happen and Minnie's plans of avenging Bowman had met a dead end. And what should he do about the key? Everything was a mess. He wondered if he had been fooling himself by thinking he could change the way things were, that he could do something that made a difference. Maybe it was just a vacation fantasy. Minnie admitted to himself that he had wanted to be a hero, especially in Kiko's eyes, but that now all that was over and they were heading home.

As if that weren't enough, he wondered what he was going to do about the IRS. What if Ed didn't buy this stuff? He began to worry again about his tax bill. There was no way he could come up with that much money and Ed, even with his good points, was not about to forgive a debt like that. Minnie shuddered as he thought about the prospect of jail. It just wasn't his style.

Kiko turned to him with a pained expression on her face. This did nothing to diminish her looks, but it did indicate to Minnie that she, too, was feeling bad.

He smiled at her and said softly, "Okay, shoot."

"Oh Min, what a failure I am. I've let everyone down. Everyone in the village and everyone I've worked with on this coffee business. It's like nothing happened."

He let her get it all out.

"The Dead have paid for all this work, all of my time, and still nothing has happened. I'm disappointed in myself. I wanted to help Mariana and all I've done is get her into more trouble."

Minnie said, "Kiko, Mariana values your help enough to want you to leave. She knows you can do things that she can't."

"I hope she's right. It feels terrible leaving her there."

Minnie put his arm around her shoulder and held her tight.

A couple of hours later, somewhere over the Gulf of Mexico, over a Bloody Mary, and during the terrible movie being shown, Minnie turned to Kiko and said, "When I find myself in a situation like this, I always ask myself, 'What would Jerry do?' "

She had a lot of respect for Jerry, too, but she just shook her head. Minnie was demented.

He was cackling now. The movie watchers across the aisle gave him dirty looks and made disapproving noises.

"Okay, okay. Just kidding," he said. "But really, what are we going to do? We can't just take this crap lying down. There has to be a way to stop these guys. We need to find a way to publicize the information that exists and all the stuff Mariana gave us. Something big."

Kiko didn't know what to say. She glanced out the window, down on the earth below, the earth that was being so mistreated, and then, suddenly, she had an idea. A great idea, she thought. An idea that scared her and, at the same time, seemed infinitely appealing.

She turned to Minnie. "I've got it," she said. "We'll use the Space Shuttle."

He suspected that either the altitude or the martinis were getting to her.

"For what? And what do you mean 'we'?"

"We'll use the Shuttle to go public. We'll go into space and hold a press conference. They'll have to pay attention then."

"No one's going to let us use the Shuttle for anything. We can't convince Ed of this stuff, let alone NASA."

"We won't have to. We'll steal it."

Minnie had an awful feeling that she was serious.

"Kiko, I'm the one who's done too many drugs, remember?"

Chapter Thirty-eight - You Can Trust Me

It felt good to be back in the U.S.A. They hadn't been gone that long, but things were now very different. Minnie could feel it every time he took a breath.

Now that he was back in California and he wasn't in immediate danger except from earthquakes and fast food, Minnie became reflective again. He and Kiko had had their lives threatened and had met some of the natives on whose land this battle was being fought. He had seen Jasmine get her just desserts, although he wasn't sure that that kind of dessert was absolutely necessary. It had pained him to see her end that way, even though she hadn't had any good intentions where he was concerned. She and Sascha wouldn't have thought twice about his death. But she was a woman and he was a man (he loved this kind of talk) and he couldn't help but think about their wild night together.

This idea of stealing the Shuttle had its attractions, but only as a deranged fantasy. It was absurd. Minnie knew you just couldn't waltz in and fire it up. People trained for years to fly that thing. People who could take orders, who were actual pilots, who weren't afraid of heights. Sure, in theory, it would work. Once in space and in charge of the Shuttle, they would be able to command the attention of the entire world, probably. They'd be able to demand things, to dictate policy, to sway public opinion. But they'd probably kill themselves in the process and put the environmental movement back a couple of decades. This was not the kind of vacation Minnie wanted. He tried to put it out of his mind and hoped that Kiko would forget about the whole thing.

Despite his reluctance, Kiko took Minnie to a doctor who checked him out and wrapped him up and told him to be more careful about who he hung out with. His ribs were healing fine. Among the things that would take a little longer to heal might be his relationship with Ed.

When they returned, there had been a blistering message from Ed waiting among the more docile letters in the mailbox. It was no form letter this time, but a direct, handwritten blast about being stood up at McDonald's. He owed Ed and his friends a lot of money, but Minnie had to laugh at the concept of being stood up at the Golden Arches.

In the letter, Ed had given Minnie an ultimatum demanding his presence at a meeting on the 25th. Or else. Minnie didn't have to wonder about the what else; Ed made it quite clear: Be there or go to jail. And then Ed elaborated — go to prison, the slammer, the clink, the pen, the calaboose, the jug, the pokey, the hoosegow, the cooler, the can, the tank. Reading this, it made Minnie smile to think that it wasn't simply zeal on Ed's part, but that beneath his white, polyester-shirted accountant's pudginess, there might beat the heart of a true poet.

This was something he appreciated, but he also appreciated that Ed actually did have the power to send him to jail. So when the 25th arrived, two days after their return from Rio, Minnie waved goodbye to Kiko, started up the red Chevy, and made the trek to Mill Valley to meet Ed.

It wasn't until he got into his second QuarterPounder that Ed did more than glare at Minnie ferociously with his little eyes. Or every now and then voice a disgusted grunt across the brightly colored table. Minnie had at first attempted to apologize and explain what had happened, but when he told Ed that he had gone to Rio, Ed began choking and turned a frightening shade of red and Minnie decided that it might be better to let him conduct this meeting in his own way.

Finally, Ed coherently spat out, "Rio? You went on a vacation? You owe me $43,548.34 and you went on vacation?"

Minnie pointed out that he was already on vacation and that he didn't actually owe Ed any money personally, he owed it to the government.

Ed waved this away with his burger. "Time is running out, Mr. Minion."

"Minnie, please."

"Minnie." He said it like it was indigestible, but he continued, "I hope you had a nice time."

"Actually, I didn't, but I found out some stuff about the coffee guys that may be of interest to you."

Ed nodded in a noncommittal fashion, afraid that Minnie was about to con him out of some more money owed. He was also reluctant to commit himself because now that Minnie had confirmed Ed's opinion of his flakiness by missing a meeting, his comments were somewhat suspect.

Then he said, "Well, give me some names, some numbers, some specifics."

"If I do, will you do something about these guys?"

"Maybe."

"Maybe isn't good enough." He wasn't about to let go of this stuff unless he was sure that the Cartel would be stopped. They had been through too much for that. He began to think that maybe Kiko's idea wasn't so crazy. "You better give me a little more time."

The big accountant shook his head and then drained his shake with a noise full of meaning. He said, "You don't have that much left."

"Ed, I know you're mad and everything. I'm sorry. I really am. I should have called or at least sent you a postcard. You would have liked that, wouldn't you?"

Ed paid no attention to this and began to unwrap his Baked Apple Pie.

"Ed, I have a plan."

Ed didn't seem very interested. "Uh huh. Tell me about it."

Minnie shook his head. "You wouldn't believe it. Besides, I can't. It's secret, but I promise that you'll get this information, even if it kills me, which it might. You'll believe it then. You'll take me seriously then. If I make it, you'll be the first guy I talk to."

Minnie was getting to know Kiko more every day, but he still could not believe that they were really going to go through with Kiko's scheme. It was dangerous. It was crazy. It was impossible. And yet, here he was pleading with Ed for the time to do it. Was he really pleading? That was pathetic. Pleading with an overweight IRS accountant? He decided that he should think of it as negotiating and that it was time to get tough.

"Ed, work with me. Trust me," Minnie demanded.

Ed said, "That's against policy."

"Fuck policy. Do you want to make the biggest bust of your life or not?"

Minnie let him chew on that for a while.

Ed thoughtfully folded his napkin and said, "I'm already sticking my neck out for you."

Minnie tried to imagine the squat mass of flesh between Ed's head and his shoulders stretching at all. It was difficult. The weight of all those years behind a desk had compressed Ed into an unyielding, though flabby solidity.

"You've got a little over a month and a half to make good on this. If you don't, it's all over for you."

"Ed, you know you're not the only guy who's on my case." He thought briefly about the future and it scared him, but he said, "Don't worry, everything is going to work out fine."

Minnie wished he was as confident as he sounded. He wasn't sure of anything and here he was, about to let Kiko talk him into a course of action that was completely insane.

He and Kiko were going to go where only a few men and women had gone before: Space, the final frontier. They were going to risk it all for their world, their country. For truth, justice, and the American way. He and Kiko had the same intention as those before them — to help the people of Earth and to try to make things better. But he and Kiko were not astronauts, they were Deadheads, and they had no practical training whatsoever.

Chapter Thirty-nine -
Hemispheric Convergence

That night Kiko and Minnie discussed their plan over dinner. "Min," she said, "it's really not so crazy. I don't know why I didn't think of it before. I knew the band was going to play the big 35th Anniversary NASA show. What an opportunity."

"Oh sure." Minnie put his head in his hands.

"Think of all the attention we'll get. This will be the publicity stunt to end all stunts."

"Uh huh."

"They won't be able to ignore us once we borrow the Shuttle."

"You mean after we take it hostage."

"Borrow it. We'll give it back. The important thing is that we'll finally get someone to do something about the rainforest. They'll have to. Plus, I love to fly and this will be the ultimate flight."

It would take a little more to convince Minnie. The Space Shuttle? Actually flying it?

"Kiko, we're talking about outer space. Way out there. No parachute is going to help us up there. And I'm afraid of heights."

"Minnie, you worry too much. I'll take care of this."

He shook his head and thought wistfully about the vacation he was supposed to be on. It occurred to him that both the show at the Cape and their plan seemed totally improbable and yet completely right. It was the perfect setting for Jerry and the Boys and, he had to admit, no one would be able to ignore them if they stole it. But it was such a big if.

Space, at least inner space, was something the Dead had been exploring from the beginning. They were internal scientists and now they would be playing for a bunch of other scientists on their home turf. There were a surprising number of Deadheads among the NASA people. Not so much among the administrators and the politicos, but they had many fans within the nuts and bolts of it, the working researchers, theoreticians, and even among the astronauts. NASA was concerned with exploration — they had that in common — but it was hard to overlook the fact that it was a military-dominated operation. The Dead represented something quite different. And yet there were similarities.

They were both actively searching for possibility. They were adventurers. They were both focused on something beyond the mainstream, something out of this normal world. They just had different approaches. One was left-brained, the other right. And yet, all brains were a combination of both and here was that combination about to be played out for real. A meeting of the minds. It was perfect.

The show might never have come off. After all, these were acid-eating, long-haired, sixties radical rock-and-rollers. But the irony was that, in spite of all that, they were just like everyone else. They just had different assumptions, beliefs, opinions, and ways of working. The Dead had been together almost as long as NASA. They were a huge and profitable corporation. They were community leaders. They were parents. And despite Ed's doubts, they paid taxes. They were just part of that great American melting pot, except that they thought it was okay to smoke pot.

Even though this was all true, Kiko had told him that it was viewed, in some circles, as a strange match, an unnatural set-up, and there had been some pointed opposition to their appearance. It turned out that John Glenn, the first American to orbit the globe, now Senator John Glenn, had always secretly been a Grateful Dead fan and he used his influence to bring about a peaceful resolution. They were scheduled for a Saturday afternoon show.

As they made their plans to go to Florida, Minnie kept questioning the wisdom of stealing the Shuttle. First, there were the logistics of the whole thing — guards, security, guards. Then, the practical aspects of it — getting it off the ground, how they would fly it, how they would get back. And was it really a good idea to steal government property?

"Minnie, are you getting uptight about this?" Kiko asked.

Well, yes he was.

"Look, this is bigger than government property," she said. "Those guys in Brazil are destroying the rainforest. They're killing people. They're affecting the global environment. That's everybody. They are doing irreversible damage to the whole world."

The fine points of ownership and personal fear seemed petty in the face of all that, though Minnie thought they figured somehow.

"We have a chance to stop them and I won't pass that up," Kiko said. "I hope you come with me, because I need your help. Besides that, think of what an adventure it will be."

Minnie thought that this entire vacation had been full of adventure. Maybe a little too full.

"Haven't you always wanted to be in space?" she asked.

Minnie admitted, "I've seen every Star Trek."

144

"See?"

"Yeah, but, Kiko, this is big time. I mean, big time outrageous."

"It is, but we've got to do it. There's no other way. You have to make up your mind." She smiled at him and then said, "We could have a lot of fun up there."

He wondered what kind of fun she was talking about. He had hopes, dreams, desires that were driving him crazy. He wanted her and yet he had pushed her as much as he could. He thought she liked him and was liking him more all the time, though it was hard to tell. She had kissed him and it hadn't been on the cheek. That was something. The possibility of romance in space was winning him over to this crazy plan.

It was obvious that she was going to do this thing with or without him. And he agreed with her about the Cartel. He owed them for Bowman. They had to be stopped. He realized that he couldn't let her do this by herself.

It crossed his worried mind to ask himself what Jerry would do in a situation like this, but he took a deep breath and said to her, "Okay, okay, you're right. Just convince me that you can fly this thing and we'll suit up. T minus six days and counting."

Then Kiko told Minnie that she had already been in the Space Shuttle. He couldn't believe it. This was too much.

"What?" he croaked. "How? When? Who with?"

She was enjoying this. "I told you my brother was in the Air Force. He's training to be an astronaut. Once when I was visiting, he took me on a tour. It wasn't exactly legal, but it was a gas."

Minnie was having a hard time.

"Jesus, Kiko. You have more tricks up your sleeve than anyone I've ever met. What's next? You've spoken to aliens?"

"No, not until I met you. But check this out." She grabbed a book from the table and showed it to Minnie. "While you were meeting with Ed, I was at the library and they had this."

It was a book called The *Space Shuttle Operator's Manual*. It was filled with information, schematics, detailed pictures of the control panels, lists of procedures, everything. How to take off, land, go to the bathroom, typical menus, even what to do in emergencies.

Minnie was amazed. "Shouldn't this be top secret or something?"

Kiko shrugged and said, "I guess they figure if you don't have one, what's the difference. They're really just trying to drum up support for the program. I'm not worried about flying the shuttle. With my flying background and this book, it should be easy."

Minnie groaned. "Oh sure. Easy. But Kiko, remember, there's no air up there and it's a long way down."

"Don't worry. Once we get into space, they'll help us. They don't want us to crash their fancy car."

Chapter Forty - Ain't No Free.

Minnie grumbled for a while, but he was convinced, sort of, that Kiko could really fly the shuttle. Actually he tried not to think about it. First they had to get in the damn thing and that probably wouldn't happen. He finally gave up all but his most personal worries and their plans to go to Florida proceeded. After all, it was another chance to hear the Dead.

In the week before they flew to Florida, Kiko and Minnie pursued leads they had gathered in Brazil concerning what they now thought of as the Cartel — an organization that manipulated the coffee market through illegal means for their own benefit. Their research revealed evidence that suggested that a small number of Americans, not all of German descent, had emigrated south in the days just before World War II. These people had been outspoken supporters of Hitler and his policies and had finally decided or been forced to abandon their native country. After that, they weren't heard from very much. America was glad to be rid of them.

And now, Minnie thought, these traitors were finally taking their revenge. Their evil, caffeine revenge. That is, if all of this was really true, if these coffee guys, the people who made up the Cartel, were actually former Americans with Nazi pasts. It sounded crazy, but everything pointed to it being true.

They were armed with the picture and the name of the man in Rio, Walter Knaus — playboy, executive of Terra Gorda, coffee exporter, and Jasmine's buddy — and their research revealed that he was the son of John Knaus, who had emigrated to Rio from the States in early 1941. All signs pointed to John Knaus being the head of the Cartel. His son, it seemed, was now in charge of the day-to-day operations, which he carried out with ruthless efficiency.

After a few days, they finally were able to reach Mariana. Through the static on the phone, she made it clear that she was glad they had made it safely back to California. She and Ze hadn't had any trouble and were continuing their activities. When she learned what Kiko and Minnie had found out, she told Kiko that their investigations had uncovered a similar story. She gave her the details and urged her to make everything public. Mariana couldn't have imagined Kiko's plan to do this and Kiko wasn't about to tell her. She said only that she and Minnie had a plan and that she hoped she'd be able to give her some encouraging news soon. They made arrangements to talk in two weeks.

Meanwhile, Minnie and Ed were becoming regulars at the McDonald's in Mill Valley. They always sat in the same spot, next to the Lego table, and seemed to enjoy each other's company. They had met several times, but had not accomplished much. Minnie was beginning to think he had been there too often, because a middle-aged woman who had rung him up a couple of times seemed to be flirting with him. Middle-aged, he thought. Definitely not his type. Then it occurred to him that, in a certain light, he might be considered middle-aged. This disturbed him. He was a little sensitive about this age thing. And while his 42 years might possibly include him in this age group, it didn't take long to convince himself that a guy who had seen God, talked with the Devil, and who had once hallucinated the entire westward movement of the United States in Katie Stevens' living room was exempt from this frightening designation or, at least, had a ways to go.

"Ed, you're not gaining weight, are you?" Minnie liked to be solicitous.

"Minnie," he said. "I think you ought to take a look in your own mirror."

Minnie laughed. "Where I'm going, I'm going to need all of this."

He had questioned Kiko about what they were going to eat during their trip through space and she had shown him the page in the book titled "Typical Space Shuttle Menu." It had listed thermostabilized applesauce, beef jerky in what passed for its natural form, rehydrated granola, freeze-dried bananas, a breakfast roll also in its natural form but irradiated, and an orange-grapefruit drink. And that was just breakfast. Having seen this, Minnie had formed a plan to carry on provisions of his own.

Ed asked him, "Where are you going?"

"To Florida."

Ed hit the ceiling. "Another vacation? Are you crazy? What about the money?"

"It's a business trip. And, yes, I am crazy."

He crossed his eyes and stuck out his tongue to indicate this and a kid at the Lego table let out a cry and reached for his mother. Minnie turned and nodded reassuringly to the kid and gave the mother a big leer. She quickly gathered her things and left with the still frightened child.

Ed laughed and said, "Minnie, you charmer."

Minnie accepted the compliment unfazed, impressed with his powers.

"Now Ed, you and I are getting to be good friends..."

Ed was dubious.

Minnie continued, "And while I can't tell you my plans, be-yond the fact that I'm going to Florida, I can say that it may change everything."

"This isn't about perfecting your tan? It has to do with your coffee fantasy, doesn't it?

"It's not a fantasy. It's real and this is a business trip. It con-cerns the coffee and it's dangerous. Really dangerous." He paused for emphasis. "So, in consideration of that fact, why don't we knock off another thousand from my bill?"

Ed wasn't buying it. "For what? I don't know any more than I did at the beginning. All you've made are promises and I haven't seen one dime. Minnie, I'd like to help you out, but the Service needs real information, not promises. It requires dollars, not assurances. You better forget it."

He trusted Ed a little, but he wasn't about to give Ed's superi-ors the information he had. They would have to wait. In a mysterious tone, Minnie said, "Ed," and as he did, he leaned low across the table. Ed looked around and met him in the middle, just above a Big Mac.

"Ed, what we're dealing with here are Nazis. American Nazis."

Ed sat back up and shot Minnie a look that said: You really are crazy. Why are you wasting my time? What am I doing here? I should just haul this guy off to jail. He continued to eye Minnie skeptically and he went back to chewing his meal, shaking his head.

Minnie nodded, undeterred, and asked, "What's that worth to you?"

Ed put down a handful of fries. "You are so full of it. Even if it were true, it wouldn't make any difference. The IRS isn't inter-ested in politics. We're interested in money. That's it. Money. Hard cash. Everything else is superfluous. Understand?" He looked at Minnie with pity. "If it were up to me, I'd adjust your bill a few hundred bucks just for having come up with such an original excuse, but it's not. So forget it."

He took a long thoughtful sip on his shake and said, "Minnie, I'm worried about you. You should get a grip."

"You mean a grip on reality?"

Ed nodded.

Minnie wondered about it, but said, "That's always been a little difficult. Reality is so weird."

Chapter Forty-one - You Can't Be Too Careful

Minnie hadn't heard from Colonel Able since their flight and now that he and Kiko were planning on stealing the Space Shuttle, he was hoping he wouldn't. Every time he left his meetings with Ed at McDonald's he looked both ways before starting across the parking lot. He was afraid he would find the Colonel leaning against his car. He also checked his mail with trepidation. And he jumped whenever the phone rang, thinking it might be the Colonel, although with his history with telephones, Minnie would have jumped anyway. He did have questions about the Shuttle, but he knew the Colonel was the wrong one to ask.

So he asked Kiko. She was enthusiastic to share her book with him, but the more he found out, the less he wanted to know. They came across the section on "Entry and Landing Emergencies," and he read:

> *Many science fiction movies and novels*
> *have depicted astronauts stranded in orbit*
> *after their retro-rockets failed. Such a*
> *situation is extremely unlikely with the Shuttle.*

Such comforting words, he thought. Unlikely, but not impossible. He turned the page and read another passage which showed the authors to be masters of understatement :

> *An equipment malfunction in space*
> *can be very serious.*

At this point he closed the book and tried to put it all out of his mind. He concentrated on packing. He had seen his mother do this in times of stress and now, years later, it appeared to be a good idea. He had to get ready for their trip. Their big trip. The trip that was freaking him out. He had the Boys on the box and they were wailing on "Big River." He turned it up.

While Minnie was freaking out and packing, he knew Kiko had been doing her homework. She had gone through the book several times. She had talked with her brother, though making sure not to give their plan away. She had read up on past Shuttle missions. She had discreetly consulted her friends on the Internet. And now she was outside warming her beautiful body in the sun and probably dreaming about flying in space.

Kiko had admitted to Minnie that the whole idea excited her — the challenge of flying the most advanced aircraft in existence, the unimaginable freedom of being in space and experiencing weightlessness, the thrill of danger in stealing the Shuttle, and the hope that they would get enough publicity to force a halt to the cruel and destructive work of the Cartel. She couldn't wait to get into space. Minnie bit his tongue and simply nodded.

She filled a small daypack for the trip and went about it with an eye to practicality. Simple, comfortable clothes, tennis shoes, a hairbrush, a couple of rubber bands to tie back her hair, sunglasses, and a few other necessities. She told Minnie that she had left a file on her computer which contained instructions, in case she didn't make it back from space. She then cleaned the house. And now she was outside, dreaming and soaking up some rays. She was a practical woman.

On Friday morning, they put Kiko's small bag and Minnie's bulging backpack into the back of the Chevy. They were headed to the airport and to the Cape.

Watching him heave his big load, Kiko asked, "Minnie, what's in there? I didn't know you had that much junk."

"It ain't junk. I need this stuff. I'm the kind of guy who likes to be prepared."

"Prepared." Kiko said it as if it were a magic word.

"Yeah. Like a Boy Scout."

"Minnie, somehow I can't picture you as a Boy Scout."

"Well, I wasn't. But I always admired Girl Scouts."

He wiggled his eyebrows and gave her a wink.

A few hours later, they were flying over Oklahoma on their way to Miami. Kiko was napping and had her head on Minnie's shoulder. Minnie looked out the window at the thinning clouds and realized that this view and this flight were nothing compared to what they were about to do. Was he still worried about the scheme? Well, no. Not really. He had developed a cautious kind of fatalistic optimism around their plan and, when he could, he kept it out of his thoughts.

He trusted Kiko, he admired her energy, he had great faith in her talents and abilities, and he thought he might even love her. Why else would he be doing something so obviously insane? He looked down at her, sleeping against him. Could he really love her? In a way that involved more than just a hope for passionate smooching and good times?

This thought scared him more than the idea of stealing the Shuttle. It was easy to see why he might love her, but that kind of feeling was just as dangerous as what they were about to attempt. He flashed on the evil Jasmine and other disappointments. He knew that for all his big noise and big attitude, his heart was a tender thing that didn't want to be hurt again, and to be even thinking about this stuff was to be crossing over into unknown territory where anything could happen, but probably wouldn't.

He didn't feel himself to be a proper match for a girl like Kiko. She was beautiful, brilliant, and young. And he was... He stopped and considered. He was just a guy. A regular guy. And, as he sighed, he thought, a regular guy who was getting older every minute. What she needed was someone her own age, someone her mom would approve of, someone she could really love — not an old fart like himself.

While he was lost in these thoughts, he felt Kiko move against him and he turned from the view of the clouds and looked at her. Her large brown eyes were open.

She considered him for a long moment in sleepy silence and then said, "What are you thinking about, big guy?"

He gave her a smile and said, in a quiet voice, "Oh, nothing. You know, space."

She smiled back and then put her head down and snuggled closer. In a minute, her soft breathing told Minnie that she was once again asleep.

Chapter Forty-two - This Is It

Their arrival in Florida went smoothly and the night before the show they looked out at the ocean from the balcony of their hotel. The scent of seaweed and salt water and exhaust from the highway below wafted up to them. Minnie had his arm around Kiko and was breathing quietly, taking in the beauty of the scene, and watching the stars pop out of a huge, darkening sky. The moon was just past its first quarter and appeared to be peering down at them in a kindly way from behind a curtain.

He couldn't believe it. How had this happened? She was acting as if they stood like this all the time. It was a moment of peace that Minnie was savoring, until he heard Kiko say, "Just think, tomorrow night we'll be up there."

Minnie's heart started beating faster. His rate of breathing increased. Despite the cool evening breeze, he began to sweat.

In a hoarse, somewhat strangled voice, he said, "Ah yes, just us two grand larcenists in the airless depths of space, orbiting a beautiful blue planet."

She gave him a playful elbow in the ribs. His good side. His Brazilian rib had almost completely healed.

"Minnie, you worry too much."

Maybe he did, but he was still able to worry and that was the important thing. He tried to deny, ignore, and postpone the reality of what awaited them the next day. They might be shot by security personnel ignorant of their altruistic mission. The Shuttle might blow up before they even got off the ground. Their oxygen might be cut off at any moment by accidently flipping the wrong switch. At the very least, they might be arrested and placed in solitary confinement for the rest of their lives.

A single cot, a single blanket, bad food, the lonesome echo of the guard's footsteps outside in the empty hallway. He would count the days with little marks on the wall, until he had lost track and it no longer mattered. His hair, what was left of it, would turn white. He would be forgotten by everyone, even Cowboy. Time would have no meaning and he would be alone, forever, with his thoughts of impossible freedom and impossible love and one day, the guard would arrive with lunch and find him hunched over in a corner, incoherent and irretrievably mad.

On the other hand, they might make a successful takeoff, convince the world to renounce those, like the Cartel, who were destroying everything, explore the outer limits of space together, and return as heroes, acclaimed by all. NASA would sign them up for another flight. They would sell their story to *Life* magazine. They would make something up to satisfy *The Enquirer*. The Dead would write a song about them. With little or no encouragement, the guys back at the Moonbeam would toast them constantly. Their future would be a gridlock of opportunities. The fact that they had actually stolen the Shuttle would be forgotten, a small detail beside the huge accomplishment of their mission.

"Minnie? Minnie?"

It was Kiko calling him back from his reverie. He looked down at her in the moonlight. She was so close. He pulled her even closer and kissed her. How could space top this?

"We're going to have to stop kissing like this," she said.

"Or what?"

"Or I might lose control."

"How much control do you have?"

"Not much." After giving him a second to contemplate this, she said, "Tomorrow's a big day. We better get some rest."

She smiled at him and kissed him sweetly, and then went inside to her room. He took a deep breath as he looked out at the beauty of good, old Earth and, for the moment, counted his blessings and forgot his troubles. He winked at the moon as if it were a fellow conspirator and turned in for the night.

The next morning they didn't say much. Kiko stuffed things into her small backpack and got ready for the show. Minnie looked at her and could see that she, too, was nervous. All the same, he drew confidence from her. He knew how strongly she felt about this and he was beginning to understand how strongly he felt about her. He saw that his imagined jail time and hero fantasy were meaningless next to the actuality of being here with Kiko, now, in this moment. Maybe she loved him and maybe she didn't, but that didn't make any difference. They were together right now.

It was a revelation to him. A kind of acid breakthrough. It was what the Dead and all the hippies and saints and madmen had said all along: There is only this moment. It is all that really exists and matters. Your worries and hopes and fantasies are like snow on the water, like syrup on the waffle, like sweat in the river. Passing clouds against a sky of blue. You are alive in this moment and no other.

He strode across the room to Kiko, took her in his arms, tilted her backwards like they do in the movies, and gave her a kiss she would never forget. When he released her, she was breathless.

She appeared startled, then quickly checked her watch and said, "We better get going."

Minnie's face fell, but then he heard a laugh that warmed his heart. She looked at him and he saw that she was glowing from the embrace. She had been teasing him. An easy thing. The electricity of his feelings had been communicated to her through the kiss. He could see it, the way her eyes and her smile sparkled.

She put her arms around him and said, "Minnie, you're the greatest."

Chapter Forty-three - And Pink Shoelaces

They arrived at the Cape early and even at 9:30 in the morning there were thousands of people milling around, coming together, looking for each other, finding a seat, and getting ready for the concert. There were lots of Deadheads in wild tie-dyed costumes and other Dead fans in jeans and t-shirts. There were also a surprising number of families dressed in Bermuda shorts who looked like they had never even heard of the Grateful Dead. They had cameras hanging around their necks and were carrying video equipment. They were tourists, not music fans, and most seemed somehow oblivious to the weirdos around them, although a few had expressions of distaste and horror.

It dawned on Minnie that these were people who had come not to hear the band, but to see the Shuttle launch which was to take place at the end of the concert, a fitting cap to the 35th Anniversary celebration. That was okay with him. There was room for everyone. It was a free show and the concert site was huge. But, boy, would they be surprised when they found out that it was he and Kiko waving down at them as the Shuttle blasted off.

The stage was set up at the edge of the endless acres of the public viewing area beyond the long runway where the Shuttle would land after its time in space. The towers of speakers, at opposite ends of the stage, framed the distant spire of the Shuttle, its rocket boosters, and the superstructure that serviced it.

The reality of it was beginning to get to Minnie. He was excited and nervous and his thoughts were a mess. He tried not to think beyond the moment. This wonderful moment of being with Kiko in the warm air. He was hoping that if he kept it to that, he would be all right.

Then Kiko said, "Min, this weather is perfect for a launch." She leaned closer to him and, smiling, said in a quieter voice, "In a few hours, you and I will be on our way to the stars."

It wasn't what he wanted to hear.

He didn't answer her and kept walking toward the stage, afraid of the future, uncertain about the past, but rooted firmly in the moment. Desperately in the moment and momentarily in torment. A moment full of doubt and apprehension.

Minnie turned to Kiko and said things like, "What do you think they'll open with?" and "Did you bring the sunblock?"

He saw that on either side of the stage there was an immense expanse of fabric, fluttering in the breeze, which covered the wide 40 foot tall wall of speakers. On each one, near the bottom, was a tie-dyed representation of the Shuttle blasting off, the white smoky steam boiling beneath it with just a hint of fiery flame. Above it, the sky faded from a bright blue into the deeper, richer blue of space and at the top of all this was a star.

This star was the focus of the scene and embodied a degree of mystery and attraction that was overwhelmingly powerful. Tiny shafts of brilliant light shot out from its center. It was otherworldly. It was inspiring. It was an indescribable combination of color that both disturbed and calmed anyone who saw it.

Then Minnie realized that this was Dark Star. The Dark Star. The one that was pouring its light into ashes. The searchlight casting for faults in the clouds of delusion. The one that hung in the transitive nightfall of diamonds.

As he stood there looking at it, Minnie was moved in a way that, just moments ago, he wouldn't have believed possible. This depiction inspired in him a sense of mission that transformed him. It was as if the Dead and the entire vibe and intention behind all of that miraculous, drug-induced, music-fueled vision of an open, honest, and goofy love was now flashing before him. Every time he looked up toward the stage, there it was. In stereo.

It was a sign, a serendipitous message which existed not just to entertain the crowd, but that spoke directly to him. It confirmed his plan, it acknowledged his purpose, it strengthened his resolve about going into space. Stealing the Shuttle seemed now merely a stepping stone toward the real goal of liberation, redemption, and expanding his consciousness. He and the cosmos became one. All his extremities began to vibrate.

He turned to Kiko, passed a hand across his forehead, and said, "I think I should have brought my hat."

He was glad to find he was still on Earth. He noticed the crowd again and mentioned to Kiko to keep an eye out for Colonel Able.

"But I've never met him. What's he look like?"

"He's in uniform. Looks like a Colonel. Uptight, doesn't smile, always looking around defensively. I hope we don't run into him because if we do, we'll never get to hear the show. He'll keep bugging me about the tape."

She gave him a skeptical look. "Is it really the only copy?"

"It can't be. Could it? It must be part of his delusion. His tie is tied too tight, his shoes are too heavy, his buttons too bright. It's got to get to him after a while. All that shouting and ordering and obeying. The poor guy. No wonder he's nuts."

They found a place to sit for the show, near the front, but on the side. A place from which they could slip away at the proper time and make their way across the runway, through the jumble of official looking buildings, and into the jungle of equipment that was centered around the Space Shuttle. From their spot, they could see that the Shuttle waited, alone and imposing, and to Minnie's active imagination it seemed to quiver with an anticipation that was palpable.

He turned to Kiko and wiggled his eyebrows. "Baby," he grinned like a fool, "You and me are going places." He jerked his head upwards.

"You're not scared?" she asked.

He shook his head. "Not right now. I'm crazy."

Just then he heard a voice call his name. A female voice that was familiar. He turned and he saw a girl, a child really, with a great tan, who seemed to be wearing only an oversized white t-shirt and dark glasses. Before he could figure out what was happening, she ran up to him and threw herself into his arms. It was Susan. She gave him a big kiss that slid off of him and she was jumping up and down with excitement.

Minnie looked at Kiko, who was smiling at his embarrassment and who stood to one side, not wanting to interrupt this tender reunion.

Minnie had turned beet red and sputtered a few incoherent words.

Susan gushed, "Oh Minnie, I missed you so much. I was worried about you."

Minnie nodded a couple times.

She continued, "You were so sweet to me back in Oregon." She smiled at him with affection. "I know you were only thinking of me."

He wasn't sure what she was talking about, but he became aware that this encounter was being watched closely not just by Kiko, but by a young guy with dreadlocks down past his shoulders who stood by with a funny expression on his face, looking completely stoned.

Susan pulled her gorgeous little body away from Minnie and turned toward the dreadlocks.

"Minnie, this is Rainbow." She blushed just a little. "My boyfriend. You remember him from the concert, don't you?"

Minnie now saw that he did and he felt an immediate relief that he was off the hook and that Susan was happy and that she was with this guy, this guy with the incredible dreadlocks.

Chapter Forty-four - Hubba, Hubba

Minnie introduced Kiko and Susan. They liked each other immediately and were all set to sit down and yak, probably about him, when Minnie asked Susan what she was doing so far from home, all the way in Florida.

"I couldn't miss this show. I mean, the Dead and a Space Shuttle launch? How many times is that going to happen? It's awesome."

The dreadlocks nodded in agreement.

"What about you guys?" she asked.

"Well," Minnie looked at Kiko. "It's the same with us. We wouldn't miss it for the world."

Kiko smiled and said, "This show is going to be a real trip." Minnie groaned a little and she glanced at him out of the corner of her eye.

They talked some more and then Susan hugged Kiko and turned and gave Minnie another big kiss. She and Rainbow waved goodbye and walked off into the crowd.

"She's sweet, Minnie."

He was still watching the back half of her.

"Yeah," he said dumbly.

Kiko banged her shoulder into his to get his attention and then she said, "I'm a little worried about the weather." She gestured toward the ocean. A fog was beginning to drift in toward them over the dunes and the runway.

"Hmm," he said. He was still thinking about Life and Love and the great mysteries. When he finally realized that Kiko was staring at him, he abruptly cleared his throat. "Uh, yeah." He inspected the white fog. His attention returned fully to the moment. "I don't think it's anything to worry about. It looks like it will burn off."

The sound of Robert Johnson singing "Steady Rolling Man" began to float over the crowd and Minnie and Kiko noticed that the place was becoming packed. The show might start at any minute. They watched the frisbees and balloons fly over the huge gathering, while they ate a light lunch. Minnie wasn't very hungry for a change. He kept looking nervously in the direction of the Shuttle and around at the crowd. He was afraid someone would be able to read his thoughts or tell, just by looking at him, that he was about to embark on a crazy venture with Kiko. A venture from which they might never return.

A man came out onto the big stage. He walked slowly until he stood before the center microphone. He looked quite out of place and Minnie pegged him for someone from NASA. He was short and was wearing dark slacks, and a white short-sleeved shirt. It looked like he had pens in the pocket of his shirt and glasses with thick black rims. The man repeatedly clasped and unclasped his hands in a nervous gesture. If he hadn't been so slight, Minnie would have taken him for a relative of Ed's. What a weirdo, he thought. But then it occurred to Minnie that people like Ed and the little guy on stage were the normal ones on this planet and that he, with his straggly beard and lingering hair and old sixties' notions about the cosmos, was the oddball.

The man began speaking, but nothing came out. An equipment guy with a ponytail crossed the stage in a couple of discreet bounds, flipped the switch on the microphone and suddenly the man's voice boomed forth in mid-sentence.

"On behalf of..."

The short-sleeved man stopped in stunned reaction to the sound of his own voice coming from the huge speaker towers.

"Wow," he said in wonder. This wonder was amplified a hundred times. The crowd laughed and beamed good-naturedly at him.

"Thanks for coming out today for what is surely one of the most unique afternoons we've had at the Cape in a long time. On behalf of NASA and everyone in the program and on behalf of the astronauts, I want to welcome all of you and the Grateful

Dead to our 35th Anniversary celebration."

There was applause and whistles and a lot of whooping going on. It eventually subsided and he continued.

"First, I want to thank all of you taxpayers."

That stirred up a huge self-congratulatory response. Kiko nudged Minnie, laughing.

"...and Bob Douglas, the Director of NASA, Sandy Rogerson, Coordinator of Public Relations, and especially Senator John Glenn for making all of this possible."

Another round of applause and good cheer.

"We're happy to mark this special occasion with a launch. It will be our 64th of the Shuttle program and one which will continue to add to our knowledge of this beautiful planet and stand as an expression of Man's inextinguishable appetite for adventure."

The crowd responded warmly and Minnie and Kiko looked at each other, for the moment forgetting all danger and feeling a part of that great appetite.

"Finally, I want to thank all of you for your goodwill, support, and the constant exercising of your imaginations. Our world is just one of an infinite number that exist in the universe and I am glad that, instead of pursuing isolation, we can turn ourselves, our best selves, to the stars and reach out into the darkness with hope, determination, and, ultimately, love."

The great crowd was silent. Then the man broke into a huge grin.

"And now it is my pleasure to introduce those other astronauts. Great musicians and a great bunch of guys. The Grateful Dead."

The crowd erupted and went wild. They were on their feet, clapping and shouting — for the Dead, for the sentiments that had been expressed, and for themselves. This wonderful little man walked toward the wings, waved once, and disappeared. The hubbub continued for several minutes. Everyone was getting excited. Finally, Jerry came out from behind a bank of amps and the crowd turned it up a few notches.

He had his back to them and was fiddling with his guitar, turning the tuning pegs and making adjustments to several of the knobs on one of the amps. Then Weir came out and did the same, but where Jerry seemed solid and deliberate, Weir appeared agile and excited. He made similar small adjustments, but he was all over the place. He crouched down, he jumped up, he danced up to and back from the amps in back of him. He floated to his microphone and repeatedly touched it to make sure it was there and steady and grounded.

Jerry examined the ring of devices that lay at his feet — wah-wah pedals, volume controls, and other mysterious objects. Phil walked on with his bass and Minnie was surprised when Mickey tested a tom-tom and the big sound rushed out in a huge sharp wave that broke over all of them. Kreutzmann was behind his set too, and they were just about ready to roll.

Jerry strummed a few chords and looked out over the crowd for a brief moment. Then Bobby walked to his microphone. They gazed at each other and because he was so close, Minnie could see them smile. Weir counted off the time and they started into "Eyes Of The World."

> *Wake up to find out*
> *That you are the eyes of the world*
>
> *The heart has its beaches*
> *Its homeland and thoughts*
> *Of its own*

Everyone went crazy and everything fell into place: the Shuttle, the show, the world, everything.

Chapter Forty-five -
Approaching The Infinite

The crowd was on their feet, dancing. Minnie wailed on his air guitar, eyes closed, in sympathetic assistance to the band. Kiko, when she wasn't dancing her beautiful bottom off, marveled at him from time to time. Even the tourists began to get into it. They swayed and tapped their feet as the band moved from song to jam to song. Bright balloons with pictures of the Shuttle bounced gracefully through the crowd and Minnie noticed an unlikely couple nearby whose eyes appeared to glaze over as the music took possession of them.

The band began to play "Alligator." They were in Florida and it made sense. Minnie hadn't heard it in years. Jerry went into a solo that gave the crowd goosebumps and began to wring a series of notes from the guitar that increased in urgency and improbability and beauty and power, bringing thousands of waving arms into the air. The crowd was howling.

This was definitely a show. Later, Jerry sang,

> *Wouldn't you try just a little bit harder*
> *Wouldn't you try just a little bit more*

And everyone was willing.

> *You can't go back*
> *And you can't stand still*
> *If the thunder don't get you*
> *Then the lightning will*

Everything about the show excited and strengthened Kiko's and Minnie's resolve about their plan. Off to one side of the stage, Minnie could see the little man who had introduced the band. His body moved in time with the music and Minnie could tell that despite his straight appearance, this man and Kiko and himself and the crowd were all together in this wild thing that was taking place.

As the show went on, the fog, instead of burning off, increased. It was eerie. The band picked up on it and began playing "Mountains of the Moon," which seemed about right. Kiko nudged Minnie and, cupping her hands around his ear, said, "Min, I'm worried about the fog. We won't be able to take off."

Minnie tore his attention away from the stage and the music

and checked it out. He looked at her watch and leaned close to her. He was tempted to kiss her ear, but instead said into the lovely receptacle, "Gorgeous, this is perfect. It's the perfect cover for us. Let's go."

They grabbed their packs and headed for the edge of the crowd. No one noticed them. The band played on and Minnie and Kiko disappeared behind a booth where a guy with a big red beard stared in the direction of the band, forgetting the orange juice and smoothies he was supposed to be selling. The fog swallowed them up as they made their way toward the Shuttle.

It was tricky. The distance they had to cover contained a variety of landscapes: hard concrete, treacherous swampland, dark lagoons, and soft spots that might be quicksand. He took her hand and they picked their way through it. The fog was thick but, miraculously, it thinned out when they needed it to. Sometimes it hung in an impenetrable wet mist and at others it grew less dense and they could see their destination towering far away.

As they started out, they had the band for accompaniment. They could still hear them. Minnie had to laugh. At one point, the Boys were playing "Franklin's Tower" and as he and Kiko traveled down the long runway through the thick fog, Jerry was singing about rolling away the dew. On their way, they heard frogs croaking and birds calling to each other. For all its concern with technology, the Cape and its big open spaces were also home to much wildlife. By the time the music faded away, Minnie and Kiko had gone the length of the runway and were at the edge of the official NASA working area.

Great buildings loomed out of the grayness at them and they huddled against a wall while Kiko consulted a hand-drawn map. Only a few buildings had real names. Most were marked simply AE-121 or Compound C-34.

They had to be more careful now and Minnie about had a heart attack the first time they rounded a corner and saw two workers. The implications were huge and scary. Kiko and Minnie looked at each other. Kiko appeared concerned, but Minnie had recovered and said, "Babe, we're not turning back now. This is going to be great." He even meant it this time.

They were on a mission and their first job was to get to the Shuttle. They put all other thoughts out of their minds as they made their way closer and closer. As they were passing one building, they looked into the window of what was a small office. No one was there. Kiko tried the door and found it was open. Inside, hanging on hooks, were three lab coats and a couple of hardhats. Names were stitched on the left breast of each coat. Kiko became Appleton and Minnie was Mollenhauer. They put them on and kept moving.

At various times, they darted between trucks, they slunk along the sides of tall buildings, they ran when the coast was clear, and they ambled with seeming nonchalance when necessary. Once, when they were cautiously walking toward a large open area, they were startled by the opening of a door close behind them.

A man came out and called to them. "Hey," he said. They froze. "What time is it?" He was consulting a clipboard and shaking the wrist to which his watch was strapped.

Minnie, who never wore a watch, panicked, but Kiko looked at hers and spoke to the man in a clear voice, "1300 hours, on the dot."

The man nodded. He turned and started off in the other direction.

They took a deep breath and moved past the Vehicle Assembly Building. It was a huge nightmare of a building, especially in the odd light of the dense fog. Their footsteps sounded loud to them, attracting attention, though they were actually deadened by the thick air.

Minnie was disoriented, but Kiko led straight on without much hesitation. She gave his hand a squeeze. "I remember this part from the time with my brother. We're almost there."

Minnie was glad they were hiding under hats and coats. Even with his backpack, they seemed to fit in. The closer they got to the Shuttle, the more people they saw. Not just others in similar coats and headgear, but uniformed personnel and soldiers equipped with sidearms. The fog cleared, suddenly, and they saw it just up ahead — pad 39A —and there, bigger than they possibly could have imagined, the huge rocket-booster assembly, pointing straight up at the stars, with the smaller Shuttle vehicle clinging to its side.

As Minnie put his head back in an attempt to see the top of the Shuttle, his hat fell off, revealing his bald dome and long curls. It hit the concrete with a loud bang. He looked around, quickly replaced it, and Kiko pulled him toward relative safety just to the side of an overhanging platform.

Her eyes were wide and glowing with the excitement of it all. It was as if she had a fever. She might as well have. Any doctor would have put them both away. Her voice shook a little as she pointed upwards and said, "Now all we have to do is get up there."

Chapter Forty-six -
The Many Moments Of Weakness

Minnie had a moment of weakness. There seemed to be people everywhere — soldiers, technicians, mechanics. It was still foggy, but how much help would that be now that they were right there in the thick of things? Holding on to his hat, Minnie looked up again at the towering mass of metal and fuel. It was huge. And cold, even in the Florida heat. And forbidding. He looked over at Kiko, who was concentrating on the activity at ground level. He saw no weakness in her and tried to put his own away.

"So, what's the plan?" he asked in a calm manner that surprised him.

"Well, the elevator's out. Too many people around. We'll take the stairs."

Minnie exploded. "The stairs!?" He looked up again and his hardhat fell. He ignored it. "Look at that thing. It's 20 or 30 stories. We'll die before we get to the top." He turned back to her and said, "I always take the elevator," as if that should have explained and settled everything.

"We don't have to go to the top. Only to the door of the Shuttle."

"Oh, fine."

"Well then you stay here and I'll go. We don't have time to argue."

She started toward the tower. Minnie grabbed her arm. "Okay, okay, okay. You're not leaving me here with all these weirdos. Let's go."

He jammed his hardhat back on his head and, without waiting for her, began to stride purposefully across the concrete. Kiko had to run to catch up with him. As she did, she noticed a guy in uniform who stood between them and where they thought the stairs were. He was examining them closely.

Kiko bent toward Minnie, checked his name tag, and began speaking in a loud voice.

"Mollenhauer, how many times do I have to tell you? When the MPS engages, it's helium, you nitwit, not hydrogen. The external tanks are not a big concern. It's the ratio between gravity and..."

The man smiled and nodded at them as they walked past, deep in their conversation. They were getting closer to the stairs and what they hoped would be safety.

They kept walking and Minnie, out of the side of his mouth, said, "Appleton, was 'nitwit' really necessary?"

She smiled. "Oh Min, don't sweat it. But it really is helium, you know."

He was amazed. He stopped her.

"Helium? You mean they get this thing off the ground with helium? Like a balloon?"

He couldn't believe it.

She nervously looked around. "Minnie, this isn't the place for this."

"But helium?"

"They pressurize it. It's one factor, one ingredient. Don't worry, they know what they're doing."

He rolled his eyes and nodded. Then he asked, "But do we?"

"Minnie, we settled all that before."

He shook his head to clear it of doubts. "You're right. Forget it." He laughed. "What are we standing here for? We've got a lot of stairs to climb."

They finally made it to the bottom of the gigantic superstructure which surrounded the Shuttle and its rockets. They tried to blend in with the shadows as they sneaked around and checked it out.

"Okay," Kiko said. "The elevators are over there where those people are. The stairs should be around to our left. If we're lucky there won't be any guards."

She took his hand and they started off. They were well hidden by the steel girders and metal panels. They located the stairs, which were deserted. They took one last look over their shoulders and began the long climb.

The first few flights weren't bad, but by the time Minnie had given up counting he was soaked in sweat and out of breath. He stopped and leaned against the railing.

Kiko said, "We're only about a third of the way." She kept climbing.

"Wait a minute," Minnie said. "I've got to rest."

"We'll get plenty of that once we're inside."

"I know, but if I don't rest, I'm not going to get there."

In the stairwell they were hidden from observation but they could still see outside. While he was recovering, Minnie took a peek. The fog was holding, but it seemed a little thinner. Then he made the mistake of looking over the side.

"Jesus!"

Over her shoulder, Kiko said, "Whatever you do, don't look

down. Let's keep going."

They did. Up and up and up. There were "No Trespassing" signs on every landing. The words "Warning - Restricted Area", blared out at them repeatedly, but they paid no attention. Minnie's legs felt like lead. He considered abandoning his pack and his coat and his hat and although it was cooler in the shadows of the stairway, all he wanted to do was to lie down and sweat to death. But he kept going. Kiko was amazing. It didn't seem to bother her. She looked just as fresh and as beautiful as she did at the start. Their steps echoed in the hollow space. They continued climbing. Minnie had no idea how close they were. All he knew was that they had gone a long way and that they were way up there. He didn't dare look.

They took the turn for yet another flight of stairs and saw above them a platform — an end to the countless stairs. Minnie gasped with relief. Kiko whispered to him that they should be quiet. It wasn't necessary. Minnie didn't have the breath to speak.

The platform appeared to encircle the Shuttle and Minnie and Kiko crept along, as silently as they could, as they explored it. Up ahead, they heard conversation and they stopped in their tracks. They could see three men in white uniforms. One of them was finishing a joke. They weren't aware of the two intruders.

"So the second question was 'How do you spell it?' And the guy said, 'That's easy. E-i-e-i-o.'"

One of the men laughed and the other said, "That's stupid." The man telling the joke shrugged and said, in a different tone, "Well, that should do it. All systems are go. Everything secured. Clean carpets, empty ashtrays, coffee pot going." The others laughed.

Minnie turned to Kiko with his eyes wide and whispered, "Coffee?"

Kiko put her finger to her lips and gave him a fierce look.

The men got into the elevator. One said, "First floor, Eleanor," and the door shut on more of their laughter. It was suddenly deathly still on the platform. All they could hear was the breeze coming through the steel girders. A seagull squawked somewhere below them. In the quiet, it felt as if the whole structure were swaying.

When they were sure they were alone, they walked toward where the men had been gathered. There was a door built into the crisp whiteness of the Shuttle's skin. A small circular hatch. It was closed. Minnie and Kiko looked at each other and Kiko said, "Here we go."

She gripped the handle and pulled. Nothing happened. She tugged some more, with the same result. She looked for a lock or a switch or something that would trigger the door. She was getting nervous and frantic. The elevator might open at any moment and all would be lost. She looked to Minnie for help.

He had had conflicting emotions about this whole thing from the beginning and he shrugged and said, "Hmm. I don't know why we didn't think it would be locked. I guess we'll have to bag it. Going down will be much easier."

He turned to go.

Kiko grabbed him by the lapels of his scientist disguise.

"Minnie," she said, struggling to bring her anger under control. "Maybe it's just stuck."

He wanted to humor her so he stepped up to the door and pounded on it. To their surprise, it sprung open.

They exchanged glances. Minnie recovered, took a deep breath and stepped to one side. It was meant to be. He smiled and said, "After you, sweetie."

Chapter Forty-seven -
T Minus 48 And Counting

"This is just like the book. It's all here." Kiko was excited.
They had ducked through the small opening in the side of
the Shuttle and had begun to orient themselves. It was just as the
Space Shuttle Operator's Manual had predicted: the large control
panel below the windshield in front of the two pilots' seats; the
three video screens in the center of the panel; rows of switches
and knobs and buttons. Very utilitarian. The whole arrangement was disconcerting because everything was on the vertical
for takeoff, not the horizontal as it would be in flight. It was all
tilted upwards, 90 degrees from normal.

Minnie had closed the hatch behind him and locked it. He
crawled through the passageway, complaining. "Couldn't they
have made it a little wider. This is for midgets." He let out a yell
as he hit his knee on a protruding bolt. "My taxes go for this?"

He stuck his head out into the cabin of the ship and took a
long look in silence. Kiko was already in her seat fiddling with
some knobs.

He began again, "I'm sorry, Kiko, this is not Star Trek. I've seen
diesels that were a lot more inviting than this. And look, a fire
extinguisher." He pointed to the small red canister attached to
the wall. "That's going to do a lot of good."

"Oh Minnie. Don't worry. This is going to be great."

"Uh huh. Couldn't they have put a few pictures up? Maybe a
calendar?"

He set his pack down and steadied himself against the wall.

"Minnie, don't knock against those switches."

"Kiko, it's all turned around. Can a guy get seasick in something like this?"

"Just sit down and strap in. It's a lot better than standing and
trying to make sense."

He threw his pack in a corner and climbed over and around
the various obstacles and then he lowered himself into the seat
on the right. It was more comfortable than it looked and he
adjusted his position as he wiggled out of his lab coat and removed his hat.

"I'll put those away," Kiko said.

She took them and stashed them and the pack in a cabinet in
the wall above them. She went back to twirling knobs and
flipping switches. The book was propped open on her lap to a

page which began to detail the procedures for liftoff. Minnie looked over at her and was not reassured by this sight. The blood was going to his head.

"How long are we going to have to hang here like this?"

"Usually it's two hours, but we're going to bypass a lot of stuff. We need to get out of here before they're onto us."

"It's going to be safe, right?"

"Don't worry." She went back to the knobs and switches.

There was a jolt and the Shuttle moved slightly for a second. Minnie gripped the side of his seat. He looked over at Kiko in wordless shock.

"That's our stairway retracting. So we can take off," she explained.

Minnie smiled weakly. "I can't believe this is really happening."

Kiko leaned over and motioned him closer. They were straining at their seatbelts and their lips just met over the SRB separation switches.

"I can't believe it either." She gazed warmly into his eyes. "I'll never forget you."

"Forget me? What do you mean? I hope not. And don't worry, I won't let you. Stop talking like that. Just fly this thing."

As he put his helmet on, he resigned himself one more time to the insanity of their plan and said, "Warp 2, Mr. Sulu."

Kiko laughed and concentrated on the panel before her. As she flipped one switch, a voice broke out over a console speaker.

"Discovery? This is Control. Do you read me? Over."

Kiko smiled at Minnie as she said in a low voice, "Roger, Control. We copy." She flipped the switch and giggled.

"Discovery?" It was a voice with a flat western accent. The accent all pilots and flight personnel seemed to have. "Discovery, you're a little ahead of schedule. What's going on? Over."

"Roger, Mission Control. Crew-access arm retracted. Cabin pressurization initiated. I would advise clearing the area. Over."

Minnie was sweating again. "Aren't they going to figure out it's us and not their guys?"

"Not yet," Kiko said. "Not before we blast off."

The way she said 'blast off' scared him.

The voice of Mission Control came back on. Minnie could hear the tension fighting with the customary calm of the voice.

"Discovery? This is Control. Over?"

It was a tone of command. Kiko's hands were all over the control panel. She was making adjustments and flipping the pages of the book.

"Minnie, this is getting a little difficult. Will you read the directions to me? Starting here."

She pointed to a spot in the book that read "MPS He isol (isolation). A, B, switches (all six) — open." He could barely pronounce it, but he called it out to her. She flipped the appropriate switches.

"That's our helium," she said.

Minnie groaned a little.

He read out, "AC Bus Sensor switches (all three) - off for one second, then monitor."

"Discovery?" The voice was now obviously agitated.

"Keep reading," she said.

"Auxiliary Power Unit pre-start. Prepare the three APUs, which power the orbiter's hydraulic system for operation."

She did. "Okay. I mean, A-okay. Minnie, we're going to manual control." She flipped a bank of switches.

He was getting into this. "APU fuel tank valves — open. APU control 1 — start. Hydraulic main pump, press 1 — normal."

A moment later, he said, "Orbiter main engines gimbal to launch position."

"Discovery, goddamnit. This is Control. What the hell is going on? Over."

Kiko answered them this time. "Roger, Control. We have switched to manual override. Preparing for liftoff in ...," she checked the clock, "...in T minus 48 seconds."

Control lost it. "Discovery, are you crazy? Identify yourself." Then an entirely different voice broke in. It was deeper, bigger, used to being obeyed. "This is General Stewart Wickes, U.S. Air Force. I command you to shut down immediately. I'm going to court-martial your ass."

"Control, we're a little busy here. We'll talk again after we've achieved liftoff. Over."

She flipped a switch and the two hijackers smiled at each other.

Minnie called out, in rapid succession, "External tank hydrogen vents - close. Solid Rocket Booster APUs - start. Space Shuttle Main Engines - start."

Kiko yelled out over the noise that was increasing every second, "First Engine - ignition. Second Engine - ignition." She flipped another switch. "Third Engine - ignition." She checked the gauges and the clock. "Five, four - main engine start - two, one, zero - SRB ignition - liftoff."

The lights on the control panel burned green and were flashing. The noise was deafening. They could feel the takeoff build from below them as the cabin and the entire Shuttle began to vibrate. The anticipation was almost unbearable and then, as if in the slowest of slow motion, everything began to move.

Chapter Forty-eight - Out Of Control

Minnie couldn't see it, but the launch pad far below them erupted into flame. Huge clouds of smoke and steam billowed around the base of the Shuttle and its attendant engines. The sound was an amazing roar of thunder that only decreased as the Shuttle rose into the air and blasted away from the Cape, from Florida, and from Earth.

They couldn't have planned it better if they tried. Back at the viewing area, the show was in the middle of the second set. There was only a lingering haze of fog. The band had been playing a version of "Dark Star" for the last fifteen minutes. Everything had come together — the fact that they were playing with the Shuttle as a backdrop, the haunting representation of Dark Star that decorated the stage, the crowd's complete identification and involvement with the music, the band going beyond whatever anyone could remember. And now this.

The song had been building in tension for a long time and was just about at the place where Jerry's guitar would take them out of the darkness and into the light. That burst of notes that would liberate everyone from their minds, their bodies, their worlds. Just as they were reaching toward this point, Minnie and Kiko blasted off, completing the sequence.

The noise of the liftoff blended in with the sound of the band, but the sight of it stopped the crowd cold. Their heads moved as one as they followed its progress upward, between the two Dark Stars on stage and above the towers of speakers and into the blue. The band played on, with their backs to this impressive scene, oblivious to all but the music. All events meshed together as the band went into a cathartic passage, the crowd got their breath back, and Kiko and Minnie cleared the tower and shot up into the sky. It was a moment no one in that audience would ever forget. Later, some would wonder if it really had happened, but no one would ever forget it.

Inside the Shuttle, Minnie and Kiko were being smashed into their seats. They couldn't move. It wasn't only the ever increasing gravitational pressure that pinned them there, but also the sheer enormity of what was happening. They held hands until the G-force became too much.

The tower and the Florida coast dropped away beneath them. The Shuttle made its 120 degree roll, accelerating all the while. In less than a minute they were traveling at Mach 1, the speed of sound, and if they could have looked, they would have realized that the ground had already disappeared. It would have been too much for Minnie.

They were shaking in their seats and not from fear alone. Having just ignited this bomb beneath them, a bomb still attached to them, they rode the wave of its explosion. Despite the fact that they were new at it, their ascent was flawless and unhindered.

"Discovery?" The voice was still panicked, but trying its best to work with the situation. "This is Control. Please abort manual override. You need our help." There was a short pause. And then, in a different tone of voice, "And we need yours."

With the G-forces acting on them, it was all Kiko could do to raise her arm and flip the switches which allowed for joint control of the ship.

The voice of General Wickes broke in. "Goddamnit, mister. If you ever get back, I'll see to it personally that you never fly again. I'll roast your ass and feed it to the sharks."

"General, this is not helping." It was Mission Control again. "We've got to save the ship."

Kiko and Minnie could hear a scuffle over the speaker and heard the shouts of the General as he was taken away.

"Okay. Discovery, this is Control. We need to work together on this." Control was recovering its breath. "Right now, we've got to separate the Solid Rocket Booster."

Minnie answered them, in a tone completely unofficial. "Go ahead on."

Back on Earth, they had to think about that response for a moment and wonder just who had control of their Shuttle.

"Discovery, this is Control. Go for Main Engine cutoff. Over."

Kiko gave Minnie a look that told him she was in charge and answered, "Roger, Main Engine cutoff on schedule. Out."

They had reached an altitude of 75 miles and were moving at almost 65,000 mph. The fuel in their external tank was almost gone. They had been burning it at a rate of 60,000 gallons a minute. Then, with a jolt, they separated the tank and coasted for a while. The Shuttle was now flying more forward than upward. Below them they could see the blue of the planet. All they could do was stare. Nothing could have prepared them for such an incredible sight.

Minnie broke this emotional silence. "Far fucking out."

They had barely registered this glimpse of Earth before they were interrupted.

"Discovery, this is Control."

Minnie made a face and said, "Like who else would it be?"

"You are go for OMS - one burn. Do you understand our instructions? Over?"

Kiko smiled and said, "Roger, Control. I've got the book. Over."

"The book? Over."

"Roger. Don't worry. Where are we now?"

"OMS - one burn. Over."

"Roger, OMS-one, out."

This was the first of two engine bursts that would ease them into orbit. Weight was becoming a negligible factor and Minnie had to hang onto the book to keep it from floating away.

"Discovery, this is Control. Coming up on OMS-two. Over."

"Roger, OMS-two."

Minnie could almost believe that Kiko was the real pilot. Everything had gone according to plan. Nothing had blown up and they were both still breathing. Back on Earth, the people at NASA weren't happy, but at least they hadn't lost their ship. He thought they might even learn a thing or two from this mission.

Kiko then announced, "OMS-two cutoff. We have achieved orbit. Over."

"Roger, Discovery. We're glad you made it. Over." Their relief was audible.

Even though they were now in weightless orbit, neither of them wanted to move. They simply couldn't believe it. As they looked through the windshield of the Shuttle, they saw the blackness of space studded with impossibly more stars than they had ever seen from Earth. And, when they looked down, they were met with a scene so bright, so blue, and just so clean that at first, they involuntarily turned away. Later, they would have to force themselves from the hypnotic power of their beautiful native planet.

Kiko beamed at Minnie, "Well, big guy, we did it. We're here. In space."

He beamed back at her with love, admiration, and wonder. "You are too much, baby. Too much."

Chapter Forty-nine - Did I Forget Anything?

Minnie was the first to undo his straps and safety belts. Once free from these restraints, he floated upwards from his seat. He started laughing. He couldn't help it.

"This is incredible," he said.

There was a loud clunk as he hit his head on the cabin's ceiling. He was glad he hadn't taken off his helmet. He waved down at Kiko.

"You've gotta try this."

He removed his helmet and fastened it with velcro to the back of the co-pilot's seat. His movements were awkward, but he was already beginning to get the hang of it. Then he found that Kiko was floating beside him.

For a moment, they didn't know what to do. They looked down at their seats and the control panel with disbelief. They looked out the windows in wonder. And they began to look at each other with something that began to absorb all of their attention and made their bodies tingle. This weightlessness was a completely new feeling and was exciting them.

Minnie pushed off the wall and gently collided with Kiko. He admired her soft skin and deep brown eyes. Her expression was one of amazement at her new weightless state. He reached out and touched her face. Their lips met and their blood, unhampered by Earth's gravity, increased its flow and temperature. The Touch had never been like this.

He adjusted the headset behind his ear. "Do you think the normal astronauts feel like this?" he asked in a hoarse voice.

"Minnie, they're professionals. We're the ones who are normal."

He thought her smile even more beautiful here in space. Her hair was floating out from her head and she made an effort to collect it and tie it back.

Then they were interrupted by, "Discovery, this is Mission Control. What's going on up there? We don't seem to be reading video transfer. Haven't been. Over."

They had forgotten all about Control.

Kiko answered. "Roger, Control. Video transfer disabled. Over."

"Disabled? Over." They were outraged.

"Roger, Control. We require a little privacy. Over." She looked over at Minnie.

The voice couldn't disguise its frustration. "Privacy? Uh, Roger, Discovery." Control took a big breath and said, "What are your intentions, Discovery? Is this a hijacking for ransom? Or what?

What is going on? I think you owe us an explanation. Over."

Kiko looked at Minnie and thought about it. The silence of space was soothing.

"Discovery? This is Control. Do you read me? Over."

Kiko finally spoke, "Roger, Control. We copy. No ransom required. Well, not money anyway. We want you to do something for us. I'll download a file I've prepared to your computer. It's got our whole proposal and all the information you need. We hope that you'll agree with us that something must be done. Our immediate intention is to continue orbit for the time being. We'll be discontinuing ship-to-Earth communication for a while. Over."

"Discontinuing?" Control was freaking out. "What are you talking about? This is our Shuttle. We require continuous contact. Over."

She winked at Minnie. "Control, we're not going anywhere."

Minnie laughed. "Oh, sure. Not much," he said.

Kiko went on. "Study the information. Think it over for a while. Take all the time you need to make a decision. Right now we want some privacy. We'll be scrambling internal communications for some time, but we'll call you back. Discontinuing contact now. Over and out."

"Discovery, wait a min..."

She punched a couple of buttons which returned the cabin to silence. They were finally all alone. The lights still flashed, the dials and gauges still registered, and yet this silence held them as they floated and their lips met. Their kiss was all the communication they needed.

It was Kiko who first came back to the reality of the situation. She knew that if they started down this romantic path, they wouldn't come back for a long time.

"Min, we've got to get to work."

"That's right, gorgeous," he said in a dreamy voice.

She could tell they were thinking of different things.

"There's a lot to do. We need to send the file and..." Her voice trailed off and she looked at him. The intensity of her feelings showed on her face. After a moment, she said, "I don't know what will happen if we get started. We have a plan, remember?"

"Kiko." Minnie felt lightheaded.

"Min, you devil. Come on. Let's get this stuff done first. Then we can really do some exploration."

He knew she was right.

They had begun to control their movements, if not their

emotions. Kiko folded up the seats and, with those out of the way, they floated freely. Terms like up and down were meaningless. The idea of a seat or a chair was also meaningless. It was the most amazing feeling. Not sitting. Not resting on anything. Not straining against the gravity they had taken for granted since birth. This was Space. It was unbelievable.

"Okay," Minnie said. "What's the plan?"

Kiko looked around the cabin and inspected the communication controls — the links to various satellites and telescopes, the ship's data facilities, computers, recording devices. She consulted the book.

"Well, the first thing is that we go to DAP."

"Kiko, it's me, remember? Speak English."

"Digital Automatic Pilot. Next, we need to open the cargo bay doors or we'll begin to boil in here."

She flipped a switch and then they floated, coasted, drifted, whatever it was, to the back of the cabin to watch. The long bay doors parted at the middle and the pure white of the cargo bay unfolded into the endless black of space, like a beautiful silent flower.

They just stared. They could have stayed that way for hours. Finally Kiko shook her head. Bringing herself back to the matter at hand, she said, "Okay, enough. Let's get to work."

She returned to the main part of the cabin and began to organize. She flipped some switches, twirled a few knobs. She downloaded the file to NASA. She then punched at the number pad on a keyboard and was speaking into her headset.

"Francisco? This is Kiko. I need your help. Yeah, this is it. We're really up here. I know. You're a genius and a sweetheart."

Minnie cocked his head in her direction.

She continued speaking to Francisco, a computer hacker she had met back in California. "Can you reroute calls from these two numbers to this one? Thanks, I know it's illegal. This is about the Cartel. This is our chance to bust them."

She smiled at Minnie, who had opened his pack. Things had begun to float out of it and he was trying to retrieve them and shove them back into it. He was swearing.

"Right. If it works, I'll have some more numbers for you. We'll build a network and I'll record it all from here. Great. And what's the address of your friend, the astronomer? No, the internet address." She wrote it down. "Okay. Thanks. When I get back I'll tell you all about it."

She turned to Minnie, who was still struggling with his pack.

"Minnie, this is great. If it works the way I think it should, we'll be able to listen in on the Cartel down in Brazil. It will add to our information. And, with a little help, we'll get the pictures we want."

"Fine," he muttered.

He was surrounded by things floating in the air — a bag of Fig Newtons, a loaf of bread, a jar of peanut butter, band aids, cassette tapes, a red crayon, condoms, a paperback copy of *The Big Sleep*, shoelaces, and a toothbrush.

"Minnie?" Kiko started laughing.

"I told you I was prepared. Now if I can just get this shit back in the pack..."

"What else is in there?"

"Don't worry, you'll be glad we have it."

CAUTION: BiG View

Chapter Fifty - Hotel Discovery

Kiko was more than organized. More than efficient. She was more than beautiful. She was amazing and Minnie was torn between staring at her and staring out the window. They both had the same infinite appeal.

She was listening in on phone conversations from Brazil.

"Can you believe it?" she said. "They're ordering a pizza."

Minnie couldn't help himself. "What kind?"

She was communicating not only with Francisco's buddy on the Internet, typing furiously and getting endless printouts, but also with her many contacts around the globe. And what better place to do it?

"Minnie, all of this work of ours is paying off. It's all coming together."

There were moments when she was quiet and tense as she listened in on conversations that took place far below them. She would excitedly say, "Min, listen to this," and she'd switch it so that they came out over the speakers and filled the cabin with sinister voices.

"Yeah. What? Only 600 kilos? Look, you tell that Texas son of a bitch what's what. And make sure he understands. This is business."

Or, in a tone more suited to discussing the weather, "Well, just have them take it the Pacific route. Up the coast. Use the Sea-Tac setup."

Or, completely the boss, "Call Behr and have him and Fritz meet us at John's at 9:30, sharp. I want a report on the new arrangement. Those guys are squeezing us and I don't like it. We've got some tricks of our own."

And so on.

Just as Kiko had predicted, she was now monitoring eight different numbers and getting names, dates, places, and amounts on tape. She was amassing evidence that would make Ed's mouth water. Of course that wasn't so difficult, but she knew that recording these conversations from the Shuttle would cement their credibility and convict many of the Cartel's most important members. With luck, they would bring the whole thing to a sudden halt.

She was getting advice and instruction over the internet from Henry, the astronomer. He was directing her use of the powerful photographic imaging devices available to the Shuttle. As they orbited above the west coast of Africa, she had been able to bring pictures of land formations up on the screen which were remarkable.

Minnie was impressed.

"You can almost see the grass. Or count the trees. They never told us they could do this."

Kiko said, "There're a lot of things they never told us."

"If they wanted to, they could read the label on your coat." He thought for a moment. "They probably do. Not only intelligence, but marketing information."

While they were passing over South America, Kiko trained the lenses on the rainforest and they both became silent. It was night down there and they could see how much of what should have been dark and sleeping was on fire, being cleared for cultivation. How much of this, they wondered, was the Cartel's doing? How much the oil companies? The others? It was frightening.

Later, when they flew over in the daytime, they were able to see just how bad it was. This part of the Amazon basin was a huge place, but they could tell from the previous data they had studied how much it had changed in the last two years. The detail they were now seeing was even more disheartening than they had expected.

"Holy shit," Minnie said in a way that mixed shock and prayer.

They transferred the digital images of this destruction to the hard drive for later use.

"Kiko, I was into this before, but now..." He didn't have the words. He threw his hands up and yelled, "Fuck!" He tried to stomp around but he was weightless and it didn't work. This added to his frustration. "They're killing us or they're sure as hell trying. It's like we're cutting our own throats."

"Min," her voice was quiet. She kept looking at the screen in horror. "We'll get these guys. Now that we have the Shuttle they'll hear us out. They'll have to release our findings."

On their second day in space, Kiko opened communication with Earth.

"Control, this is Discovery, do you read me?"

They waited a moment and then the radio crackled with static and the voice of Control said, "Discovery, we read you. We've been following your progress and so far everything is on target, but this is an outrage. Do you hear me? It's crazy. You must return at once. Do you understand the gravity of what you're doing? Over."

"The gravity?" she laughed. "Control, what a sense of humor. I assure you we are well aware of our position and purpose. Did you read our proposal? Over."

There was a silence on the other end.

"Control? Do you read me? Over."

"We read you and, yes, we've studied it. We think it's a lot of horseshit, but we read it."

"Control, you can deny the truth all you want, if that's what you need to do, but we can see it from up here. The destruction is appalling and obvious. Now are you going to fulfill our requests or are we going to crash your Shuttle?"

Minnie's eyes went wide and his mouth dropped open. She looked like she meant it.

"I want you to let everyone know that we have taken the Shuttle as a way of publicizing, of presenting the full information about what the Cartel, the oil companies, and other big-money interests are doing to the environment. This was a last alternative on our part."

"Discovery, we will not be blackmailed."

"Control, we will not let this planet be murdered. Now either do it or say good-bye to the Shuttle. Over."

It was quiet. A long silence began during which Minnie looked at Kiko, who returned his look without saying anything. As the moments passed and he thought it over, the more sure he was that she was right. He agreed that desperate situations called for desperate measures, but he worried that NASA wouldn't go for it and they would be required to go through with their threat. Then he realized that he and Kiko might crash this thing anyway. They were a long way from Earth and solid ground and anything could happen. He looked out the window. It was black out there and colder than he could imagine.

Mercifully interrupting his anxiety, Control was back. The voice was clear, unemotional. "Discovery, we agree to your demands. The broadcast is set for 1900 hours EST, today. We'll release the presentation section of your file. Over."

Kiko smiled over at Minnie, who let out a big breath, shook his head, and rolled his eyes.

"Discovery, what are your current plans? Over."

Minnie thought they were taking this a little too easily, but he was relieved. Then Kiko said, "We'll continue orbit and check back later. Over and out."

After all their negotiations they had worked up an appetite. The pickings were slim. They made brave attempts at rehydrated shrimp cocktail and thermostabilized chocolate pudding, but so far, they had mostly relied on Minnie's peanut butter and jelly and Fig Newtons.

Minnie was always happy when he was eating. "See, it's a good thing I brought this stuff. I just hope we have enough."

They both had to think about that for a moment.

Minnie asked, "How long are we going to stay up here?"

"You're not getting bored, are you?"

"Bored? Are you crazy? All I have to do is look out the window and I'm gone for a couple of hours. I don't know what I was thinking when I packed that book. And, you know," he wiggled his eyebrows at her, "you're kind of cute too."

Kiko blushed just like she might have on Earth. "Oh, Min."

She reached over and touched his arm. She leaned closer to him. Her eyes were shut and her lips were taking on great importance when they both heard a voice over the cabin's speaker. It was a voice they recognized.

"Minnie, this is Cowboy. Pick up the phone. This is serious."

Minnie couldn't believe it.

He shook his head and said to Kiko, "I can't ever get away from that place."

"Minnie?" Cowboy sounded desperate.

Minnie floated over to the controls and patched himself into the line.

"Jesus, Cowboy, how'd you get this number? Don't you know I'm on vacation? What's the problem now?"

"Well, Beaver says he's going to New Orleans and just when Bubba quits, too. He says he's going anyway. He says you've had your vacation and now it's his turn. He says not to worry, the bar will run itself, but I don't think so. When are you coming back?"

"Cowboy, you take that place too seriously. It's a long trip back and it's going to take me a while. You need to relax. Maybe you should go on vacation."

"Oh, right." Cowboy was quiet for a moment. "Well, maybe I will. I don't know why I care about this stuff if you guys don't."

"I don't either."

"Just hurry back, will you? You know, it's been a while."

"Tell me about it. It's like another lifetime. Just keep doing whatever it is you're doing. We're still making money, aren't we?"

"Well, yeah."

"Okay. No problem. Talk to you later."

Chapter Fifty-one - Love Me Do

They worked all afternoon and had just finished a light lunch of Fig Newtons. They had gathered an amazing amount of data. They had pictures of the rainforest and could identify the areas that were under cultivation. It was awful. Minnie thought about his last cup of coffee, about the many coffee places he knew in Boulder, about Bowman. The whole thing was crazy.

The recorded conversations of the Cartel were safely stored on the hard drive. Their evidence showed that the Cartel people actually were Nazis. Minnie and Kiko had gathered a record of transactions, shipping routes, connections, and even names of some of the Brazilian and U.S. politicians who had smoothed the way for the Cartel's illegal and destructive schemes. All of this reinforced the information that NASA had and was about to release.

It was nearing time for the broadcast. Kiko fiddled with the communications gear. The sound of static filled the cabin. She pushed buttons and flipped switches, changed channels and still all they heard was static.

"Min, this is awful. I can't get any reception."

"Try calling the operator."

She was able to get through to them. "Control, we have a problem with the radio. We are not receiving transmission. Over."

"Affirmative, Discovery. We're working on it."

"Control, if you're thinking of trying to pull a fast one on us, I'd like to remind you who's flying this thing."

"We copy, Discovery. Broadcast will continue as scheduled. We're checking the problem and will get back to you ASAP. Over."

Kiko tried to get in touch with Francisco with no success and 1900 hours came and went and still all they got was static. All the communications in the ship were down, with the exception of their link with Control. Her conversations with Control informed them that the broadcast had indeed been made and that reaction to it had been immediate and considerable. Control was working on the radio problem, but now that they had fulfilled their part of the bargain, they kept asking when they'd get the Shuttle back.

Minnie lost his patience. He broke into the conversation and had the last word. "You guys keep working on it. We'll be back when we get there. Over and out."

Later, when things calmed down a little, Minnie was drinking a plastic-encased orange-pineapple drink, one of the few consumable things on board that wasn't rehydrated, thermostabilized or irradiated.

He lifted it in a toast to Kiko and said, "Here's to you, Kiddo. I have to admit that I had my doubts..."

"No kidding," she said.

"But you did it. You stole the Shuttle. You flew it into orbit. And you got the goods on the Cartel."

"We did, Minnie," she said softly. "We. You and me."

"Well, hmm." He wasn't sure. "Maybe, but it was a great thing. And you're the greatest."

He took a long drink and then said, "Okay, we got the info. We got them to broadcast it. That about does it." He paused.

"We assume they broadcast it."

Minnie nodded. "Yeah, we didn't hear it, but," he waved the printouts about the broadcast that Control had sent them, "it shook them up down there. It worked. We did it." He was proud of her. Then he said, quietly, "Kiko, don't you think we should go home? You know, while our luck is running the right way?"

"Minnie, are you homesick?"

"No way. Here in space with a beautiful babe like yourself? What do I care? I just wonder, that's all."

She gave him a mysterious smile and said, "Min, there are a couple more things we have to do before we go back."

She floated over to him and gave him a kiss that would have lifted him off the ground if he hadn't already been weightless. He got the idea. They had done all that they had set out to accomplish. The work was behind them and now they looked at each other without saying anything. They didn't have to. They had been building up to this for a long time. This time he kissed her. Her lips were warmer than anything in space had ever been. She reached over and turned off the lights of the cabin. Their eyes adjusted to the glow that came through the windows from Earth.

In the soft light, they floated close together with only their fingertips touching. He had never seen her look so beautiful.

Music was playing at low volume in the background and this moment was more romantic than either could fully admit. They began a slow dance that they both knew from past experience, but in this weightless environment it required a new level of cooperation.

As he struggled with the enviable job of freeing her of her pants, Minnie began laughing. "Wait a minute. I've got to get a little leverage."

"Minnie, grab onto the ladder so I can help you."

Each action had an equal and opposite reaction and it wasn't as easy or as smooth as they had imagined. The force of his Touch, gentle and loving though it was, caused her body to move through space in a graceful, but frustrating way. She had to hold onto his shirt to remain close, but what she really desired was to remove it. Clothes were now unnecessary and unwanted.

Their struggle continued in carnest. Kiko had pinned Minnie against a control panel and the knobs were digging into his back. He tried not to complain.

They wanted to stretch out, but were afraid of snagging loose wires or accidently flipping a crucial switch. Although their time together these past weeks and the restraint Kiko had imposed on them urged them to a faster pace, they now found that they needed to take things a little slowly here. Caution was in order, but after such a build-up, it was difficult. Their touch was as light as weightlessness could make it and this was driving them crazy.

Eventually, various articles of clothing floated nearby. The music was slow and sultry. Pigpen was singing. It was the infamous Pigpen tape providing a background for their movements.

Minnie said, "If only the Colonel could see me now."

Kiko laughed. "It's a good thing he can't."

The Colonel had been right after all. They were levitating.

Minnie stroked her hair, which was floating out from her head.

"Gorgeous," he said, "this is a new kind of space exploration. Your kisses are out of this world."

She was holding him as close as she could. She could feel his laughter.

He said, "Captain, initiating rotation. Shifting to manual control."

She began giggling.

He continued. "Prepare the landing site. Extending probe, now."

She laughed out loud.

"You have a heavenly body," he said.

"You too, Min."

"Kiko, I'm about to fire my thrusters."

She entered into the spirit of the thing. She answered, "Roger, sensors are reading off the scale."

He warned her, "Prepare for re-entry."

They both cracked up. They held on to each other, until their laughter died down and their passion took over. As time went on, they found themselves in positions neither could have imagined before. It was a tender dialogue between two sensitive instruments that registered each kiss, each touch, each caress. This was the Touch raised to the ultimate level.

The action had heated up to such a pitch that all concern for tubes, wires, and switches was forgotten. There was no pilot, no co-pilot in this engagement, only the two heavenly bodies in sweet constant motion, in synchronous orbit.

After a while, Minnie laughed again and exclaimed, "Maximum transmission," and then, "Mission accomplished."

Kiko pulled him closer and said, "You goofball, just kiss me."

It was sweet. Minnie was left breathless.

She said, "Mister, we're giving you a promotion."

Kiko then looked him in the eye and, as if stating a sad truth, whispered, "Minnie, it will never be the same after this."

Their laughter filled the cabin.

Chapter Fifty-two -
Daydreaming At Midnight

After this romantic earthquake, Minnie was exhausted. He drifted off into a nap. In his relaxation, he naturally adopted what is known in space as the neutral body position. This consisted of being bent slightly at the waist, arms floating away from and just in front of the body. His knees were flexed and his toes pointed a bit.

His body was at peace and his mind was dreaming. He lay on a beach. It was warm and though there was a breeze, the air gently rushing over him was also warm. The waves washed up against the white sand and the sound of it lulled him into deeper sleep. He was in the shade of a single palm which towered over him and curved gracefully toward the sea. Far above him, it ended in a lush green headdress.

Around the point sailed a boat. Its white sail was taut with the force of the wind and as he watched the small red boat against the infinite blue of the ocean, he softly sang the words to a song.

Paradise waits
on the crest of a wave

Poised for flight
wings spread bright
spring from night
into the sun

He was giving it a calypso twist and was quite impressed with his own singing when he saw the little boat go into the wind. Its white sail began to flap. The wind picked up, his vision magically zoomed in on the sail and he saw it in detail as it began to shred into many pieces. In alarm, he involuntarily called out to the little ship and woke himself up.

He was sweating. His heart was pounding. Then he heard it. A strangled voice over the speaker.

"Minnie. Minnie. Help."

He was somewhere between the beach and the Shuttle.

"What the fuck?"

He looked around for Kiko, but all he saw was the empty cabin. It wasn't that big a place, but he looked again. Nothing. Then, once more, that scared voice.

"Min..."

He looked out past the windshield into nothingness. Then he shoved himself at full speed toward the back of the cabin and peered through the window there. One of the spacesuits was floating far to the right of the cargo bay. He blinked his eyes and then he saw it move.

He adjusted his headset and said, "Kiko?"

"Oh Minnie, help me. I'm having trouble breathing."

There wasn't time for conversation. Minnie's mind became suddenly focused. His movements were precise. He felt as he imagined a surgeon must — a complete concentration on the business at hand. A cessation of all thoughts not pertinent to the immediate crisis. An eerie calm that makes everything possible. He knew exactly what he had to do. He went and got the book.

He hurried back with it and frantically flipped to the pages marked "Extra-vehicular Activity." There he found instructions on how to prepare. He took it with him into the airlock between the cabin and the cargo bay.

He pulled the bulky pieces of the suit from their storage space began to struggle into them. First the cooling and ventilation garment, then the huge lower torso section with its large feet. Next he wriggled into the ungainly upper torso, connected the cooling mechanism, and then joined the suit halves.

He put on his communications carrier so that they could talk once again. As he adjusted the oxygen flow in his suit and put on his gloves, he heard Kiko's labored breathing. He knew every second counted and yet he could not hurry his preparation. It had to be right.

"Kiko, I'm on my way," he said. "Hang on."

He fastened the helmet to the suit and climbed into the manned maneuvering unit. He pressed the buttons on the airlock control panel and could hear it decompress. The door slid open and he looked out into a blackness unimaginably endless and real. He looked down and below him shone the Earth he and Kiko both loved. He had a stab of fear that lasted only a moment and then, with a deep breath, he pushed off into space.

"Kiko? How are you doing?" he asked.

Her voice was small. "I'm sorry, Min." She was crying.

"Sshh," he said, trying to soothe her. "Tell me the problem."

She pulled herself together and, in short gasps, began to speak.

"The maneuvering unit...is broken...so I'm just drifting. There's something wrong with my oxygen...I can't get enough."

"I'm coming. As soon as I can figure out how to work this thing."

He experimented with the handheld controls. He pressed a button with a stiff gloved finger. A small jet of air issued from somewhere on the unit and he shot slowly, but steadily, backwards and banged against the side of the ship.

"That ain't it," he said.

He pushed a few more buttons and he yawed and rotated and stopped and started until he finally got the hang of it. He began to make his way toward her.

"Okay," he said. "Stay relaxed. We'll be back in the ship before you know it."

"I can't relax...I'm scared."

"I know, kiddo. But try. It's important."

He was worried that all his preparation and the time spent figuring out the suit would make him too late to help Kiko. The thought of something happening to her shivered through him. He hoped he would be able to maneuver the two of them to the ship without too much delay.

One more burst from the right side of his pack brought him within arm's reach of her. The white of her suit stood out against the darkness and she shone like an odd-shaped moon. His arms moved with robot deliberateness and then his big gloves clamped onto her.

Peering through the faceplate, he saw how pale and scared she was. Her eyes were wide with terror and her lips were parted and, in that light, appeared to be blue. He checked the display on the front of her suit. Lights were flashing and it took him a minute to figure it out. There was a digital readout that suggested appropriate corrective actions. He tried them. He adjusted a valve in back. He punched a couple of buttons in front. It wasn't making any difference.

"Shit. Kiko, I'm taking you back now. But you have to try to control your breathing. Your air is way low."

"Oh, Min." Her face was contorted with fear.

"We'll make it. Just try to breathe slowly. Like this."

As he pulled her toward the ship, he began a steady rhythmic pattern.

"Min." It was a strangled cry. She was panicked and hyperventilating.

He looked slyly at her and gently said, "Don't distract me. I'm trying to count to four."

She had to smile, in spite of herself.

Chapter Fifty-three - Say Your Mantras

Kiko was freaking out. Her oxygen was almost gone. It was imperative that she conserve what was left. And so while Minnie carried her, pulled her, pushed her closer to the ship, he talked to her in a way he hoped might calm her down or distract her and slow her oxygen loss.

"This is an old trick I learned from Swami Eddie back in Boulder. You concentrate on the bridge of your nose and you place your forefingers against your thumbs. I know you've got those damned gloves on, but it's the principle of the thing."

He made an adjustment to their course. Her fingers tried, despite the gloves, to carry out his instructions. He looked in on her and saw her attempt a smile.

He kept talking. "You close your eyes and as you gently increase the pressure on your fingers, you transfer the feeling of it to your nose. Then, while all this is going on, you say your mantra."

He thought for a moment.

"You can use mine, which is Uh, uh huh. Uh, uh huh. Don't laugh. Swami Eddie said that mantras can't be imposed on you, they come from within. Anyway, it works. Now try it."

He looked and saw that her eyes were closed. He checked the readout on the front of her suit. The oxygen was running out and it was cold out there, despite the suits. Minnie was scared but he couldn't allow himself to panic. He brought her steadily closer to the ship and the lifesaving airlock.

He felt he could hear the slowing of her breath. Was it too slow?

"Kiko, keep breathing," he said.

Finally they were at the airlock. It was a little cramped with the two of them and their bulky suits. Minnie had to remove the maneuvering unit and leave it as another bit of space debris, but at last they were both inside. He hit the controls which closed the door and began to pressurize the airlock.

It seemed to take forever and Minnie kicked the wall with his big boot.

He said, "Come on already." And other things.

Kiko was not moving. He peered into the helmet. Her eyes were still closed, but whether from the meditation or the lack of oxygen, he couldn't tell.

Finally, there was a beep signaling that the airlock now had an atmosphere similar to that of the cabin. Minnie attacked the connections between Kiko's suit and her helmet, wanting to get her into the air immediately.

His gloves made this difficult and it was a confusion of undoing, but at last he succeeded. She had lost consciousness and Minnie attempted to lay her down on the floor. He had his helmet off too. Putting his CPR training to good use, he breathed into her, pulled back, and helped her exhale. He sent his breath into her again. There was no response.

"Kiko," he cried. "Oh, Kiko."

He continued the CPR for what seemed like hours and wished they'd never had this bright idea to go into space. Tears appeared on his cheeks and he wiped them away with one hand. Nothing was working. It seemed that nothing would.

His grief burst from his heart and he lay his body, still in its suit, across her chest and wept.

A moment later, through his unbearable despair, he felt a hand clumsily playing with the curls on the back of his head and he heard her voice again, as she said weakly, "Min, you've got to move."

He sat up like someone had stuck him with a pin. He saw her face. All of its native color had drained from it and it was almost as white as the suits. But her eyes were open and she gave him a weak smile.

"Oh." She heaved a great sigh. "That's better."

He threw his awkwardly suited arms up in the air and gave a wordless cry that mixed relief, hope, and gratitude. For a moment, he didn't know what to do for her. Talk to her? Move her? Kiss her?

She smiled and blinked her eyes, as if she couldn't believe she was here, still alive and safe.

Her small voice said, "Swami Eddie..." Then she rolled her eyes. "And that Minnie," she smiled again, "what a guy."

He brought her into the cabin where she floated quietly. Her color was returning and besides the big scare, no permanent damage seemed to have been done. She was slowly recovering. Minnie was beaming. He was so glad she was back and that she was okay that he kept trying to get her things. He was fidgeting in his desire to do something for her. He kept up a stream of words, afraid to lose contact with her again.

"A drink? A Fig Newton? God, I was so scared. I am never getting into that bag of junk again. I could barely move."

He gently smoothed her hair back.

"Kiko, don't ever do anything like that again. Are you warm enough? How about some more mouth-to-mouth? I mean, when I had to step out of the airlock into nothing it was too much. No acid, no drug, nothing, was ever like that. I couldn't believe it."

He took a breath.

"And when I saw your face...you didn't look good. Well, you know what I mean. Your lips were blue. Oh, God. But now you're back. You're here. Are you sure you don't need anything?"

She reached out and put her finger to his lips. Her touch stopped him and softened him. All the fear and tension seemed to leave his body. He gave a great sigh.

He smiled and, with tears starting in his eyes, said quietly, "Kiko, I'm so glad you're safe."

Then he made a loud, unheroic sniffle.

She gazed at his face. He started up again, but she touched his lips.

"Minnie, I'm so sorry."

He began to say something, but she shook her head and continued.

"I'm sorry I scared you and that I did something that dangerous without telling you. You looked so sweet floating there asleep, I didn't want to wake you. I was curious and thought I'd just go for a little walk."

Minnie snorted.

She said, "You are so brave and so wonderful. What would I have done without you?"

She smiled and he was finally quiet. She sat up and kissed him tenderly. As they contemplated each other in silence, the ship continued its orbit. Far below them, the Earth kept turning. And calling to them.

She took his hand. "Minnie, let's go home."

Chapter Fifty-four - Back At The Ranch

They spent the next two orbits looking out the windows at space and at the stars and at that glowing blue globe. They let the vision of this beautiful universe soak into their bodies and minds. They had learned much in their short time in space and these last orbits were a present they gave themselves.

They were torn between wanting to stay in this quiet, wondrous place and knowing that their lives were meant to be lived out on Earth where there was still sweet air and warm breezes and friendship. They missed the Earth. They wanted to feel its solidity and gravity once again. They wanted to hear the ocean and the birds and the wind. They longed for the smell of flowers and grass. They realized how much they needed the sight of colors and mountains and creatures like themselves.

"This is just like every other vacation," Minnie said.

Kiko looked at him as if he were crazy.

"I mean, you're gone for a short time, but it feels like forever. Time practically stops because everything's new, everything's different. The mind has to catch up, but it's difficult. If we wanted to have the longest life possible, we'd travel constantly."

She nodded. "Uh huh. Should we keep going then? How about Mars? Or Jupiter?"

He smiled. "No, we should go home. We just won't take any of it for granted."

They began to make preparations for re-entry. They were back facing the windshield and the control panel was spread out before them. Kiko was flipping switches and twirling knobs like an expert. Minnie had the book in his lap and was giving her directions to prepare for landing.

She flipped a switch and said, "Control, this is Discovery. Do you read me? Over."

There was no response. They looked at each other.

Minnie shrugged. "Maybe they forgot about us," he said.

"Sure," she said, but they knew better. She repeated, "Control, do you read me? Over."

There was a burst of static and then the voice of Control came out of the speakers. It struggled to present its cool twangy demeanor, but they could hear relief and frustration in the transmission.

"Roger, Discovery. This is Control. We read you loud and clear. And about time, too. We were worried." Control then became sarcastic. "Have you had a good flight? Over."

"Affirmative, Control. Never a dull moment. Over."

"Discovery, would you care to discuss your present plans?" Control's voice was rising. "When the hell, uh, I mean, when do you propose to return? Over."

"Control, we'd like to return as soon as possible." She paused. "But we're going to land at Edwards. Over."

Control blew up. "Edwards? What's wrong with Florida? The weather's fine. Do you realize the trouble and expense that will cause? Over."

"Roger, Control. We'll be landing in California. Do you want us to come back or not? Over."

They were thinking about it.

She turned to Minnie and said, matter of factly, "California's home. It's so much simpler."

He nodded, in the same spirit.

After a minute or so, they heard, "Discovery, this is Control. You are go for Edwards. Let's coordinate our plans. Over."

There was a lot to do. Kiko and Minnie floated around the cabin straightening up and securing everything. They gathered together their data and copied it to Kiko's computer in California for safekeeping.

"Don't you think they're going to be a little upset with us?" Minnie asked.

"Well, yes, but we'll reason with them. And anyway, all the reporters will be there."

"Kiko, we stole their Shuttle."

"Well..." she said and gave a guilty smile.

They knew they'd just have to wait and see and react accordingly. So they left it at that.

Minnie read about the re-entry process until he felt he might be able to do it himself. They strapped themselves in again. They were still going 17,000 miles per hour and were orbiting 200 miles above the ground. They looked at each other. Finally the time for return had come.

One last kiss in space and then Kiko said, "Okay, co-pilot, let's bring this crate back to base."

With the help of Control, they did the de-orbit burn which reduced their speed and started their descent. They reached an altitude of 400,000 feet — the entry interface. The atmosphere began to drag on the Shuttle and dissipate its tremendous energy and slow it down. Heat was building up as the Shuttle encountered this resistance.

Kiko, with the skill and calm of a professional, put the Shuttle through a series of banking maneuvers — S-turns — which kept their descent under control. The Earth was growing bigger and they could see the California coast in the distance.

Minnie was singing a Beach Boys song until Kiko said she needed his help. Between Minnie and Control, Kiko was guided toward touchdown. She checked the various meters and indicators on the control panel to determine the precise heading, glideslope deviation, and altitude as they came closer and closer. In due time, they arrived at what was called Waypoint One and then, within a minute, the runway entry point.

Minnie was gripping the armrests as the ground came up at them at an unbelievable speed. Kiko finally pulled the nose up and deployed the landing gear.

"It's about time," Minnie squawked. He was freaking out.

They were only seconds away from landing and maybe 90 feet off the ground. The runway was stretched out before them. The sun was shining.

Kiko said, "Minnie, let's do this again sometime."

He didn't answer. He just looked straight ahead, hoping they wouldn't smash to bits on the runway.

"Discovery, this is Control. Main gear at ten feet...five feet....four feet...three, two, one, contact. Nosewheel at five feet, four, three, two, one, contact. Over."

"Roger, Control. Out."

There was the gentlest of bumps and Kiko applied the brakes. About 7000 feet later, they rolled to a stop.

Kiko and Minnie stared at each other in silence. They had made it. They were excited, relieved, and safe, but there wasn't much to say. Minnie said something anyway.

He said, "Welcome back, baby."

They weren't sure what would happen next. They had completed their mission. They had their data. And they had their memories. For the moment, that was enough.

Chapter Fifty-five - Book 'Em, Danno

Through the windshield they saw the ground support trucks moving in. It was their job to drain the excess fuel from the Shuttle to make it safe. One of the trucks, with a stairway attached to it, drove right up to the Shuttle. They felt it nudge the side of the ship.

Their bodies were strangely heavy and unstable now that they were back in the gravity of Earth and after traveling so fast for so long, it was odd to be still and unmoving.

Minnie stood up and stretched as if it had only been a long nap.

"Okay, kiddo, it's showtime. You look great. The press is going to love you. We're going to be heroes."

They took one last look around the cabin and then undid the hatch and stepped through it into a small enclosed area at the top of the stairs.

"I guess I better straighten my tie," he said, laughing.

"Min." Kiko gave him a kiss. "I'm a little scared."

"Kiko, this is the easy part."

He gave her hand a squeeze and then pulled the door to one side. The light rushed in on them. It was a bright, clear morning and they stepped out onto the top of the stairs. They were smiling. Minnie winked at Kiko and they started down the short stairway to Earth.

They immediately saw that it wasn't going to be a very friendly reception. Not a hero's welcome, not one smiling face. Kiko and Minnie exchanged disappointed glances. To their surprise, there was no press, just technicians and a large troop of MPs, each wearing a gun and carrying a big stick.

As Minnie got to the bottom, one of the goons reached for him. Minnie put up a hand in a forbidding gesture that stopped him in mid-reach. Minnie stepped onto the Earth unassisted. He knelt down and ceremoniously kissed the runway.

He stood up and proclaimed, "My fellow Americans, that's one small kiss for Min. And one giant smooch for mankind."

Then they grabbed him.

The head goon said, "You, both of you, are under arrest."

"Where are the reporters, the welcoming committee, the dignitaries?" Minnie asked.

"This is it. There's no press. This whole thing is top secret."

Minnie looked over at Kiko, who had gotten over the shock of it and didn't seem surprised.

He said, "What about the broadcast? Our revelations? The information?"

The big policeman shook his head.

"You mean we believed those bozos and they double-crossed us?"

The policeman shrugged. "You're lucky you made it back. What the hell were you thinking?"

"We had a good reason," Minnie said.

"Sure." He laughed. "Tell it to the judge."

Despite the disappointment, it was good to be back on Earth. Minnie took a deep breath of the sweet air and turned to survey the solid horizon.

The goon said, "Take a good look, Space Boy, this will be the last time you see it. They're never going to let you out of jail."

"We'll see about that," Minnie said.

They walked, surrounded by the MPs, to a waiting unmarked truck. They got in and sat next to each other on a hard bench.

"Kiko, I'll explain everything."

She smiled at him. "Min, maybe I should do the talking."

He shrugged. "We'll both explain. They're mad, of course, that we stole it, but once we can get what we know out to the world, it'll be okay."

"Maybe."

Neither of them felt very sure about anything. They rode for a short time and none of their guards spoke. The truck crossed the huge runway, zipped past a collection of hangars and buildings, and made its way to the heart of the base, where it pulled up in front of the biggest official-looking building in that whole official-looking place.

They were marched in a back entrance and down to a harshly lit basement. There they were questioned briefly and simply — names, ages, addresses, occupations, etc. The process didn't take long and didn't allow for any explanations on their part.

Then the goons respectfully indicated that Kiko was to go with them and they started down a long hallway. Kiko looked back over her shoulder, blew Minnie a kiss, and called to him, "Don't let 'em break you, Rico."

Minnie laughed but was interrupted by two big guys who weren't very respectful, who dragged him by the arms and took him down a hallway in the opposite direction. He didn't have an opportunity to make a return remark to Kiko and this angered him almost more than the fact that they were trying to pull his arms out of their sockets.

In the three days that followed, he and Kiko sat in their separate cells and thought about what might happen to them. They had plenty of time to think. They were assigned an Air Force attorney to represent their case and he went back and forth, pretending to confer with his clients.

The lawyer was not sympathetic to either of them and they began to lose heart. He laughed when they each, in their turn, tried to tell him about the Cartel. They had transferred all the data from the Shuttle to Kiko's hard drive in Bolinas, so they had no evidence on them. Evidently, the data they had transmitted from the Shuttle to NASA was under lock and key. It was only their word against everyone else's and this jackass in brass was not about to believe them.

When Minnie said he would expose the Air Force to ridicule by going public with the story that an old hippie had stolen the Shuttle, the uniformed lawyer just snorted and said that even if he ever got any word out, which was unlikely, no one would believe it. He said it as if even he didn't believe it, though he knew they had.

The two hijackers, at either end of the lonely basement, sat on their narrow beds and stared at the wall. What had started out as a vacation had long ago turned serious. That he could handle. But jail? Here was Minnie's dreary fantasy come to life — the guard outside in the hallway, the lonely meals not much better than those in space, counting the days of his imprisonment as they piled up. He worried about Kiko and missed her terribly.

No news or communication with the outside world was allowed. Hope dwindled and the prospect of spending the rest of his life in jail depressed him. And yet, he kept thinking, trying to figure out a plan for their release or, failing that, escape. He cursed, he paced, he slept.

Kiko, for her part, tried to convince the lawyer not of their innocence, which didn't exist, but of their reasons for being forced to their extreme actions. He laughed at her. He wasn't buying it. It was so frustrating that they had risked their lives to get the information, actually had it, and now no one would believe them or do anything about it. They couldn't contact anyone and they couldn't use any of it. As they sat idle in prison, the Cartel and the others were clearing more of the rainforest and getting away with everything.

It was all over for them, the lawyer said. The government couldn't let anyone know that its security had been breached in such an outrageous way. He said this was one cover-up he was glad to be a part of. A few more formalities and they would be transferred to a maximum-security prison from which they would never emerge. It served them right, he said, as he slammed the cell door behind him.

Minnie heard the same speech from the lawyer and neither he nor Kiko could get the sound of the slamming door out of their heads that night. In the darkness, they both tried to send a silent message to the other, but no message was received. Much later, after a long night of tossing and turning, they began another day. Each day was beginning to take on a sameness that should have been unnerving and frightening, but Minnie had always been contrary. It was making him mad.

Chapter Fifty-six - Take Me To Your Leader

Minnie banged on the bars of the cell with his tin cup, just like in the movies.

"Hey, asshole," he said to the guard. "Who's in charge of this dump?"

The guard, a guy about 6' 4" with a buzz cut and dead eyes, walked slowly over to where Minnie waited.

Minnie looked up into the dead eyes and asked, "Hey, are you awake?"

The guard just stared back at him.

"Well, I've been locked up here for four days now and the only guy I get to see is that ding-dong who says he's my lawyer. I want to talk to the head ding-dong. Okay?"

There was no response. Minnie raised his voice.

"Hello? Minnie to Earth. I want some action around here. I want to talk to the boss."

Still no change. Minnie tried another tack.

"Look," he said confidentially, "we're friends, right?"

Nothing.

"Do me a favor and let someone on the outside know just what the fuck is going on here." He looked at him for a moment and then gestured for the guard to come closer. "You know, I've been in space. Not spaced out, but..." He pointed a finger and the guard followed. "Up there."

His audience was not impressed. Hell, the guy might not even be breathing.

"Goddamnit, this is no way to treat an American."

The guard's mouth twitched in what might have been a smile. He turned and without a word walked down the hall and out of sight.

Minnie wanted to scream and he did, but no one heard him. He kicked the bars, he hit the wall, he paced, and he muttered. Finally he sank onto the bed and tried to think what his next move might be. He and Kiko hadn't gone through all this just to be locked up. And not only locked up, but separated. He couldn't stand it.

After what passed for lunch in that place, the lawyer came by. Minnie looked on with contempt as his smug legal representative reiterated, with much apparent glee, the fact that Minnie and Kiko were in deep shit, as he called it, and were soon going to a real jail from which they would never leave. No end to their sentence, no visitors, no hope of parole.

Minnie had had it. "Cut the crap, jerkface. I've heard enough of this shit."

He stood up and walked over to where the lawyer was sitting. He towered over him. The lawyer looked out nervously for the guard but didn't say anything.

"I want to see someone in charge. I want to see someone other than your unpleasant, unhelpful self. And I want to see him now."

Minnie glared down at the lawyer, who just smiled an oily smile back. He stood up now and looked Minnie in the eye. He had fully regained his insolent, unfeeling manner and told Minnie that that was the very reason he had come to visit this afternoon. He had been instructed to bring him to the officer in charge for a last interview before transfer. He repeated the phrase "before transfer" just in case Minnie didn't get it.

Minnie ignored the implications and said, "It's about time I got some response around here. What are we waiting for? Let's go."

The lawyer and the big guard escorted Minnie through the maze of endless hallways and up and down stairs until, finally, they turned a corner and he saw Kiko waiting outside a door. She had her own guard.

Minnie lit up and ran over to her. He took her in his arms and kissed her. For a moment, time stood still. The bars and bad light and the dim future vanished. He was lost in the kiss. Then he felt a heavy hand on his shoulder. It wasn't Kiko's. The guard separated them — not unkindly, but firmly. The lawyer had a look on his face as if he had just walked out of a bad movie.

"Jealous," Minnie said to him.

The guard knocked and opened the door. Minnie, Kiko, and the lawyer entered. It was an office with a window that opened on to a parking lot. Its only furnishings were gray filing cabinets and a large desk with two chairs in front of it. A picture of the President gazed blankly down on them from the wall.

An officer was bent over some papers. He didn't look up. He addressed the lawyer and ordered him to leave the prisoners and retire. He obviously had rank because the lawyer left immediately and without a word.

"Sit down," he ordered.

He flipped a couple of pages and then raised his head.

Minnie's eyes bugged out and then he broke into a big smile. Kiko could not figure it out.

"Colonel, you devil," Minnie said.

The Colonel leaned back in his chair, enjoying Minnie's surprise. Then he leaned forward, extending a hand toward Kiko.

"Ma'am, Colonel J. M. Able, U.S. Air Force. Pleased to meet you."

Now she got it. She shook his hand, smiled, and said, "My pleasure. I've heard a lot about you."

He wasn't so crazy that he didn't notice her beauty.

"I just want to say that you are a beautiful young woman and that was a hell of a piloting job you did up there."

"Thank you, Colonel." Kiko was pleased.

The Colonel looked at Minnie and then his expression became serious, professional, and full of authority.

"You two are in hot water. You trespass on government property. You steal the most expensive piece of hardware we have. You go off on some kind of damn joyride and won't talk to anyone. And then you expect us to welcome you back with open arms."

Minnie interrupted what promised to be a long lecture. "Colonel, we had a good reason."

"What was it? Bored with Earth? High on drugs?"

"No," Kiko said. "It was serious. Let me tell you all about it."

"Oh, sure. I heard all about your file, but nobody's buying that story."

"Colonel, you've got to listen to us, to me." Kiko pleaded.

She gave him a look that must have done something to him, because he relented as much as a military man can and said, "Okay, Miss, you can run it by me, but that's it."

She did. They had nothing to lose at this point. They were headed for jail and finally they had someone besides the lawyer to tell their story to. She told him everything — Minnie's problems with the IRS, their meeting, the trip to Brazil. And all about the Cartel, their plans and history, their methods of shipment, the huge profits, the destruction of the rainforest, their Nazi past, their use of intimidation and murder.

"You expect me to believe this?" the Colonel asked.

"You think we'd go into space on top of that bomb for the hell of it?" Minnie was losing patience. "You're not going to believe us either? Colonel, think about all you and I have been through together. You can trust me."

The Colonel got a good laugh out of that one.

"Minion, you are pathetic. In all of our encounters you have shown yourself to be an unrepentant, uncooperative, self-absorbed hedonist."

Minnie was smiling and nodding in agreement.

"Jesus," the Colonel muttered. He went on. "I'm not sure you understand your position here. You stole the damn Space Shuttle. Mister, that is serious business. We're going to throw you both in jail. Forever. Do you read me? This fairy tale about Nazis and coffee is not helping." He collected himself. "Now do you have anything else to say for yourselves before we haul you away?"

Minnie smiled into the Colonel's grim face. He spread his hands out on the desktop and leaned forward.

"Colonel, I think it's time we cut a deal."

Chapter Fifty-seven - Deal

The Colonel had been waiting for this.

Minnie said, "Do you still want that tape?"

"What tape?"

"Look, Colonel, I know you want it. The tape of Pigpen. The tape with the 23-minute Dark Star. The tape where everyone levitates. The tape that will reveal the true source of Hippie power and insight."

Kiko warned him quietly, "Don't overdo it."

Minnie held up his hand. "Okay. The tape you've been bugging me about ever since I met you. You want the tape, right?"

The Colonel had a feeling he wasn't going to like this.

"Yes, I want it."

"Okay. Here's the deal. We've got it. You've got us. Sounds bad, but it's good. You let us go and we give you the tape."

"Let you go? That's ridiculous. You two are the biggest crooks in history and a pain in the ass to your government. You give me the tape and I'll make sure you don't hang."

"Not good enough," Minnie said. "Colonel, this tape is important to the national interest. Vital. You told me that. It could give our armed forces the edge they need. The preparation and knowledge they require to prevail over our enemies. Our many, many enemies."

"That's all true, Minion, but obviously I have you at a disadvantage."

"What disadvantage?"

"You're in my custody, you bonehead. I'm going to send you to jail and throw away the key. And speaking of keys, Minion, do you know anything about a key and a guy named Bowman?"

Minnie almost jumped out of his chair. He had almost forgotten about the key Bowman had given him. He had no idea what it was to and Bowman was dead. How did the Colonel know about all this? Evidently he was more interested in the Cartel than he was letting on.

He could feel Kiko staring at him. He knew she was wondering what was going on, but he was in a difficult spot. She didn't ask the questions she had about it and he completely ignored the whole issue.

"Jail doesn't mean shit, Colonel. You don't have the tape."

Negotiations had reached a standstill. Minnie sat back in his chair, stuck his legs out, folded his hands on his belly, and appeared unconcerned. The Colonel sat in his usual ramrod posture and bit his lip. Kiko watched the two of them and looked as if she didn't know whether to laugh or to continue to worry about her future.

The Colonel made what he thought was a big concession. "Okay. Maybe we could let you out in 20 years."

"Colonel, get serious. I'm not getting any younger. Life is short. I'm old enough as it is. Either you let us go or you're never getting this tape. The Russians or the Chinese or someone else, one of our many enemies, will get a hold of it and they'll figure it all out."

"You'd sell your country down the river? That's pathetic."

"Colonel, I'm not selling anything, but my country looks like it doesn't value me very much. And just because I'm a little different. Look, we try to get the goods on criminals, we save you guys the expense of paying astronauts — remember we were volunteers — and we want to help you protect America's goddamn physical and psychic borders and you're hung up on putting a couple of heroes like us in jail. That's not very nice."

"Heroes?" The Colonel was incredulous.

"Well, at least we didn't hurt anybody."

Kiko said, "I'm getting tired of listening to you two argue. I think I'd rather be in jail."

"Young lady, you are in jail." He turned back to Minnie. "How do I know you've got the tape?"

"I've got it."

"I've heard it," Kiko said, smiling at the memory. "It's pretty good."

The Colonel struggled for a minute and then slammed his fist down on the desk. "All right. I want that tape. I need that tape. I've got to have it. It will take some explaining, but I'll let you go. Jailing you would only be a big expense anyway. Now, where is it?"

"You let us go and I'll tell you."

The Colonel shook his head. "I'm not that big an idiot. Why should I trust you?"

"Well, you can't really. Except that I'm an American like you. You'll just have to take my word for it."

"Not like me, Minion. You're the weirdest American I've ever had the misfortune to encounter. You're hardly fit to carry that honor. Like I said before, it's a technicality."

"Well, being the CIA, you'll always know where I am and if you don't get the tape, you can kill me. Deal?"

The Colonel stared across at the two of them. He looked as if he thought this might be a mistake, but he stood up and put his hand out. "Deal."

They shook on it.

The plan was for the Colonel to drive them to the San Francisco airport, where they had left their car before their trip to Florida. Before their trip to space and to jail. It was a lifetime ago. Once there, they would tell him how to get the tape and he would let them go.

That would be the end of their deal. From then on, everyone was on their own. The Colonel asked some more questions about the Cartel and said that even if there were any truth to this coffee fantasy, no one would believe them. The government would deny any knowledge of it and of the Shuttle affair. They would just be seen as two drug-deranged weirdos. Kiko and Minnie took no offense, agreed to the plan, and their release was set for that night.

It was late and it was dark when the Colonel showed up at Minnie's cell. The guard was nowhere to be seen. He led Minnie down the echoing hallways.

Minnie asked, "Where's Kiko?"

The Colonel, without looking back, said, "She's in the car."

They went out through a thick steel door into the parking lot. The Colonel's sedan was waiting. It was empty.

Minnie stopped as soon as he saw Kiko wasn't there.

"Colonel, what the fuck is going on? Where's Kiko?"

"We couldn't let both of you go. And she's the one who actually flew the Shuttle. You might be able to operate a dishwasher, but I doubt it."

Minnie didn't have a dishwasher, but there were more important things to think about.

The Colonel stood next to the open car door and continued, "Look, Minion, you're free. Isn't that enough? She's cute, but forget her. You're only getting out because you've got the tape."

"Fuck you, Colonel. I'm not leaving her." Minnie stared him.

The Colonel closed the door. "If that's the way you want it, you can both stay in jail. It might take a week, it might take a year, but you'll give me that tape."

Minnie watched as the Colonel waited impassively. The situation was looking desperate. It seemed that the Colonel meant what he said. Minnie decided to play his last card.

Minnie asked the Colonel, "How'd you know about Bowman's key?"

"Minion, you need to revise your opinion of military intelligence. It's no secret that key is worth a fortune. Everyone's been looking for it. They killed Bowman for it, but never found it." As a joke, he said, "Maybe you have it."

Minnie played along. "Valuable, huh? And just who killed him?"

"Who cares? He's dead. The important thing is that tape. You're free. We've made our deal, now let's get out of here. If you do have that key, you're a lucky guy. You can get any girl you want."

Minnie remembered Bowman's words — never tell anyone, never give it to anyone. Bowman was dead and he had no idea what the key was to. It meant nothing to him, but it obviously did to someone.

"What if I offered the key to you?"

The Colonel exploded. "Goddamnit, Minion, don't play with me."

"Look, you're the double-crosser. I've got the fucking key. Go back in there and get her and I'll give it to you."

The Colonel thought for about three seconds.

"You've really got it?"

Minnie nodded. "But, Colonel, we don't say anything about it to Kiko."

Everything was quiet except for the buzz from the lights in the deserted parking lot which cast a sickly glow over the scene. They stared at each other.

"Okay. You stay here."

Minnie said, "I'm not leaving without her."

Several minutes later, the Colonel returned with Kiko. He watched for a moment as they embraced and then dumped himself behind the wheel. He waited a moment and then rapped insistently on the window for them to get in.

The Colonel's driving hadn't improved and Kiko and Minnie found this trip up the freeway much more frightening than the takeoff and landing of the Shuttle combined. Kiko, in the front seat, braced herself against the dashboard and stared at the highway in silence, eyes wide with alarm. Minnie was in the back, leaning forward, thinking that he could somehow shield Kiko from the imminent accident. He called out warnings and instructions to the Colonel, who kept ordering him to shut up and sit back. The drive seemed endless to all of them.

The Colonel was the calmest of the three. He, after all, had the wheel to hang on to and was nominally in control. He showed an interest in the Cartel, especially in its profits, and asked them some more questions. Once that was attended to, he kept up a running commentary on the state of the world and emphasized his paranoid observations with elaborate hand gestures and pointed looks which distracted him from driving and threatened their lives. The other cars on the road did what they could.

At last they squealed to a stop in front of the airport terminal.

"Okay," said the Colonel. "We're here."

Minnie and Kiko could barely move.

"Now, where's that tape?"

Minnie had the door open, just in case. "It's in the tape player on board the Shuttle. I left it there to blow their minds and because I knew if I had it with me it would be confiscated."

"On the Shuttle?"

"That's it."

"Mister, if it's not there, you better start saying your prayers."

"Colonel, it's there. Don't sweat it. You can trust me."

Minnie made a move to leave. The Colonel wouldn't let him go. He had Minnie's arm in a grip that could crush bones. He wanted the key.

Minnie stuck his hand out to shake and the Colonel saw the light flash on the key hidden in Minnie's hand. He looked up at Kiko, who was already out of the car, and then back at Minnie. He nodded and shook hands, taking the key from Minnie. No words were spoken between them.

He looked again at Kiko and said, "Ma'am, you seem pretty level-headed. I'd ditch this fruitcake if I were you."

"Thanks for the advice," she said. "He's not so bad, once you get to know him."

"Sure. Well, another time."

Minnie joined Kiko on the curb, as the Colonel peeled out without looking back.

Minnie was staring at Kiko. "Thanks for the glowing testimonial."

"Oh, Min." She took his arm, pulled him close, and said, "I didn't think we were ever going to get out of there. You're no fruitcake, big guy, you're my hero."

Chapter Fifty-eight -
The Big Guy Wants The Skinny

Kiko and Minnie couldn't believe it. They had to hug each other. Back from space, out of jail, and free. They breathed in the exhaust-filled air from the airport traffic and felt lucky and wonderful.

After searching the parking lot and finally finding their car, they hopped in the red Chevy and headed out for the bridge and Bolinas. Kiko was exhausted, but Minnie was all revved up and sang, in his unique voice, about leaving his heart in San Francisco and about wearing flowers in his hair and about knocking on California's golden door.

Kiko commented that his driving wasn't much better than the Colonel's, but that she was too tired to do anything about it. He leaned over and kissed her forehead, almost sideswiping a Toyota in the process.

He continued to sing as they crossed the Golden Gate to Marin. "If you want to know where it really is, it's in his kiss, that's where it is, oh yeah." "Baby, It's You" and "Wake Up Little Susie," but it wasn't doing any good. Kiko was asleep. He kept singing anyway, though softly, and from time to time he looked over at her sweet face, smiling as it leaned against the window.

He thought about the key. What the hell was it to? How valuable was it? At that moment, it didn't matter. It had sprung Kiko from jail and they were on their way home. That was plenty. It was like the song said, you had to pass it up or pass it on. As far as he was concerned, he was done with it. The secret of the key, as far as he knew, had died with Bowman. It was time to go on living.

Kiko woke as they began to go down the curves on the other side of Mt. Tamalpais. The ocean was a black void in front of them and further on, Bolinas and the house were waiting. In the darkness, it was hard to tell which were lights and which were stars.

Kiko said, "Minnie, as great as space was and as many problems as there are down here, I'm really glad to be back." She put her hand on his leg. "I want to stay here." Everything had shifted between them.

He looked over. Her face was lit by the lights of the dash.

"I like it here too," he said softly. "Plus, I don't think they'll ever let us have the Shuttle again."

They laughed and cruised through Stinson Beach. Nothing

and no one was stirring. At last they pulled into the little lane outside Kiko's house. Out there, they could smell everything — the ocean, the red dirt beneath their feet, the eucalyptus, and all of the flowers. A night bird somewhere welcomed them and they could faintly hear the waves crashing on the shore down below the cliffs.

With his arm around her, Minnie guided a sleeping Kiko through the yard and into the house. As they stretched out in the big bed, Kiko put her hands beneath the pillow and sang, in a faint voice, "It's in his kiss. That's where it is." This was a confirmation that she was as goofy as he was. He turned toward her and felt her warm breath on his face. He closed his eyes and then he too was asleep, at home, back on Earth.

The next day turned out to be a busy one. Minnie woke to the smells of a real breakfast. No more rehydrated oatmeal or bland prison food, but three eggs, toast, and juice. This was more like it. They checked the computer and were relieved to find that the data had all been transferred without any problem.

It was all there. And as they reviewed it and organized it, they were constantly amazed and appalled at what they had collected. They thought that this information was conclusive and damaging. It had everything — names, dates, and numbers. Even if NASA and the Air Force wouldn't believe them, they had faith in Ed's sense of duty and his greed and they felt confident that he would see it for what it was. That he had the means and the organization to do something about the Cartel. That he would take the data and use it.

Kiko made a few calls to her connections and got the latest on what had happened since they were gone. People asked where she had been and she smiled and told them, "On vacation." The call to Mariana went through and Kiko found that she and Ze were safe. She told her she had found out information that corroborated the evidence they had given her and that she would check with them later. She left e-mail for Francisco and Henry thanking them for their help.

Kiko put their information into its final form and transferred it to three small disks. She held them up and waved them at Minnie, who was on the couch reading the sports section of the newspaper.

"This is it," she said. "We've got 'em. Maybe our plan with the Shuttle didn't work, but this has got to convince someone".

"Okay. I'll call Ed and set up a meeting."

The meeting was scheduled for lunch the next day at the usual place.

On the way over, Minnie wondered if Ed really would believe what was on the disks or not. He was hard to figure out, but at least he still wanted to meet with him. Then Minnie remembered the $43,000. He laughed. No wonder. But here was another deal to be made and he wasn't going to blow it.

Ed was in his usual seat by the Legos. He greeted Minnie with a grunt. He was halfway through the first QuarterPounder.

As Minnie sat down, he said, "Ed, it's good to see you." He meant it. He liked the big square.

Ed, cheeks bulging, nodded his head and tried to smile. With his mouth full, he mumbled, "You too."

After some chewing, Ed said, "Well, do you really have the dope on these guys? Are you ready to tell me the truth?"

Minnie was relaxed. After recent events, it even felt good to be at McDonald's. He nodded and asked, "Are you ready to believe it?"

"Where'd you get it? I was beginning think you skipped out on me and were never coming back from your damn vacation in Florida."

"Ed, it came from space."

Ed looked at him as if this confirmed all of his doubts about Minnie. He made a resigned noncommittal movement with his head and brought the straw of his shake to his small red lips.

Minnie said, "I'm going to tell you because I know you'll believe me."

Ed looked at him with concern.

Minnie leaned over the immovable plastic table. "We stole the Space Shuttle and got the information in space. Well, some of it."

Ed started choking. Minnie smiled. Ed continued choking.

It seemed serious and Minnie said, "I know Heimlich. I know CPR." The thought of performing CPR on this guy, even though he liked him, was a little scary.

So he said, "Put your arms up."

Finally, Ed recovered. He gasped, "Minnie, don't do this to me. You're full of it."

"No, it's the truth and I'm going to give you all the info we have." He paused. "But first, we have to make a deal."

Ed held up some fries defensively. "Uh oh. This sounds like trouble."

"Relax, Ed. It's simple. I'll give you this stuff on the Cartel and you can take it and check it out. If it's as good as I think it is, you'll find you have enough there to bust the Cartel and make more money than you can imagine."

Ed was intrigued. He was also worried, because he could feel conditions bubbling to the surface, about to be mentioned. He met them head on.

"And if I do," he said, "and we do recover considerable cash, what do you want in return?"

Minnie smiled. This didn't reassure the big accountant.

"Ed, compared to what you're going to get, what I want is laughable."

Ed nodded, but he wasn't laughing. He had a feeling it was going to cost him.

"How laughable are we talking?"

"Okay. You get the coffee guys and all of their dough and in exchange you forget and forgive my measly bill."

"$43,548.34? You call that measly?" He almost choked again.

"And," Minnie went on, "you get off the Dead's back. They pay you guys plenty and you know it."

"This better be good, Minnie."

"Don't worry," Minnie said, "it's good. Do we have a deal?"

Ed stared at the empty wrappers on his tray as he thought. Then he looked at Minnie and smiled. He shook his head as if he couldn't figure out why he liked this guy.

"Okay, Minnie, it's a deal. But I've got to verify it. Let's meet here in three days. That should give me time."

They shook on it.

As they parted in the parking lot, Ed said, "Just remember, if it doesn't pan out, you still owe me. You don't want to go to jail, do you?"

Chapter Fifty-nine - Every Last Cent

For the next two days, Minnie and Kiko took it easy. They ate, they kissed, they slept. There wasn't much else to do. They had to wait for word from Ed. He was their best bet. They also realized that they were exhausted from their time in space and needed to recover. After what they had been through, these two days were like a vacation for them. And in Minnie's case, it was like a vacation from the vacation from the vacation. Or something like that. It was complicated, but well earned.

On the morning of the third day, Minnie began to get nervous about his meeting with Ed. He paced around after breakfast and then took out the trash. He swept the floor. He even tried to straighten the closet. It was unlike him.

"What if Ed doesn't buy it?" he said. "If he thinks we made it all up? I'll have to go to jail and this time they won't let me out."

"Minnie, relax. It's all there. He'll check it out. Everything will be fine."

"Yeah. Sure. But if it's not, I'm in big trouble."

"You've been in big trouble before."

He slumped down in a chair and Kiko came over and sat on the arm of it, next to him. She applied the Touch to Minnie's shoulders and he began to melt. Minutes drifted by. Everything was at rest. The world was quiet. Peaceful.

Suddenly, Minnie's eyes popped open and he returned to what he called reality.

"What time is it? I'm probably late."

As he went out the door, Kiko said to him, "Don't worry. Just drive safely and don't eat too much of that food."

The music was blaring and the top was down as Minnie sped toward Mill Valley. He was nervous. He was worried. And he was hungry.

When he got to McDonald's, he walked in, looked around, and immediately saw that Ed wasn't in his usual place. The table was empty. The beginnings of an awful feeling started in Minnie's stomach and it wasn't the thought of the food, either. Ed wasn't there. He had always been there. Something was very wrong. Thoughts of jail began to fill Minnie's head. He imagined that he heard the cell door slam, but it was just the cash register.

He ordered two Big Macs with the works, Super Fries, and a large Coke. As he waited, the din of the place faded and a fantasy of a prison cafeteria started up — the tin plates, no knives or forks, only spoons, food that made McDonald's seem good. He and all the other prisoners were wearing itchy drab clothing. The light came faintly through barred windows set high in the gray walls. The sound of their shuffling footsteps echoed in the large hall. Rows of prisoners at long tables were bent over their lunches, chewing and mumbling.

The whole thing turned him cold. He felt like he might snap and was about to throw his tray to the cement floor and make a desperate break for it when he felt the guard's restraining hand on his shoulder.

"Minnie." The guard's voice was abrupt.

He turned, but instead of the evil, unfeeling guard he expected, he saw Ed. And Ed was smiling.

"Minnie, this lunch is on me."

"What?" Minnie was shocked at this, almost as much as finding himself back in McDonald's.

"Minnie, are you okay? You look a little weird." This made Ed laugh. "That's a good one, isn't it? You looking weird?" He laughed some more.

It wasn't funny to Minnie.

Ed said, "Aw, come on, I know I'm late. I had to do a couple of things. That stuff you gave me was great. It all checked out. You're a hero."

They settled themselves at the table. Ed was smiling and at the same time trying to put away his QuarterPounder. Minnie was very relieved. He tried to be cool, sipping his Coke, but he couldn't help smiling too and prompting Ed, "So tell me. Tell me the story."

Ed waved his fries at him and saying, "Wait a sec," munched on. They ate their lunch.

Finally, Ed said, "Okay. Here's what happened. I went back to the office and put the disks on the box. It was unbelievable — the conversations, the transcripts. And the pictures." He looked at Minnie with wonder. "You really were in space."

"Of course I was."

"Tell me what it was like."

Minnie shook his head. "Later. What else?"

"Well, I went down the hall and showed it to my boss. He took one look at it and called in a couple of field agents. We spent the rest of the day, all night, and all of the next day checking it out. You were right. This is going to be the biggest bust yet."

He went on and told Minnie the details and said they had already made plans to pick up some of the Cartel hoods in Seattle.

Ed said he received a call from a Colonel Able, who leaned on him, first for information and then about keeping the whole operation secret. Of course, he said, the IRS wasn't after publicity, they're after money and this promised to be big. The two agencies had made an arrangement. Together, they were setting up the whole thing and they were going to Brazil to strike at the heart of the Cartel. And, in addition to all the money, there was the fact of the Cartel's Nazi ties. Extradition papers were being drawn up.

Ed couldn't contain himself. "This is big, Minnie. Huge. Everyone wants in on it — us, CIA, EPA, State Department."

Minnie was pleased. He watched as Ed licked his fingers. He hadn't known what to expect and this exceeded everything. But he was still cautious.

"So what about my bill?" he asked.

"We're going to ignore it," Ed said smiling.

"Is that the same as forgetting it?"

Ed rolled his eyes and nodded.

"And the Dead?"

"Well, that's a little bit harder to arrange, but we're going to try and settle with them. A nominal amount. So everyone is happy."

Minnie shook his head. "You guys are cold. They're the ones who helped us out, who made all this possible."

"Well, we're grateful." The big accountant laughed at his own joke.

Even Minnie had to laugh. "But you wouldn't say you owed them anything, would you?"

Ed's expression changed entirely and he became quite serious. "Minnie, the IRS is in no one's debt. Everyone owes us, get it?"

"But I'm off the hook?"

"Yes, completely." Ed paused and then said, "Of course, you'll owe on this year's income."

"Of course."

Chapter Sixty - You Da One

When Minnie got back to the house in Bolinas, he told Kiko the good news and the celebration began. She pulled champagne out of the refrigerator, saying she knew everything was going to turn out right so she had been making preparations while he was gone.

"Here's to you, Minnie," she said as she lifted her glass.

He shook his head and said, "You da one, babe."

"No, we're the one," she said and their glasses clinked for the first, but not the last time that night.

They were pretty pleased with themselves and spent the next few days patting each other on the back and making up for lost time. They walked on the beach, they danced around the house, and they smooched on the couch, in the kitchen, and in bed.

One night, they lay in the bedroom, candles burning. The music was playing softly and the sound of the breeze outside drifted through the window. Kiko pulled back for a moment, listening. Minnie was alarmed and asked her what was wrong.

"That music. That's the same music that was on the tape in space. Pigpen. The tape you were supposed to give to the Colonel."

Minnie gave her a devilish grin.

"Oh, Min, how could you double-cross him? He'll kill you."

"Kiko, he got the tape. Everything's all right."

They listened as Pigpen moaned in the background. Then the sound of his harmonica filled the room.

"But you told me it was the only copy."

"It was then, but I made another before we went to Florida. Anything could have happened to it. And it's pretty good, isn't it?" He kissed her. "Want to try a little levitation?"

Two days later, they were sitting on the front steps when the phone rang.

Minnie said, "If it's Cowboy, I'm hanging up."

"Don't worry, Min. I'll take care of it."

Minnie looked out at the yard full of flowers and green grass and was more than glad to be safe on Earth and to be with Kiko and to not owe the IRS. A lot had happened on this vacation. He began to wonder what would happen next. Or could. It probably was time to go back to the bar. His heart sank a little, but he thought about poor Cowboy.

Kiko came back. She had a big smile on her face. She said, "It's for you."

Minnie gave her a look.

"It's not Cowboy," she said.

"Who is it?"

"Just answer it."

They went inside. Kiko lay on the couch, watching him. He made a face at her and picked up the phone.

"Yeah?"

His expression changed completely. A big grin spread across his face and he looked at Kiko, who smiled back.

"Uh huh." He listened.

"Yeah," he said.

"Well..." He gave an embarrassed laugh.

"Uh huh."

This went on for a couple of minutes.

"That's great. Well, thanks. Really. Any time. Yeah, she's the greatest. She did it all. Uh huh."

Suddenly, Minnie became motionless. His eyes focused on something Kiko couldn't see. He listened for a few moments and then said, "Come on. You mean it?"

Minnie turned to Kiko. His mouth hung open. Then his face completely changed. He flashed her a huge smile. He spoke into the phone again.

"Oh man, you're not kidding, are you? I have to think about that one. Yeah, I'll let you know. Sure. Okay. Bye."

He returned the receiver to its place and sat down. The grin was bigger than ever. He looked over and was speechless for a moment. Then he stated the obvious to her.

"It was Jerry."

She nodded.

"He thanked me. Us. For everything. For busting the Cartel and saving the rainforest, for working the deal with the IRS. They settled. He went on and on. I almost forgot he could talk. I've only heard him sing. He said to come backstage and see him." Minnie shook his head. "Wow. He offered me a job working for the Dead. Can you believe it? That's too fucking much."

Kiko came over and hugged him.

"You talked to him, too?" he said.

She nodded. "I told him all about you."

Minnie was about to say something when the phone rang. They looked at each other. No time to recover.

Minnie picked it up and said, "Cowboy?" He listened. "Oh, sorry. Sure, okay." He was nodding his head. "Let me give you the directions." They were detailed. "Yeah. Uh huh. No, a right.

Okay. See ya."

Minnie filled her in. "That was Ed. He said he has some good news, but that he has to bring it in person." He laughed. "This is great. He's a trip. I'm glad you guys can finally meet."

They waited for Ed out on the steps. The sun was warm and everything was peaceful. They were miles away from all the trouble in Brazil and miles from space.

"What do you think is going to happen?" he asked.

"To us?"

"Well, yeah. But I was thinking about all the other stuff. Brazil and everything. It's kind of overwhelming."

"It sure is."

He got up and began to pace.

"No, I mean, we helped to bust these guys, but don't you think someone else will take their place? And then there are all those other assholes — oil companies, lumber conglomerates, agriculture. It drives me crazy. All of them stomping around down there like there's no tomorrow."

"Like you?"

He laughed and sat back down next to her.

Kiko was quiet and leaned her head on his shoulder as he continued to talk.

"There's an endless supply of those guys. It will be like nothing happened."

"But, Min, it did happen," she said. "We didn't save the world, big shot, but we did something. At least we did something."

"Yeah, it's a start." He shook his head. "I hope everything I'm thinking is wrong."

She laughed. "It probably is."

Then they both were laughing and that was when Ed came through the gate. He had his suit on, of course, and the collar of his shirt was pressing against his more than ample neck. His tie was tight and his face was pink and sweating in the sunshine.

Minnie introduced him to Kiko and mutual congratulations were exchanged. They took to each other immediately. She thanked him for believing them and for being so fair to the Dead and so generous to Minnie. In his turn, he said that they had done him a favor. He had just received a promotion. He gallantly said that if he had met Kiko earlier, all his doubts about the story would have vanished.

"What? Like I jived you?" Minnie protested.

"Of course not, but..." Ed just looked at Kiko as if that were explanation enough.

They went inside and Minnie brought out beers, chips, and

guacamole. Ed immediately went for the chips. Then he told them why he had come.

"I have a letter for you. A special letter."

He wiped his hands and pulled an envelope out of his jacket pocket and waved it at them. Minnie took it and, when he saw the return address, his mouth dropped open. He unfolded the letter and stared at the single sheet of paper.

"Read it," Kiko suggested.

He looked at the two of them on the couch. Beautiful Kiko and big Ed.

"This is amazing. It's from the White House." He flashed the letter at them so they could see the letterhead at the top. He cleared his throat.

November 23, 1994

Dear Friends,

Thank you for your recent contribution.

Minnie looked up, made a face, and then continued reading.

It has been my experience and I'm sure you'll agree that to bring about change one must go beyond one's own backyard.

The most direct route is often the most round-about and we must never be afraid to scale great heights in order to see things as they really are. It's all a matter of perspective.

Hillary and I commend you for your dedication, perseverance, and uniquely American sense of adventure.

Sincerely,

Bill Clinton

President Bill Clinton

There was a reverent silence after Minnie finished reading. They all looked at each other and then Minnie said, "Who cares if he didn't inhale?"

Chapter Sixty-one - Baby, It's You

Before he left, Ed said he had been authorized to offer Minnie a job with the IRS.

Minnie started laughing. "You guys too? Get serious. As what?" he asked.

"As a special agent. It's such an honor. You know, they never do this. It would mean a lot of money and a good pension. You'd be undercover and we could work together." The big accountant was getting excited.

"Would I have to wear a tie?"

"Well, of course."

Minnie stifled a snort. He looked at Ed and at Kiko. "Ed, I'm honored and it would be great to work with you. It has been great, but, you know, it's just not my thing."

Ed said he understood, but told Minnie that if he ever changed his mind, all he had to do was call.

After Ed left, Kiko and Minnie went back out to the front steps and watched as the afternoon changed into evening.

"Can you believe that? Me, an agent? For those guys?"

"It is pretty far-fetched, but you let him down gracefully. You're kind of a sweetie, you know. Now, what about the job with the Dead?"

"I don't know what to think. It's the job of a lifetime, but..." he groaned. "I've got the bar. It's a responsibility. And just think of poor Cowboy." He was quiet for a moment and then sighed a big sigh. He stared into her big eyes, made a small sound of frustration, and said, "I think you should go back to your life and I should go back to mine."

"But what about us?"

Minnie looked around at the grass and at the flowers and at the sky. It was hard for him to look at her.

Finally, he said, "Kiko, you're the greatest, but I know you couldn't really go for a guy like me."

"What do you mean?"

"You don't have to humor me. It's like I've said all along. I'm just a guy, just an old guy. And you are beautiful, sweet, talented, wonderful, and young. You couldn't really like a guy like me. I'm okay to play with, sure, but you know..." He shrugged. "I'm too old for you. I'm just a guy, babe, and you're something special."

"How old do you think I am, anyway?"

"Twenty-five, thirty?"

She shook her head. "I'm your age, you big dope. Well, almost." She put his hand in hers. "Minnie, age and looks and all the rest of that doesn't matter. What matters is your heart. And yours is huge."

She made him look at her.

"I admit that I had my doubts, at first. I thought you were a flake. Well, more than a flake, but you always came through. You helped me when you didn't have to. You cared about all those people who were being crushed by the Cartel. You went into space with me, even though you thought it was crazy and even though there was a good chance we'd never come back. You saved my life."

Minnie was quiet. After a moment, she leaned back and gave him a look. She tried to imitate his wiggling eyebrows.

"Besides," she laughed, "you've got the Touch. I love you, Min. You're not leaving me behind. If you want to go back to the bar, fine. If you want to stay in California and work with the Dead, fine. But I'm not letting you go. We're sticking together."

Minnie couldn't quite get a grip on this. Everything was so great. So perfect. Kiko telling him all this. The job offer from Jerry. Surviving all their adventures. There had to be a catch somewhere. He had always been attracted to happy endings, but they had never happened to him before.

He and Kiko looked at each other for a long time. Kiko had a smile on her face, waiting for him to say something. He knew this was no hallucination. He knew she meant it. The light had grown soft and, even though it was still warm out, he got goosebumps and found it hard to speak. He reached out and gently touched her cheek. His heart hadn't pounded like this since space.

He said, "Kiko..." Then he smiled. "There's this place down in the islands. Maybe we should go there and think things over."

She threw her arms around him and almost knocked him off the steps. He knew he was a lucky guy.

That night he made a phone call.

"Cowboy? Minnie here. I've got a problem."

He smiled at Kiko, put his hand over the receiver, and said to her, "I think he's having a heart attack."

Cowboy recovered.

"Yeah, Cowboy. I can't believe you're still there. You've gone way above and beyond the call of duty on this one. I'm giving you a raise — 50 cents an hour." He laughed. "Just kidding. Just kidding. Anyone as conscientious as you are deserves an oppor-tunity, so I'm splitting my share of the bar with you. Now it's your headache. From now on, you and Beaver can figure things out. I'm going on vacation."

He listened for a second.

"I know. This is a new vacation. A vacation from the vacation."

He listened some more. He had a big smile on his face and he looked over at Kiko. He was nodding his head, waiting for Cowboy to stop gushing.

"Well, okay. Give my best to the boys. I'll call you."

He hung up and turned toward Kiko. He thought about the future, about their future, and said, "Baby, let's start packing."

Chapter Sixty-Two - It Ain't Over

Two days later, in a gray and desolate office in Washington, D.C., a meeting was taking place. Several people were seated on either side of a large conference table, empty except for a pile of papers in front of one of the men. There were two parties at this meeting — the IRS and the CIA.

Despite the Colonel's unstable imagination, no part of what Kiko and Minnie had told him had been lost on him. NASA had ignored them, but their story meant something to the CIA. Colonel Able had turned over Minnie's key and his story to a superior officer. The Colonel's bosses already knew the story but were glad and relieved to get the key.

They were more than familiar with what it represented - evidence of their previous involvement with the Cartel's activities and documentation showing that sometimes the CIA had even provided financial support. This was the evidence that Bowman had stumbled onto in his small-scale dealings down south. Evidence that had cost him his life.

Everything incriminating had been immediately destroyed and the time had come for the CIA to act. They made their plans accordingly. This meeting was the result.

Colonel Able, by virtue of his dumb luck, had proven useful but was now unnecessary. A transfer had been arranged. He had been superseded by a grim-looking officer who was all business.

Ed was in attendance, but in a completely subordinate position. He had been instructed to keep quiet. A Washington bigwig was representing the IRS and the meeting's outcome was a foregone conclusion. The room was dimly lit and the dull noise of traffic could be heard through the thick windows.

The grim officer was speaking. His voice was professional, mechanical and efficient.

"This is something that can benefit both Agencies for a long time to come. It's an opportunity. The Nazis are a dead issue. They're too old to prosecute. What would be the point?"

No one felt the need to answer.

"We're taking over the operation. Stopping the flow would invite a caffeine crisis and it would mean chaos in the workplace. That would be a disaster."

Ed was chilled by the look of the man. This wasn't the ending he had envisioned everything.

The officer glanced around the table at all of them and, smiling, said, "Besides, why stop a good business when it can be run more profitably by real Americans?"